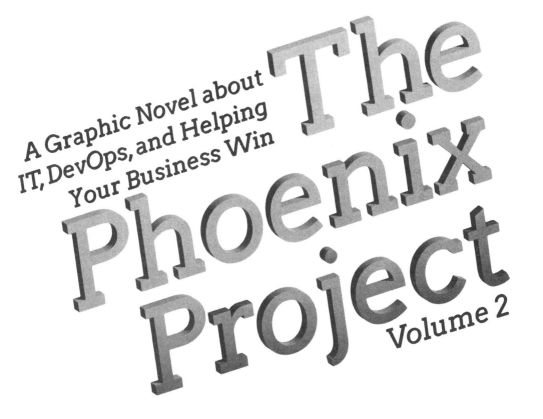

A Graphic Novel about IT, DevOps, and Helping Your Business Win

The Phoenix Project

Volume 2

Adapted by Gene Kim
Illustrated by Mike Collins

IT Revolution
Portland, OR

25 NW 23rd Pl, Suite 6314
Portland, OR 97210

Script Copyright © 2025 by Gene Kim
Illustration Copyright © 2025 by Mike Collins

All rights reserved. For information about permission to reproduce selections from this book, write to Permissions, IT Revolution Press, LLC, 25 NW 23rd Pl, Suite 6314, Portland, OR 97210.

Printed in the United States of America
30 29 28 27 26 25   1 2 3 4 5 6 7 8 9 10

Cover layout by Devon Smith
Cover illustration by Mike Collins
Lettering and interior design by AndWorld Design
Edited by Jim Spivey/Working Vacation Studios

Library of Congress Control Number: 2025940582

ISBN: 978-1950508921

For information about special discounts for bulk purchases
or for information on booking authors for an event,
please visit our website at www.ITRevolution.com.

THE PHOENIX PROJECT: VOLUME 2

About the Creators

Gene Kim is an award-winning CTO, researcher, and author. He is the founder of Tripwire and served as CTO for thirteen years. He is the author of several books, which have sold over one million copies, including *Wiring the Winning Organization* (2023), *The Unicorn Project* (2019), the Shingo Publication award-winning *Accelerate* (2018), *The DevOps Handbook* (2016), and *The Phoenix Project* (2013). Since 2014, he has been the organizer of DevOps Enterprise Summit, studying the technology transformations of large, complex organizations. Kim has a Master of Computer Science from the University of Arizona and has been studying high-performing technology organizations since 1999. He was the founder and CTO of Tripwire, Inc. for thirteen years, an enterprise security software company. In 2007, *ComputerWorld* added Gene to the "40 Innovative IT People to Watch Under the Age of 40" list, and he was named a Computer Science Outstanding Alumnus by Purdue University for achievement and leadership in the profession. He lives with his wife and children in Portland, OR.

Mike Collins recently celebrated forty years working in comics. In that time, he's drawn pretty much every major character in the US and UK: X-Men, Batman, the JLA, Spider-Man, Superman, Wonder Woman, The Flash, Judge Dredd, Slaine, and Rogue Trooper among them. Best known for drawing Doctor Who since the show's triumphant return twenty years back for *Doctor Who Magazine*, IDW, Titan, and two Dalek graphic novels for BBC Books, as well as writing and drawing Doctor Who online games for Tiny Rebel. He's also the artist on the 1970s Marvel-style Doctor Who merchandise. He's drawn two well-regarded and successful original graphic novels: an adaptation of Dickens' *A Christmas Carol* and the docudrama about the first moon landing, *Apollo*. He's married to Bernadette Vella, an IT manager at several major international financial institutions for the last few decades, who was very excited about this book happening as she'd long used it in her work strategies. Mike lives in Cardiff, Wales.

PREVIOUSLY AT PARTS UNLIMITED...

BILL PALMER, NEWLY PROMOTED TO VP OF IT OPERATIONS, FOUND HIMSELF THRUST INTO A MAELSTROM OF CRISES. A CATASTROPHIC PAYROLL FAILURE EXPOSED DEEP-SEATED ISSUES WITHIN THE COMPANY'S IT LANDSCAPE, WHILE THE HIGH-STAKES *PHOENIX PROJECT* TEETERED ON THE BRINK OF DISASTER. AS BILL SCRAMBLED TO PUT OUT FIRES, HE ENCOUNTERED *ERIK REID*, AN UNCONVENTIONAL PROSPECTIVE BOARD MEMBER WHO CHALLENGED HIS UNDERSTANDING OF IT MANAGEMENT.

INSPIRED BY ERIK'S INSIGHTS, BILL DISCOVERS THREE OF THE *FOUR TYPES OF WORK:* BUSINESS PROJECTS, INTERNAL IT PROJECTS, AND CHANGES. WITH THESE NEW LEARNINGS, BILL BEGAN PERFORMING EXPERIMENTS, AND EVEN IMPLEMENTED SOME SWEEPING CHANGES, WITH THE HELP OF HIS TEAM, *WES DAVIS* AND *PATTY MCKEE*.

HE ESTABLISHED A CHANGE ADVISORY BOARD (CAB) TO BRING ORDER TO THE CHAOS OF UNCONTROLLED CHANGES AND DEVISED A STRATEGY TO PROTECT *BRENT GELLER,* THE OVERWORKED GENIUS WHOSE KNOWLEDGE WAS CRITICAL YET DANGEROUSLY SILOED.

DESPITE THESE IMPROVEMENTS, BILL'S TEAM STRUGGLED TO BALANCE THE DEMANDS OF DAILY OPERATIONS WITH THE LOOMING PHOENIX DEPLOYMENT, ALL WHILE UNDER INTENSE SCRUTINY FROM EXECUTIVES LIKE THE FORMIDABLE *SARAH MOULTON*, SVP OF RETAIL OPERATIONS, AND THE INCREASINGLY IMPATIENT CEO, *STEVE MASTERS*.

JUST AS BILL THOUGHT HE WAS MAKING PROGRESS, A STARTLING REVELATION EMERGED. THE CHANGE MANAGEMENT PROCESS, INTENDED TO BRING STABILITY, HAD INSTEAD EXPOSED A MOUNTING CRISIS OF UNFINISHED WORK. CHANGE REQUESTS WERE PILING UP LIKE INVENTORY ON A FACTORY FLOOR, ECHOING ERIK'S WARNINGS ABOUT *WORK IN PROCESS* (WIP) AND ITS DETRIMENTAL EFFECTS.

AS OUR STORY RESUMES, BILL STANDS AT A CROSSROADS, REALIZING THAT CONVENTIONAL IT PRACTICES MAY BE FUNDAMENTALLY FLAWED. HE IS NOW IN A RACE TO FIND THE FOURTH TYPE OF WORK AND FIGURE OUT WHAT THE THREE WAYS REALLY ARE. WITH THE FATE OF *PARTS UNLIMITED* HANGING IN THE BALANCE, WE NOW JOIN BILL AS HE ATTEMPTS TO FIND A WAY TO APPLY THESE NEW INSIGHTS BEFORE IT'S TOO LATE.

CHAPTER 12 FRIDAY, SEPTEMBER 12

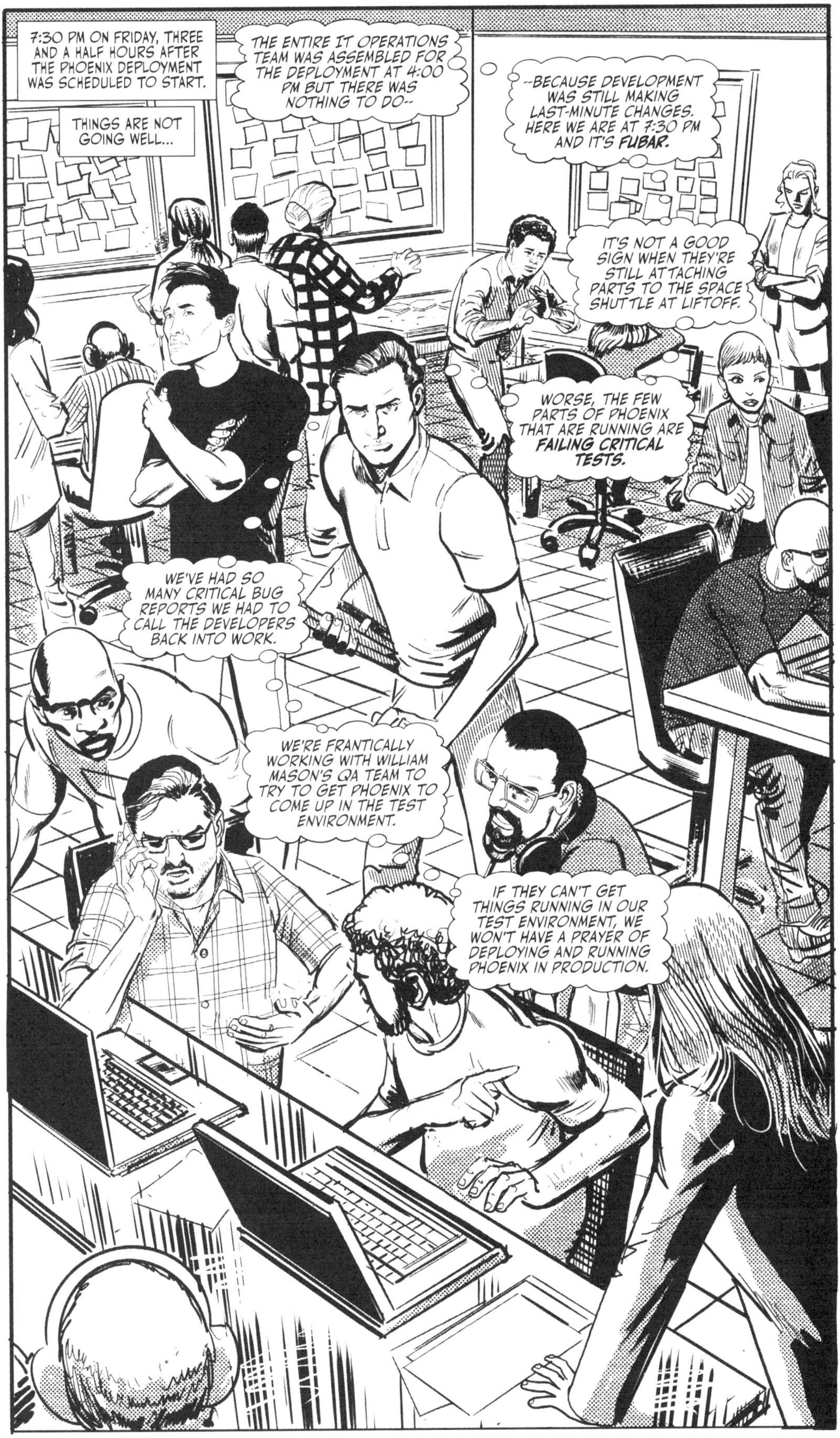

7:30 PM ON FRIDAY, THREE AND A HALF HOURS AFTER THE PHOENIX DEPLOYMENT WAS SCHEDULED TO START.
THINGS ARE NOT GOING WELL...
THE ENTIRE IT OPERATIONS TEAM WAS ASSEMBLED FOR THE DEPLOYMENT AT 4:00 PM BUT THERE WAS NOTHING TO DO--
--BECAUSE DEVELOPMENT WAS STILL MAKING LAST-MINUTE CHANGES. HERE WE ARE AT 7:30 PM AND IT'S **FUBAR.**
IT'S NOT A GOOD SIGN WHEN THEY'RE STILL ATTACHING PARTS TO THE SPACE SHUTTLE AT LIFTOFF.
WORSE, THE FEW PARTS OF PHOENIX THAT ARE RUNNING ARE **FAILING CRITICAL TESTS.**
WE'VE HAD SO MANY CRITICAL BUG REPORTS WE HAD TO CALL THE DEVELOPERS BACK INTO WORK.
WE'RE FRANTICALLY WORKING WITH WILLIAM MASON'S QA TEAM TO TRY TO GET PHOENIX TO COME UP IN THE TEST ENVIRONMENT.
IF THEY CAN'T GET THINGS RUNNING IN OUR TEST ENVIRONMENT, WE WON'T HAVE A PRAYER OF DEPLOYING AND RUNNING PHOENIX IN PRODUCTION.

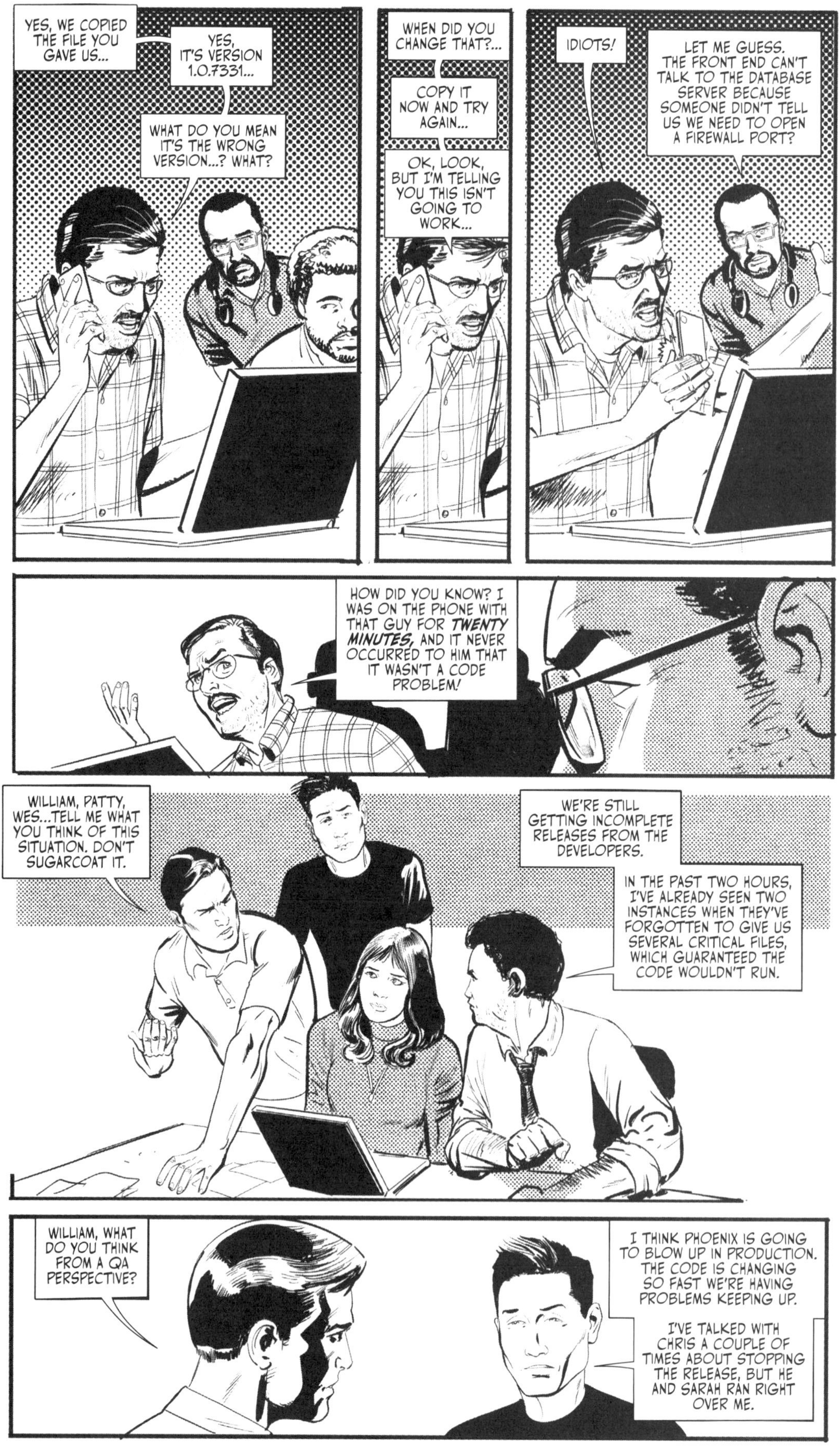
YES, WE COPIED THE FILE YOU GAVE US...
YES, IT'S VERSION 1.0.7331...
WHAT DO YOU MEAN IT'S THE WRONG VERSION...? WHAT?
WHEN DID YOU CHANGE THAT?...
COPY IT NOW AND TRY AGAIN...
OK, LOOK, BUT I'M TELLING YOU THIS ISN'T GOING TO WORK...
IDIOTS!
LET ME GUESS. THE FRONT END CAN'T TALK TO THE DATABASE SERVER BECAUSE SOMEONE DIDN'T TELL US WE NEED TO OPEN A FIREWALL PORT?
HOW DID YOU KNOW? I WAS ON THE PHONE WITH THAT GUY FOR *TWENTY MINUTES,* AND IT NEVER OCCURRED TO HIM THAT IT WASN'T A CODE PROBLEM!
WILLIAM, PATTY, WES...TELL ME WHAT YOU THINK OF THIS SITUATION. DON'T SUGARCOAT IT.
WE'RE STILL GETTING INCOMPLETE RELEASES FROM THE DEVELOPERS.
IN THE PAST TWO HOURS, I'VE ALREADY SEEN TWO INSTANCES WHEN THEY'VE FORGOTTEN TO GIVE US SEVERAL CRITICAL FILES, WHICH GUARANTEED THE CODE WOULDN'T RUN.
WILLIAM, WHAT DO YOU THINK FROM A QA PERSPECTIVE?
I THINK PHOENIX IS GOING TO BLOW UP IN PRODUCTION. THE CODE IS CHANGING SO FAST WE'RE HAVING PROBLEMS KEEPING UP.
I'VE TALKED WITH CHRIS A COUPLE OF TIMES ABOUT STOPPING THE RELEASE, BUT HE AND SARAH RAN RIGHT OVER ME.

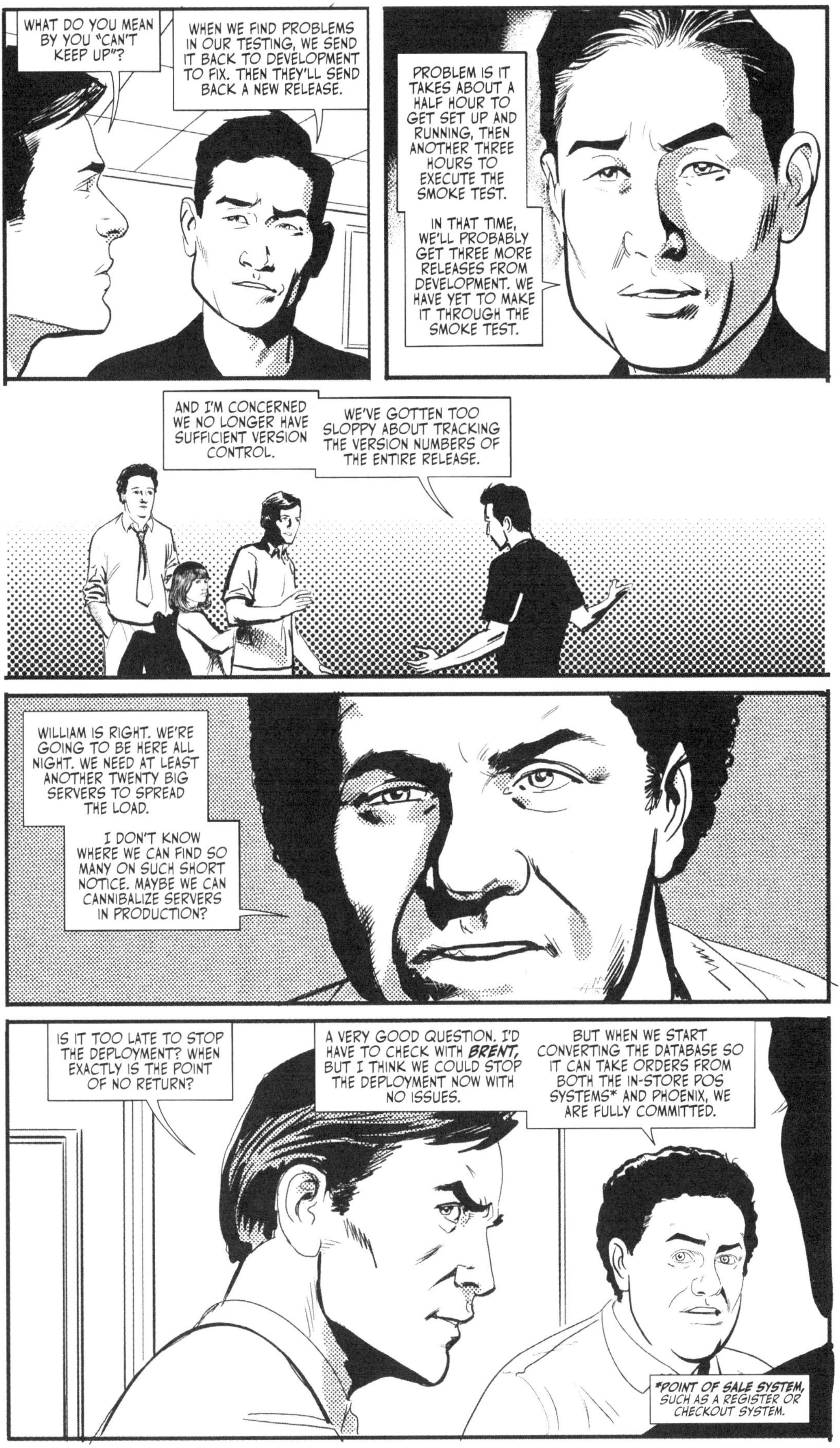
WHAT DO YOU MEAN BY YOU "CAN'T KEEP UP"?
WHEN WE FIND PROBLEMS IN OUR TESTING, WE SEND IT BACK TO DEVELOPMENT TO FIX. THEN THEY'LL SEND BACK A NEW RELEASE.
PROBLEM IS IT TAKES ABOUT A HALF HOUR TO GET SET UP AND RUNNING, THEN ANOTHER THREE HOURS TO EXECUTE THE SMOKE TEST.
IN THAT TIME, WE'LL PROBABLY GET THREE MORE RELEASES FROM DEVELOPMENT. WE HAVE YET TO MAKE IT THROUGH THE SMOKE TEST.
AND I'M CONCERNED WE NO LONGER HAVE SUFFICIENT VERSION CONTROL.
WE'VE GOTTEN TOO SLOPPY ABOUT TRACKING THE VERSION NUMBERS OF THE ENTIRE RELEASE.
WILLIAM IS RIGHT. WE'RE GOING TO BE HERE ALL NIGHT. WE NEED AT LEAST ANOTHER TWENTY BIG SERVERS TO SPREAD THE LOAD.
I DON'T KNOW WHERE WE CAN FIND SO MANY ON SUCH SHORT NOTICE. MAYBE WE CAN CANNIBALIZE SERVERS IN PRODUCTION?
IS IT TOO LATE TO STOP THE DEPLOYMENT? WHEN EXACTLY IS THE POINT OF NO RETURN?
A VERY GOOD QUESTION. I'D HAVE TO CHECK WITH BRENT, BUT I THINK WE COULD STOP THE DEPLOYMENT NOW WITH NO ISSUES.
BUT WHEN WE START CONVERTING THE DATABASE SO IT CAN TAKE ORDERS FROM BOTH THE IN-STORE POS SYSTEMS* AND PHOENIX, WE ARE FULLY COMMITTED.
*POINT OF SALE SYSTEM, SUCH AS A REGISTER OR CHECKOUT SYSTEM.

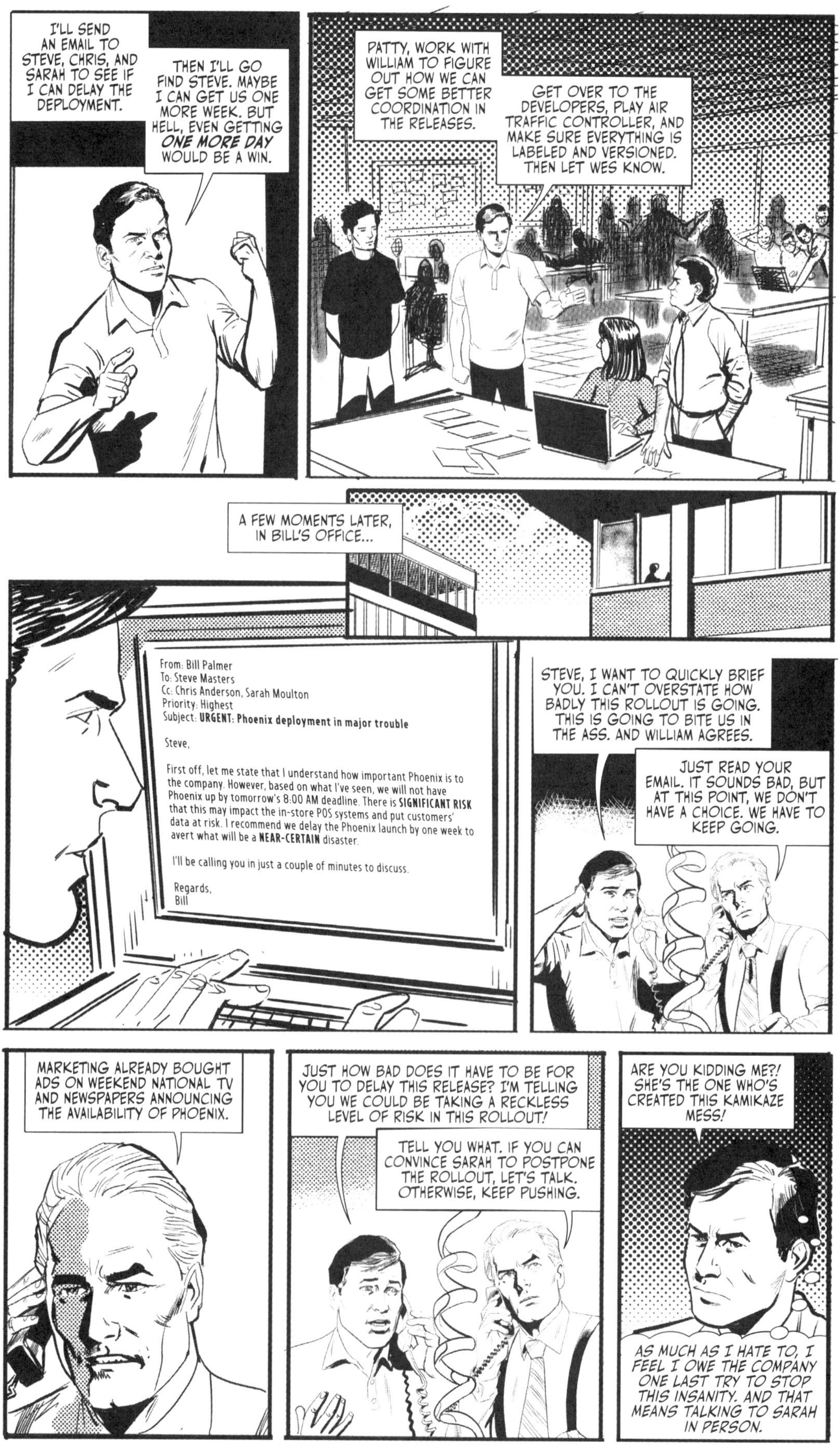

I'LL SEND AN EMAIL TO STEVE, CHRIS, AND SARAH TO SEE IF I CAN DELAY THE DEPLOYMENT.
THEN I'LL GO FIND STEVE. MAYBE I CAN GET US ONE MORE WEEK. BUT HELL, EVEN GETTING ONE MORE DAY WOULD BE A WIN.
PATTY, WORK WITH WILLIAM TO FIGURE OUT HOW WE CAN GET SOME BETTER COORDINATION IN THE RELEASES.
GET OVER TO THE DEVELOPERS, PLAY AIR TRAFFIC CONTROLLER, AND MAKE SURE EVERYTHING IS LABELED AND VERSIONED. THEN LET WES KNOW.
A FEW MOMENTS LATER, IN BILL'S OFFICE...
From: Bill Palmer
To: Steve Masters
Cc: Chris Anderson, Sarah Moulton
Priority: Highest
Subject: URGENT: Phoenix deployment in major trouble
Steve,
First off, let me state that I understand how important Phoenix is to the company. However, based on what I've seen, we will not have Phoenix up by tomorrow's 8:00 AM deadline. There is SIGNIFICANT RISK that this may impact the in-store POS systems and put customers' data at risk. I recommend we delay the Phoenix launch by one week to avert what will be a NEAR-CERTAIN disaster.
I'll be calling you in just a couple of minutes to discuss.
Regards,
Bill
STEVE, I WANT TO QUICKLY BRIEF YOU. I CAN'T OVERSTATE HOW BADLY THIS ROLLOUT IS GOING. THIS IS GOING TO BITE US IN THE ASS. AND WILLIAM AGREES.
JUST READ YOUR EMAIL. IT SOUNDS BAD, BUT AT THIS POINT, WE DON'T HAVE A CHOICE. WE HAVE TO KEEP GOING.
MARKETING ALREADY BOUGHT ADS ON WEEKEND NATIONAL TV AND NEWSPAPERS ANNOUNCING THE AVAILABILITY OF PHOENIX.
JUST HOW BAD DOES IT HAVE TO BE FOR YOU TO DELAY THIS RELEASE? I'M TELLING YOU WE COULD BE TAKING A RECKLESS LEVEL OF RISK IN THIS ROLLOUT!
TELL YOU WHAT. IF YOU CAN CONVINCE SARAH TO POSTPONE THE ROLLOUT, LET'S TALK. OTHERWISE, KEEP PUSHING.
ARE YOU KIDDING ME?! SHE'S THE ONE WHO'S CREATED THIS KAMIKAZE MESS!
AS MUCH AS I HATE TO, I FEEL I OWE THE COMPANY ONE LAST TRY TO STOP THIS INSANITY. AND THAT MEANS TALKING TO SARAH IN PERSON.

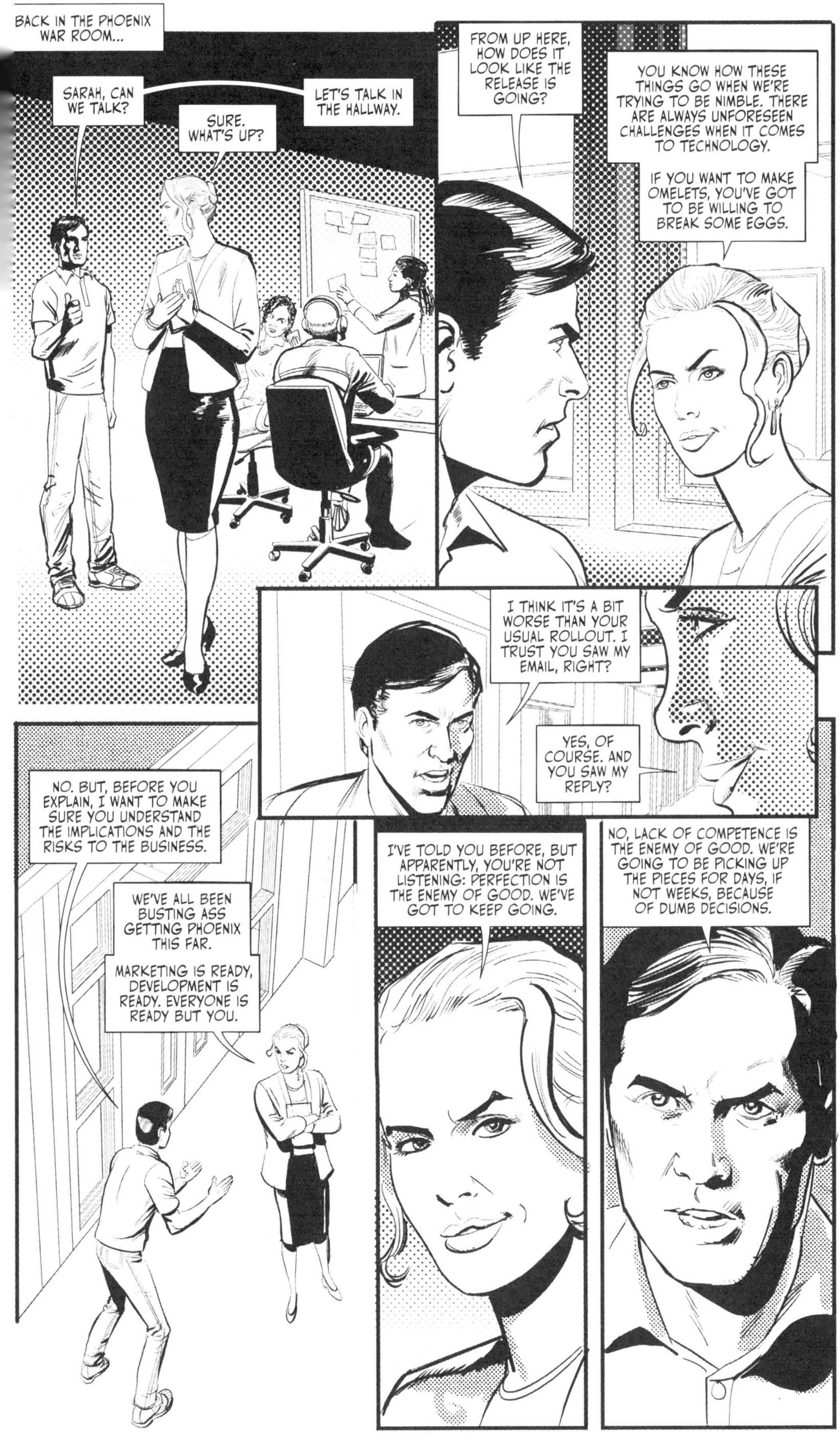

BACK IN THE PHOENIX WAR ROOM...
SARAH, CAN WE TALK?
SURE. WHAT'S UP?
LET'S TALK IN THE HALLWAY.
FROM UP HERE, HOW DOES IT LOOK LIKE THE RELEASE IS GOING?
YOU KNOW HOW THESE THINGS GO WHEN WE'RE TRYING TO BE NIMBLE. THERE ARE ALWAYS UNFORESEEN CHALLENGES WHEN IT COMES TO TECHNOLOGY.
IF YOU WANT TO MAKE OMELETS, YOU'VE GOT TO BE WILLING TO BREAK SOME EGGS.
I THINK IT'S A BIT WORSE THAN YOUR USUAL ROLLOUT. I TRUST YOU SAW MY EMAIL, RIGHT?
YES, OF COURSE. AND YOU SAW MY REPLY?
NO. BUT, BEFORE YOU EXPLAIN, I WANT TO MAKE SURE YOU UNDERSTAND THE IMPLICATIONS AND THE RISKS TO THE BUSINESS.
WE'VE ALL BEEN BUSTING ASS GETTING PHOENIX THIS FAR.
MARKETING IS READY, DEVELOPMENT IS READY. EVERYONE IS READY BUT YOU.
I'VE TOLD YOU BEFORE, BUT APPARENTLY, YOU'RE NOT LISTENING: PERFECTION IS THE ENEMY OF GOOD. WE'VE GOT TO KEEP GOING.
NO, LACK OF COMPETENCE IS THE ENEMY OF GOOD. WE'RE GOING TO BE PICKING UP THE PIECES FOR DAYS, IF NOT WEEKS, BECAUSE OF DUMB DECISIONS.

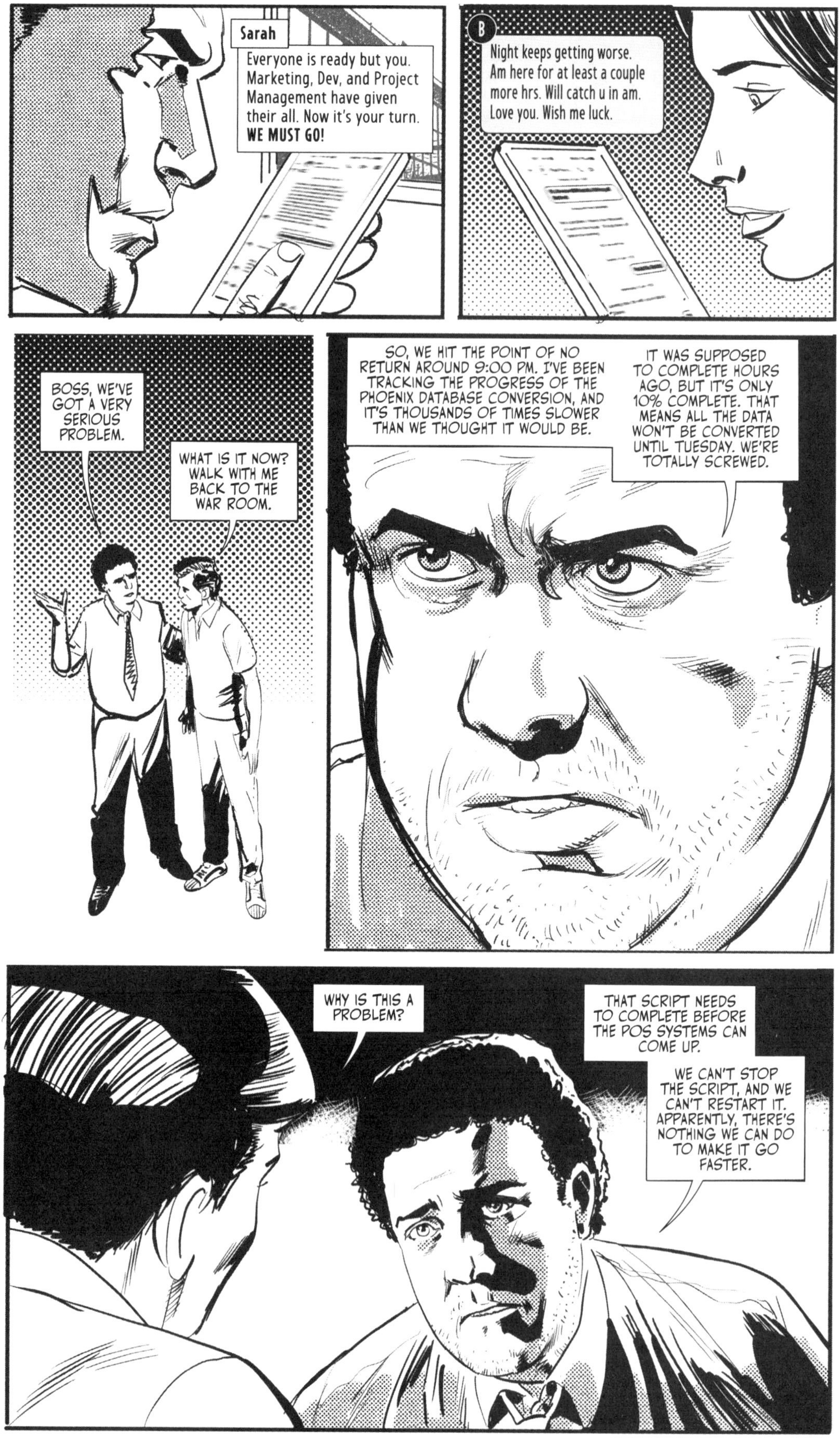
Sarah
Everyone is ready but you. Marketing, Dev, and Project Management have given their all. Now it's your turn. **WE MUST GO!**
B
Night keeps getting worse. Am here for at least a couple more hrs. Will catch u in am. Love you. Wish me luck.
BOSS, WE'VE GOT A VERY SERIOUS PROBLEM.
WHAT IS IT NOW? WALK WITH ME BACK TO THE WAR ROOM.
SO, WE HIT THE POINT OF NO RETURN AROUND 9:00 PM. I'VE BEEN TRACKING THE PROGRESS OF THE PHOENIX DATABASE CONVERSION, AND IT'S THOUSANDS OF TIMES SLOWER THAN WE THOUGHT IT WOULD BE.
IT WAS SUPPOSED TO COMPLETE HOURS AGO, BUT IT'S ONLY 10% COMPLETE. THAT MEANS ALL THE DATA WON'T BE CONVERTED UNTIL TUESDAY. WE'RE TOTALLY SCREWED.
WHY IS THIS A PROBLEM?
THAT SCRIPT NEEDS TO COMPLETE BEFORE THE POS SYSTEMS CAN COME UP.
WE CAN'T STOP THE SCRIPT, AND WE CAN'T RESTART IT. APPARENTLY, THERE'S NOTHING WE CAN DO TO MAKE IT GO FASTER.

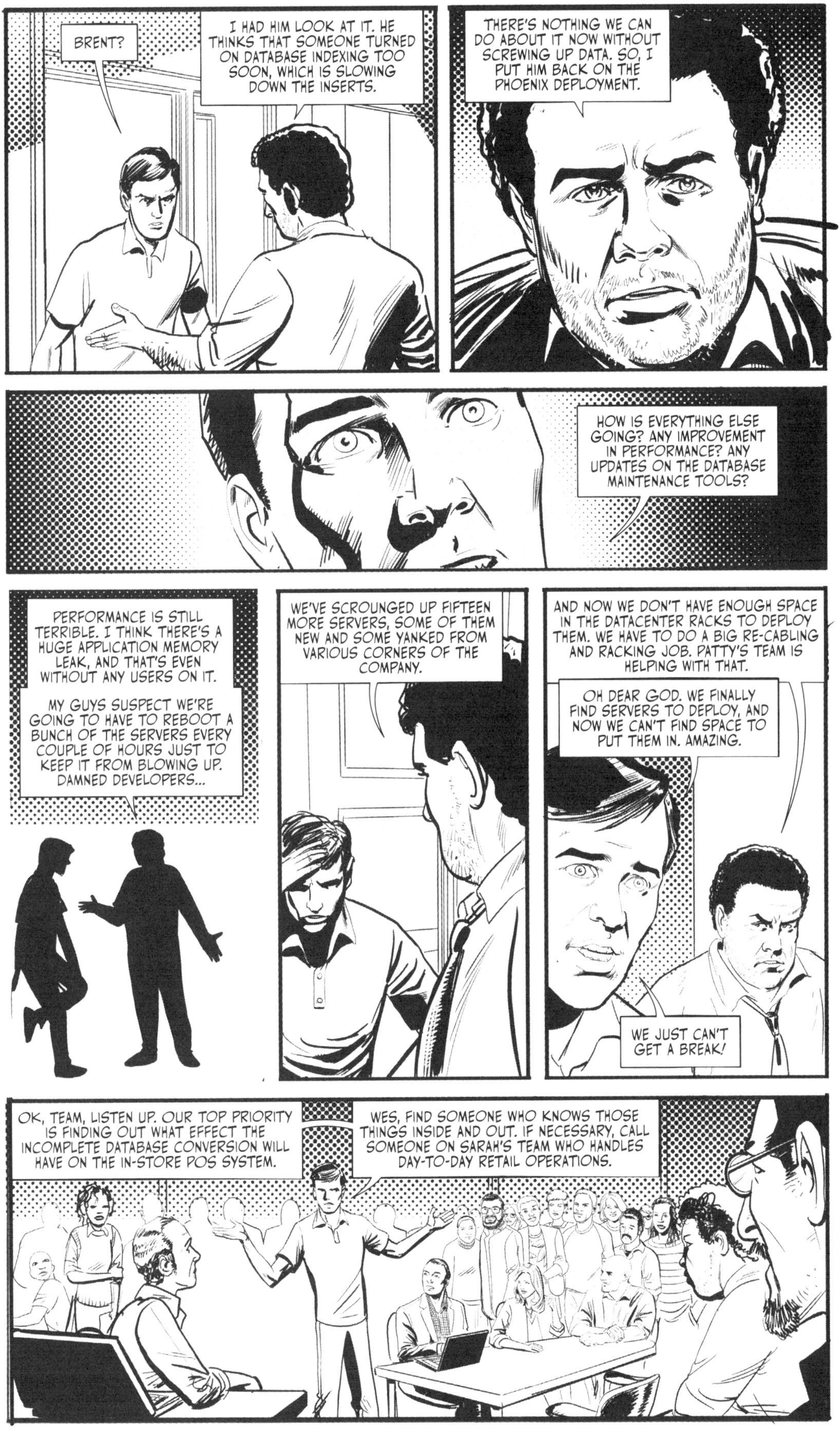
BRENT?
I HAD HIM LOOK AT IT. HE THINKS THAT SOMEONE TURNED ON DATABASE INDEXING TOO SOON, WHICH IS SLOWING DOWN THE INSERTS.
THERE'S NOTHING WE CAN DO ABOUT IT NOW WITHOUT SCREWING UP DATA. SO, I PUT HIM BACK ON THE PHOENIX DEPLOYMENT.
HOW IS EVERYTHING ELSE GOING? ANY IMPROVEMENT IN PERFORMANCE? ANY UPDATES ON THE DATABASE MAINTENANCE TOOLS?
PERFORMANCE IS STILL TERRIBLE. I THINK THERE'S A HUGE APPLICATION MEMORY LEAK, AND THAT'S EVEN WITHOUT ANY USERS ON IT.
MY GUYS SUSPECT WE'RE GOING TO HAVE TO REBOOT A BUNCH OF THE SERVERS EVERY COUPLE OF HOURS JUST TO KEEP IT FROM BLOWING UP. DAMNED DEVELOPERS...
WE'VE SCROUNGED UP FIFTEEN MORE SERVERS, SOME OF THEM NEW AND SOME YANKED FROM VARIOUS CORNERS OF THE COMPANY.
AND NOW WE DON'T HAVE ENOUGH SPACE IN THE DATACENTER RACKS TO DEPLOY THEM. WE HAVE TO DO A BIG RE-CABLING AND RACKING JOB. PATTY'S TEAM IS HELPING WITH THAT.
OH DEAR GOD. WE FINALLY FIND SERVERS TO DEPLOY, AND NOW WE CAN'T FIND SPACE TO PUT THEM IN. AMAZING.
WE JUST CAN'T GET A BREAK!
OK, TEAM, LISTEN UP. OUR TOP PRIORITY IS FINDING OUT WHAT EFFECT THE INCOMPLETE DATABASE CONVERSION WILL HAVE ON THE IN-STORE POS SYSTEM.
WES, FIND SOMEONE WHO KNOWS THOSE THINGS INSIDE AND OUT. IF NECESSARY, CALL SOMEONE ON SARAH'S TEAM WHO HANDLES DAY-TO-DAY RETAIL OPERATIONS.

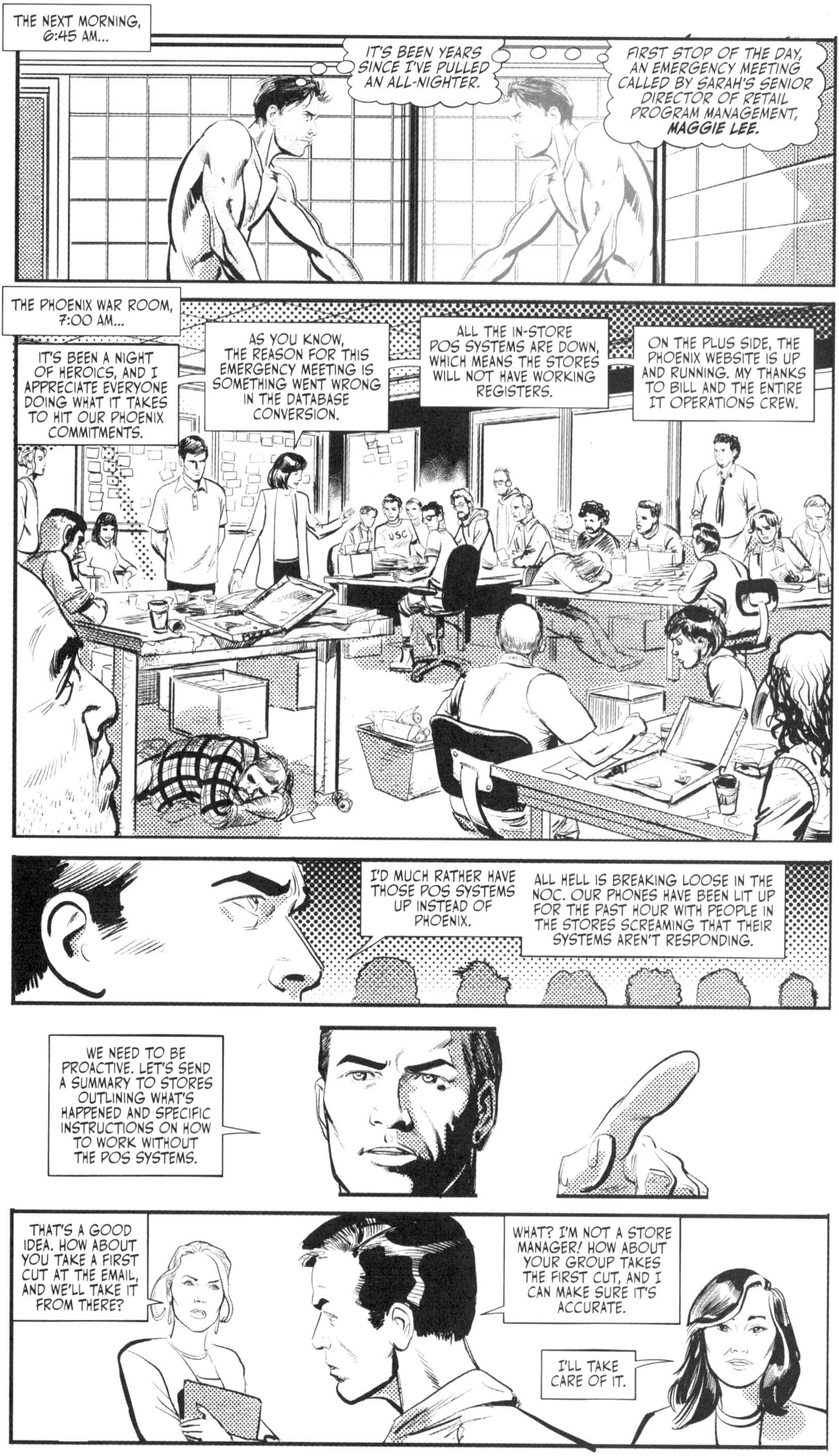
THE NEXT MORNING, 6:45 AM...
IT'S BEEN YEARS SINCE I'VE PULLED AN ALL-NIGHTER.
FIRST STOP OF THE DAY, AN EMERGENCY MEETING CALLED BY SARAH'S SENIOR DIRECTOR OF RETAIL PROGRAM MANAGEMENT, MAGGIE LEE.
THE PHOENIX WAR ROOM, 7:00 AM...
IT'S BEEN A NIGHT OF HEROICS, AND I APPRECIATE EVERYONE DOING WHAT IT TAKES TO HIT OUR PHOENIX COMMITMENTS.
AS YOU KNOW, THE REASON FOR THIS EMERGENCY MEETING IS SOMETHING WENT WRONG IN THE DATABASE CONVERSION.
ALL THE IN-STORE POS SYSTEMS ARE DOWN, WHICH MEANS THE STORES WILL NOT HAVE WORKING REGISTERS.
ON THE PLUS SIDE, THE PHOENIX WEBSITE IS UP AND RUNNING. MY THANKS TO BILL AND THE ENTIRE IT OPERATIONS CREW.
USC
I'D MUCH RATHER HAVE THOSE POS SYSTEMS UP INSTEAD OF PHOENIX.
ALL HELL IS BREAKING LOOSE IN THE NOC. OUR PHONES HAVE BEEN LIT UP FOR THE PAST HOUR WITH PEOPLE IN THE STORES SCREAMING THAT THEIR SYSTEMS AREN'T RESPONDING.
WE NEED TO BE PROACTIVE. LET'S SEND A SUMMARY TO STORES OUTLINING WHAT'S HAPPENED AND SPECIFIC INSTRUCTIONS ON HOW TO WORK WITHOUT THE POS SYSTEMS.
THAT'S A GOOD IDEA. HOW ABOUT YOU TAKE A FIRST CUT AT THE EMAIL, AND WE'LL TAKE IT FROM THERE?
WHAT? I'M NOT A STORE MANAGER! HOW ABOUT YOUR GROUP TAKES THE FIRST CUT, AND I CAN MAKE SURE IT'S ACCURATE.
I'LL TAKE CARE OF IT.

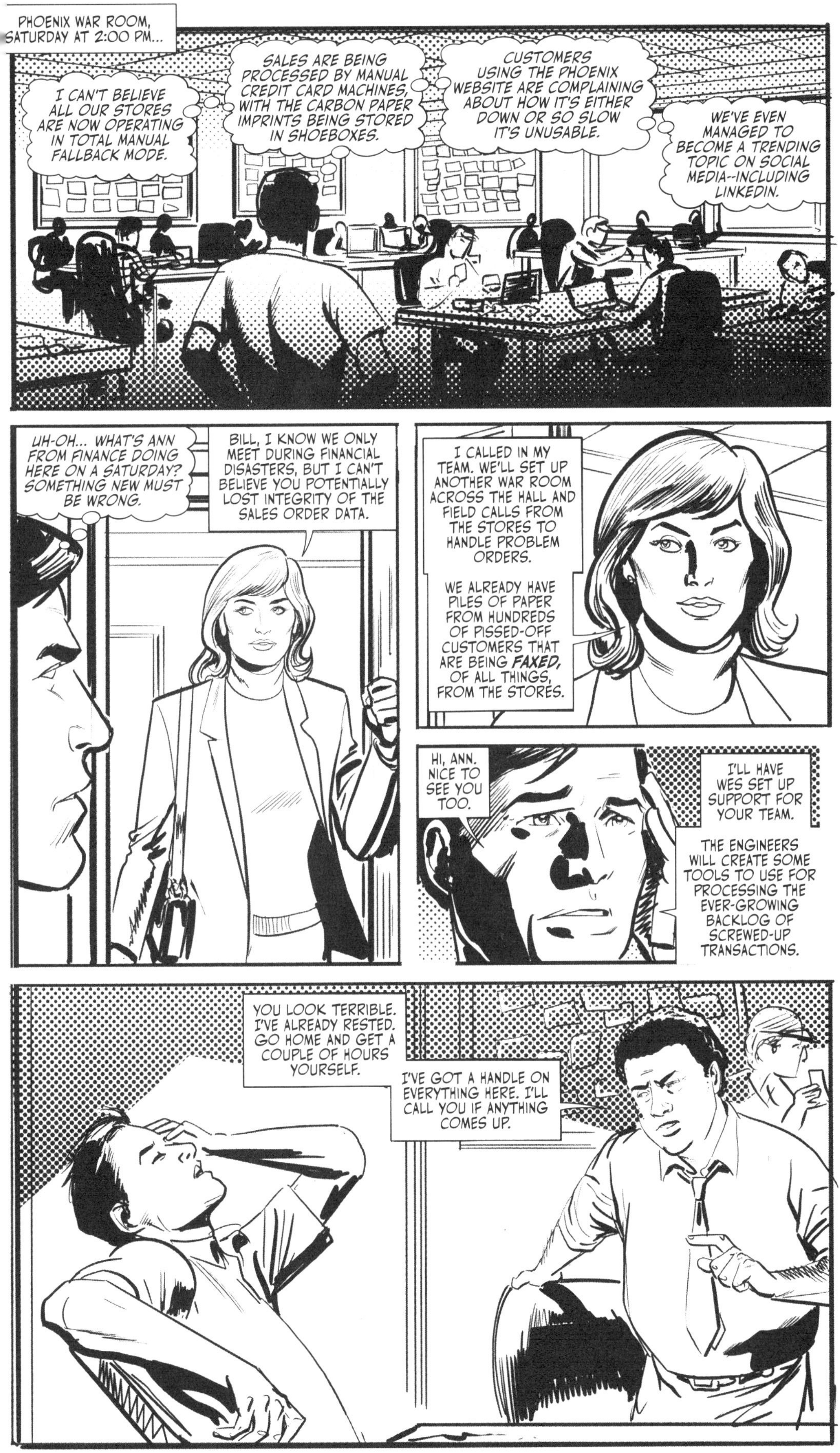

PHOENIX WAR ROOM, SATURDAY AT 2:00 PM...
I CAN'T BELIEVE ALL OUR STORES ARE NOW OPERATING IN TOTAL MANUAL FALLBACK MODE.
SALES ARE BEING PROCESSED BY MANUAL CREDIT CARD MACHINES, WITH THE CARBON PAPER IMPRINTS BEING STORED IN SHOEBOXES.
CUSTOMERS USING THE PHOENIX WEBSITE ARE COMPLAINING ABOUT HOW IT'S EITHER DOWN OR SO SLOW IT'S UNUSABLE.
WE'VE EVEN MANAGED TO BECOME A TRENDING TOPIC ON SOCIAL MEDIA--INCLUDING LINKEDIN.
UH-OH... WHAT'S ANN FROM FINANCE DOING HERE ON A SATURDAY? SOMETHING NEW MUST BE WRONG.
BILL, I KNOW WE ONLY MEET DURING FINANCIAL DISASTERS, BUT I CAN'T BELIEVE YOU POTENTIALLY LOST INTEGRITY OF THE SALES ORDER DATA.
I CALLED IN MY TEAM. WE'LL SET UP ANOTHER WAR ROOM ACROSS THE HALL AND FIELD CALLS FROM THE STORES TO HANDLE PROBLEM ORDERS.
WE ALREADY HAVE PILES OF PAPER FROM HUNDREDS OF PISSED-OFF CUSTOMERS THAT ARE BEING *FAXED,* OF ALL THINGS, FROM THE STORES.
HI, ANN. NICE TO SEE YOU TOO.
I'LL HAVE WES SET UP SUPPORT FOR YOUR TEAM.
THE ENGINEERS WILL CREATE SOME TOOLS TO USE FOR PROCESSING THE EVER-GROWING BACKLOG OF SCREWED-UP TRANSACTIONS.
YOU LOOK TERRIBLE. I'VE ALREADY RESTED. GO HOME AND GET A COUPLE OF HOURS YOURSELF.
I'VE GOT A HANDLE ON EVERYTHING HERE. I'LL CALL YOU IF ANYTHING COMES UP.

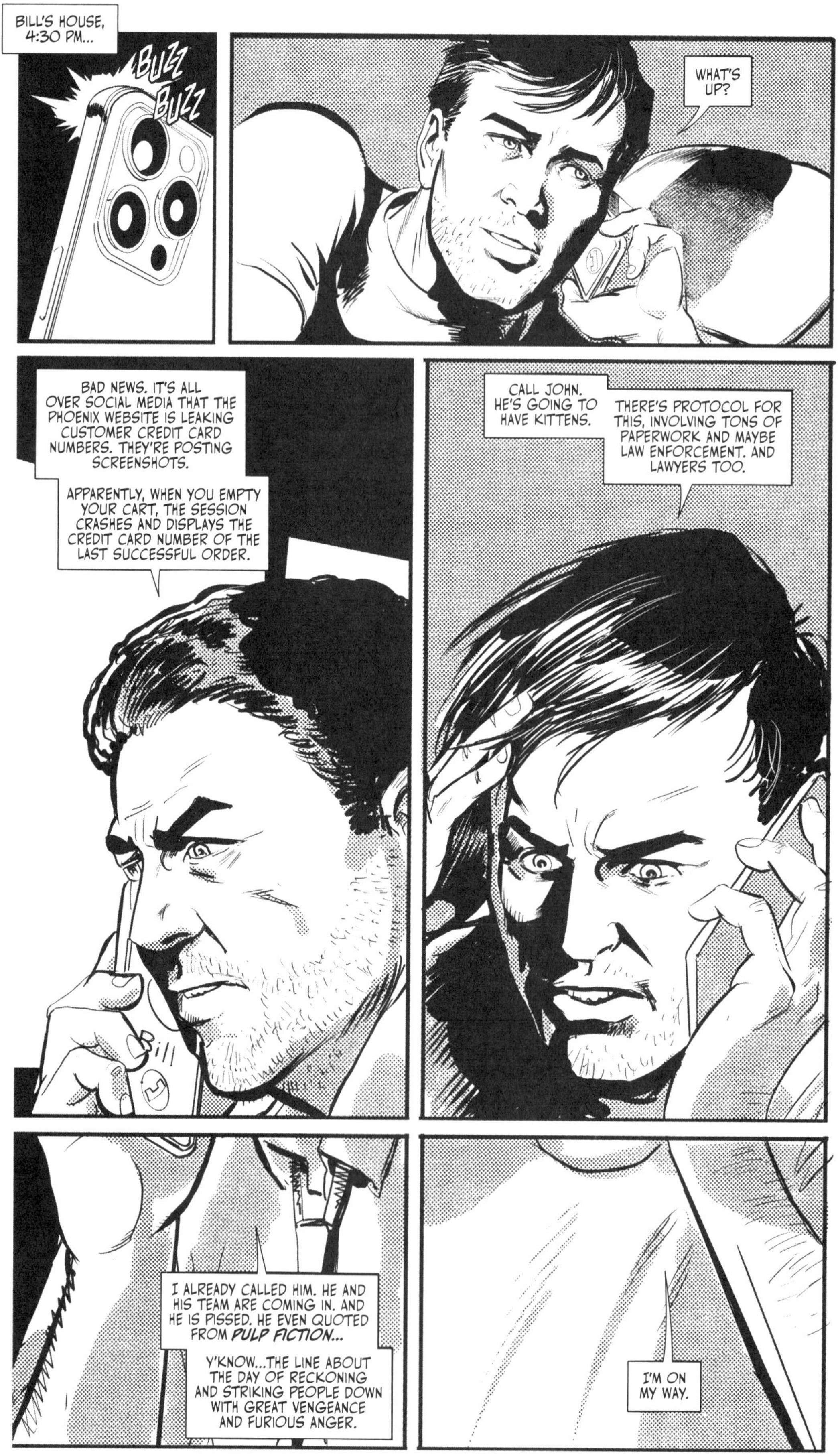
BILL'S HOUSE, 4:30 PM...
BUZZ BUZZ
WHAT'S UP?
BAD NEWS. IT'S ALL OVER SOCIAL MEDIA THAT THE PHOENIX WEBSITE IS LEAKING CUSTOMER CREDIT CARD NUMBERS. THEY'RE POSTING SCREENSHOTS.
APPARENTLY, WHEN YOU EMPTY YOUR CART, THE SESSION CRASHES AND DISPLAYS THE CREDIT CARD NUMBER OF THE LAST SUCCESSFUL ORDER.
CALL JOHN. HE'S GOING TO HAVE KITTENS.
THERE'S PROTOCOL FOR THIS, INVOLVING TONS OF PAPERWORK AND MAYBE LAW ENFORCEMENT. AND LAWYERS TOO.
I ALREADY CALLED HIM. HE AND HIS TEAM ARE COMING IN. AND HE IS PISSED. HE EVEN QUOTED FROM PULP FICTION...
Y'KNOW...THE LINE ABOUT THE DAY OF RECKONING AND STRIKING PEOPLE DOWN WITH GREAT VENGEANCE AND FURIOUS ANGER.
I'M ON MY WAY.

CHAPTER 13 MONDAY, SEPTEMBER 15

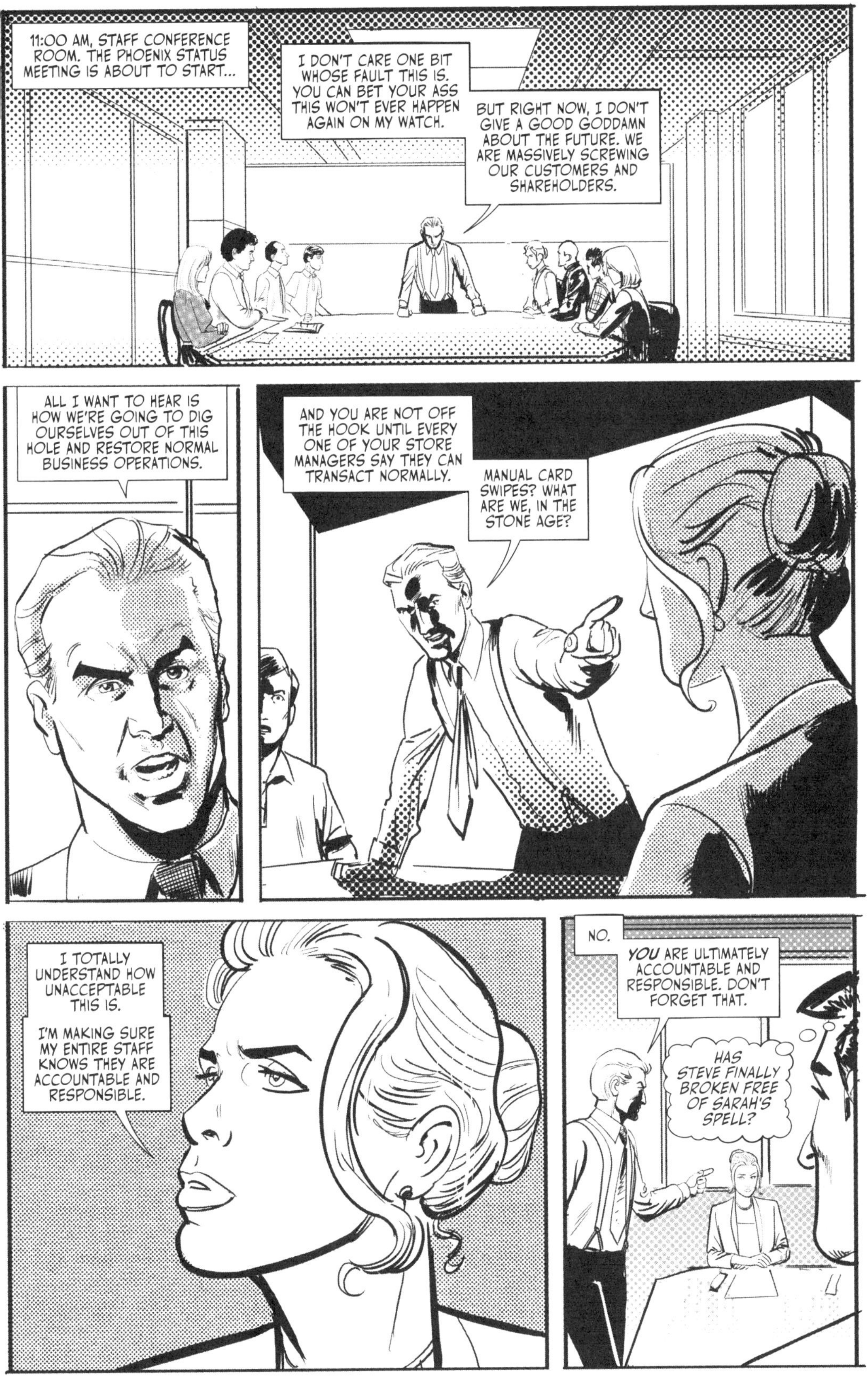

11:00 AM, STAFF CONFERENCE ROOM. THE PHOENIX STATUS MEETING IS ABOUT TO START...
I DON'T CARE ONE BIT WHOSE FAULT THIS IS. YOU CAN BET YOUR ASS THIS WON'T EVER HAPPEN AGAIN ON MY WATCH.
BUT RIGHT NOW, I DON'T GIVE A GOOD GODDAMN ABOUT THE FUTURE. WE ARE MASSIVELY SCREWING OUR CUSTOMERS AND SHAREHOLDERS.
ALL I WANT TO HEAR IS HOW WE'RE GOING TO DIG OURSELVES OUT OF THIS HOLE AND RESTORE NORMAL BUSINESS OPERATIONS.
AND YOU ARE NOT OFF THE HOOK UNTIL EVERY ONE OF YOUR STORE MANAGERS SAY THEY CAN TRANSACT NORMALLY.
MANUAL CARD SWIPES? WHAT ARE WE, IN THE STONE AGE?
I TOTALLY UNDERSTAND HOW UNACCEPTABLE THIS IS.
I'M MAKING SURE MY ENTIRE STAFF KNOWS THEY ARE ACCOUNTABLE AND RESPONSIBLE.
NO.
YOU ARE ULTIMATELY ACCOUNTABLE AND RESPONSIBLE. DON'T FORGET THAT.
HAS STEVE FINALLY BROKEN FREE OF SARAH'S SPELL?

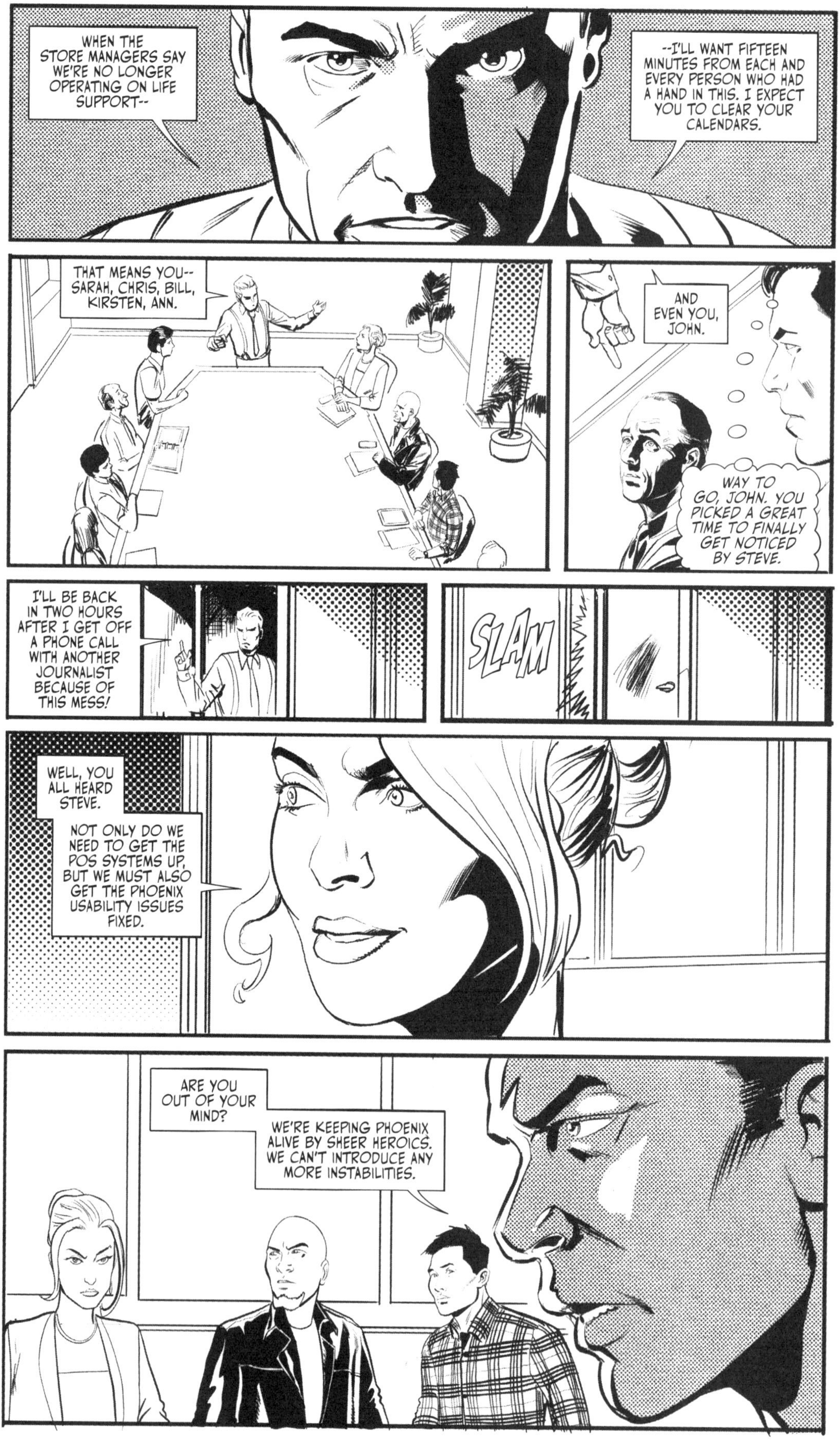

WHEN THE STORE MANAGERS SAY WE'RE NO LONGER OPERATING ON LIFE SUPPORT--
--I'LL WANT FIFTEEN MINUTES FROM EACH AND EVERY PERSON WHO HAD A HAND IN THIS. I EXPECT YOU TO CLEAR YOUR CALENDARS.
THAT MEANS YOU-- SARAH, CHRIS, BILL, KIRSTEN, ANN.
AND EVEN YOU, JOHN.
WAY TO GO, JOHN. YOU PICKED A GREAT TIME TO FINALLY GET NOTICED BY STEVE.
I'LL BE BACK IN TWO HOURS AFTER I GET OFF A PHONE CALL WITH ANOTHER JOURNALIST BECAUSE OF THIS MESS!
SLAM
WELL, YOU ALL HEARD STEVE.
NOT ONLY DO WE NEED TO GET THE POS SYSTEMS UP, BUT WE MUST ALSO GET THE PHOENIX USABILITY ISSUES FIXED.
ARE YOU OUT OF YOUR MIND?
WE'RE KEEPING PHOENIX ALIVE BY SHEER HEROICS. WE CAN'T INTRODUCE ANY MORE INSTABILITIES.

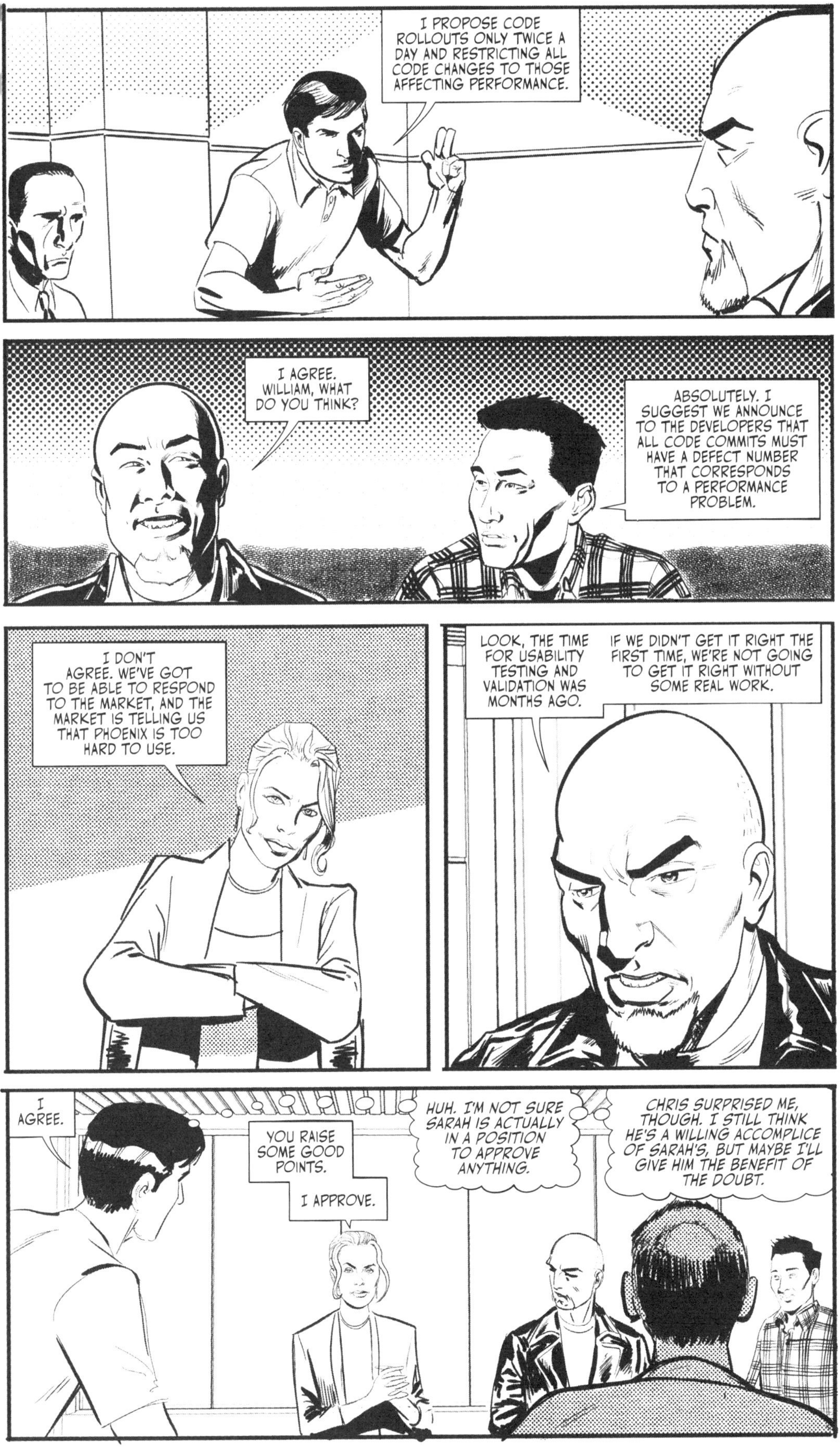
I PROPOSE CODE ROLLOUTS ONLY TWICE A DAY AND RESTRICTING ALL CODE CHANGES TO THOSE AFFECTING PERFORMANCE.
I AGREE. WILLIAM, WHAT DO YOU THINK?
ABSOLUTELY. I SUGGEST WE ANNOUNCE TO THE DEVELOPERS THAT ALL CODE COMMITS MUST HAVE A DEFECT NUMBER THAT CORRESPONDS TO A PERFORMANCE PROBLEM.
I DON'T AGREE. WE'VE GOT TO BE ABLE TO RESPOND TO THE MARKET, AND THE MARKET IS TELLING US THAT PHOENIX IS TOO HARD TO USE.
LOOK, THE TIME FOR USABILITY TESTING AND VALIDATION WAS MONTHS AGO.
IF WE DIDN'T GET IT RIGHT THE FIRST TIME, WE'RE NOT GOING TO GET IT RIGHT WITHOUT SOME REAL WORK.
I AGREE.
YOU RAISE SOME GOOD POINTS.
I APPROVE.
HUH. I'M NOT SURE SARAH IS ACTUALLY IN A POSITION TO APPROVE ANYTHING.
CHRIS SURPRISED ME, THOUGH. I STILL THINK HE'S A WILLING ACCOMPLICE OF SARAH'S, BUT MAYBE I'LL GIVE HIM THE BENEFIT OF THE DOUBT.

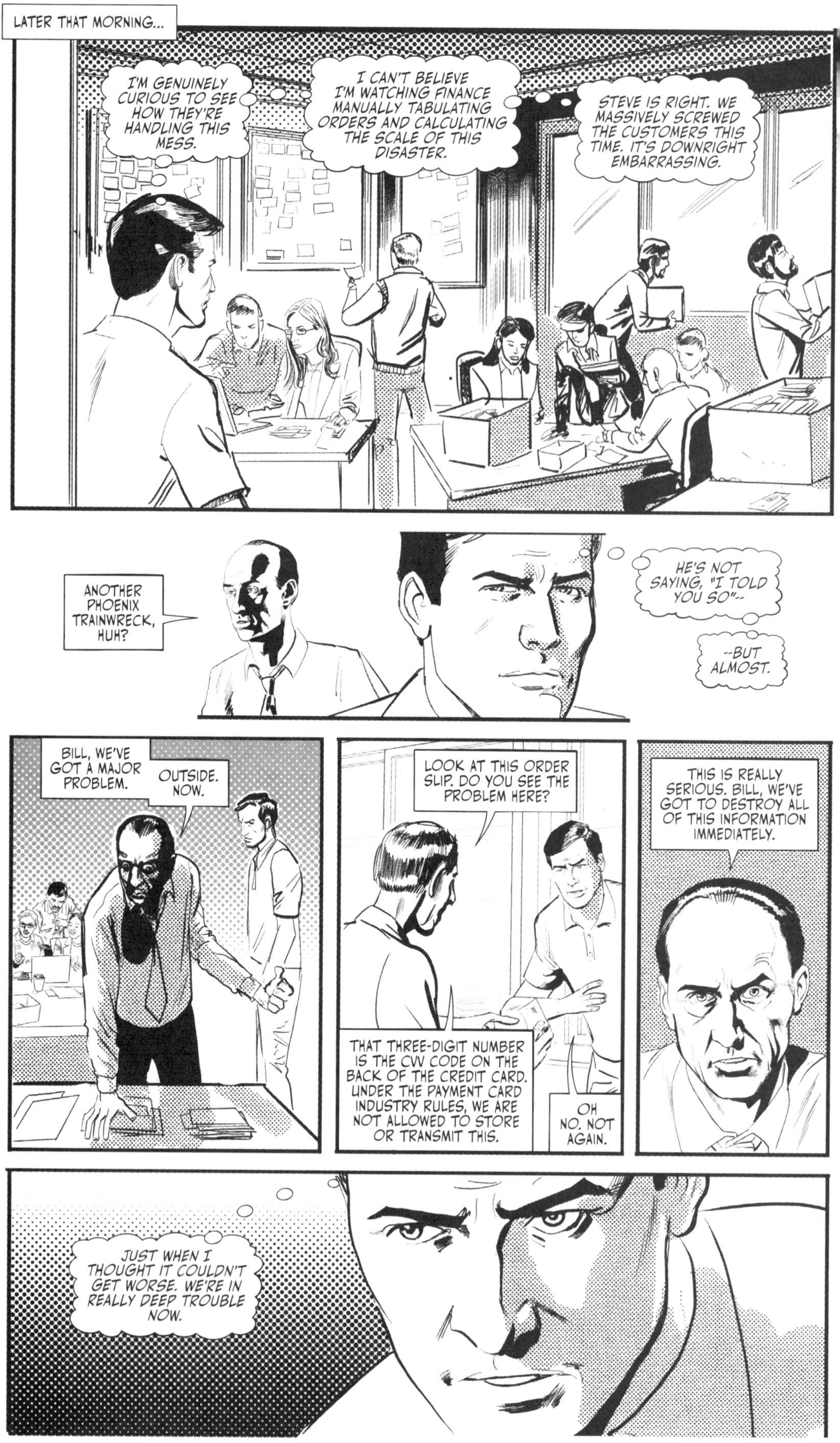
LATER THAT MORNING...
I'M GENUINELY CURIOUS TO SEE HOW THEY'RE HANDLING THIS MESS.
I CAN'T BELIEVE I'M WATCHING FINANCE MANUALLY TABULATING ORDERS AND CALCULATING THE SCALE OF THIS DISASTER.
STEVE IS RIGHT. WE MASSIVELY SCREWED THE CUSTOMERS THIS TIME. IT'S DOWNRIGHT EMBARRASSING.
ANOTHER PHOENIX TRAINWRECK, HUH?
HE'S NOT SAYING, "I TOLD YOU SO"--
--BUT ALMOST.
BILL, WE'VE GOT A MAJOR PROBLEM.
OUTSIDE. NOW.
LOOK AT THIS ORDER SLIP. DO YOU SEE THE PROBLEM HERE?
THAT THREE-DIGIT NUMBER IS THE CVV CODE ON THE BACK OF THE CREDIT CARD. UNDER THE PAYMENT CARD INDUSTRY RULES, WE ARE NOT ALLOWED TO STORE OR TRANSMIT THIS.
OH NO. NOT AGAIN.
THIS IS REALLY SERIOUS. BILL, WE'VE GOT TO DESTROY ALL OF THIS INFORMATION IMMEDIATELY.
JUST WHEN I THOUGHT IT COULDN'T GET WORSE. WE'RE IN REALLY DEEP TROUBLE NOW.

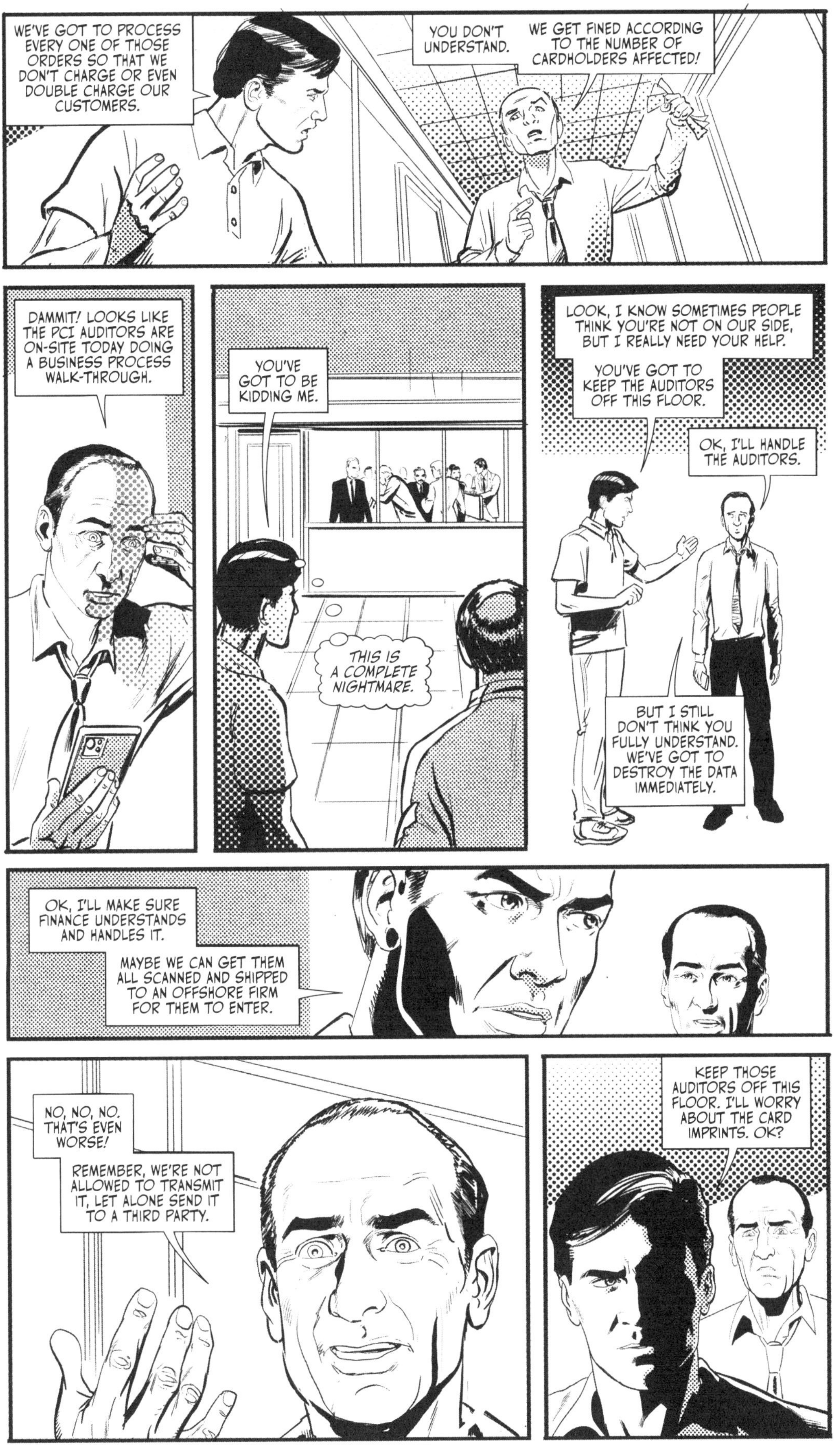
WE'VE GOT TO PROCESS EVERY ONE OF THOSE ORDERS SO THAT WE DON'T CHARGE OR EVEN DOUBLE CHARGE OUR CUSTOMERS.
YOU DON'T UNDERSTAND.
WE GET FINED ACCORDING TO THE NUMBER OF CARDHOLDERS AFFECTED!
DAMMIT! LOOKS LIKE THE PCI AUDITORS ARE ON-SITE TODAY DOING A BUSINESS PROCESS WALK-THROUGH.
YOU'VE GOT TO BE KIDDING ME.
THIS IS A COMPLETE NIGHTMARE.
LOOK, I KNOW SOMETIMES PEOPLE THINK YOU'RE NOT ON OUR SIDE, BUT I REALLY NEED YOUR HELP.
YOU'VE GOT TO KEEP THE AUDITORS OFF THIS FLOOR.
OK, I'LL HANDLE THE AUDITORS.
BUT I STILL DON'T THINK YOU FULLY UNDERSTAND. WE'VE GOT TO DESTROY THE DATA IMMEDIATELY.
OK, I'LL MAKE SURE FINANCE UNDERSTANDS AND HANDLES IT.
MAYBE WE CAN GET THEM ALL SCANNED AND SHIPPED TO AN OFFSHORE FIRM FOR THEM TO ENTER.
NO, NO, NO. THAT'S EVEN WORSE!
REMEMBER, WE'RE NOT ALLOWED TO TRANSMIT IT, LET ALONE SEND IT TO A THIRD PARTY.
KEEP THOSE AUDITORS OFF THIS FLOOR. I'LL WORRY ABOUT THE CARD IMPRINTS. OK?

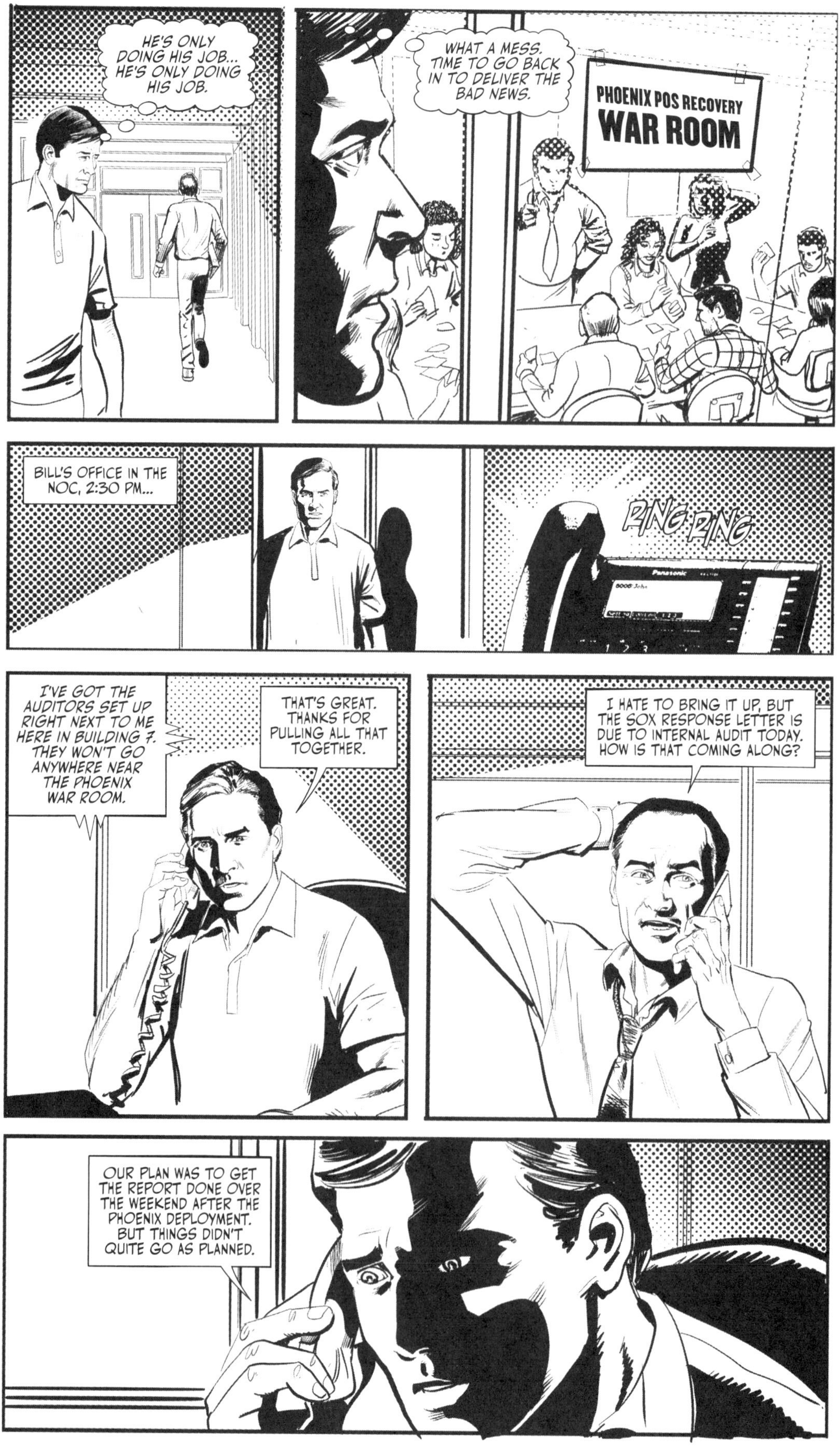
HE'S ONLY DOING HIS JOB... HE'S ONLY DOING HIS JOB.
WHAT A MESS. TIME TO GO BACK IN TO DELIVER THE BAD NEWS.
PHOENIX POS RECOVERY WAR ROOM
BILL'S OFFICE IN THE NOC, 2:30 PM...
RING RING
I'VE GOT THE AUDITORS SET UP RIGHT NEXT TO ME HERE IN BUILDING 7. THEY WON'T GO ANYWHERE NEAR THE PHOENIX WAR ROOM.
THAT'S GREAT. THANKS FOR PULLING ALL THAT TOGETHER.
I HATE TO BRING IT UP, BUT THE SOX RESPONSE LETTER IS DUE TO INTERNAL AUDIT TODAY. HOW IS THAT COMING ALONG?
OUR PLAN WAS TO GET THE REPORT DONE OVER THE WEEKEND AFTER THE PHOENIX DEPLOYMENT. BUT THINGS DIDN'T QUITE GO AS PLANNED.

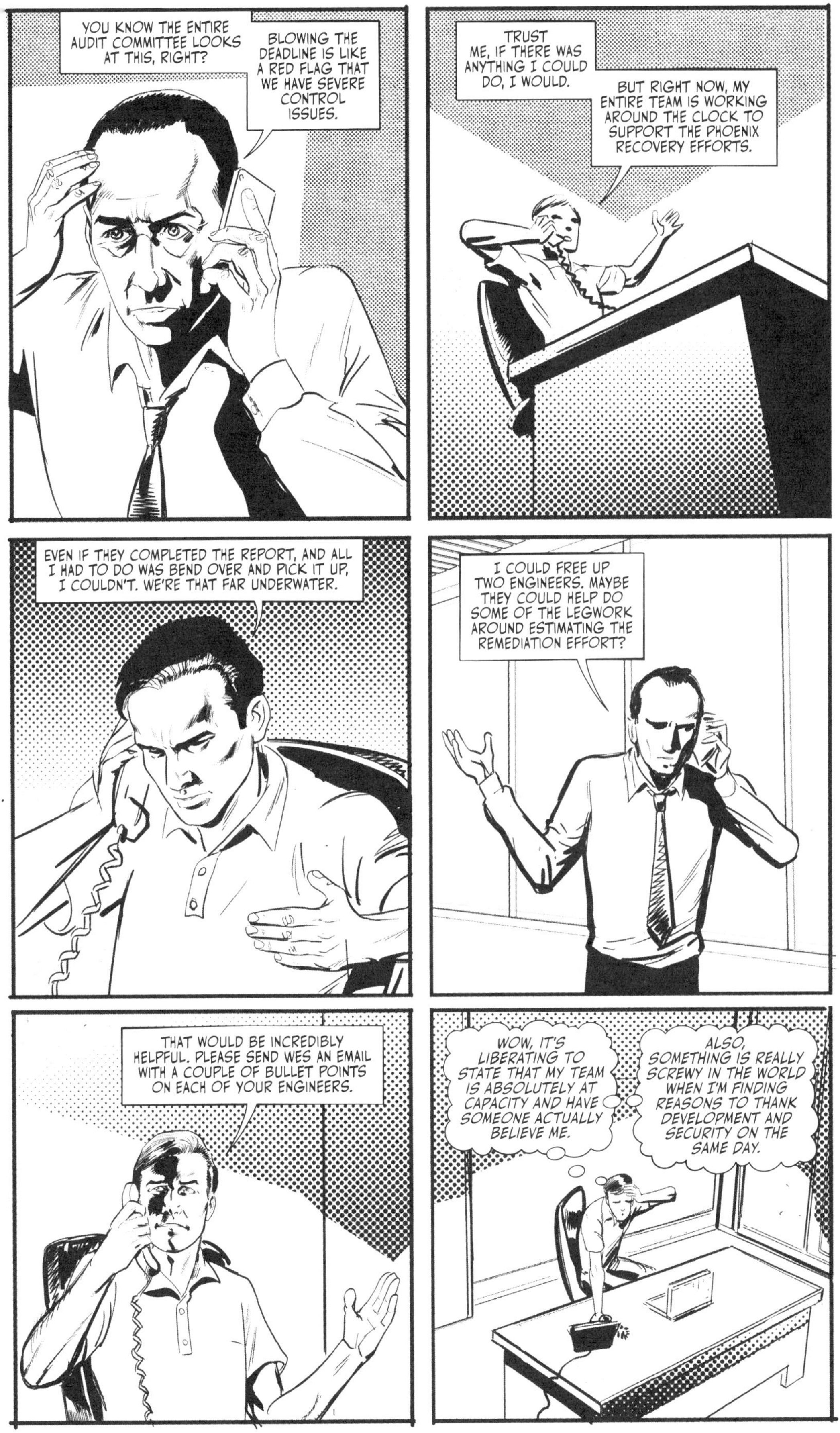
YOU KNOW THE ENTIRE AUDIT COMMITTEE LOOKS AT THIS, RIGHT?
BLOWING THE DEADLINE IS LIKE A RED FLAG THAT WE HAVE SEVERE CONTROL ISSUES.
TRUST ME, IF THERE WAS ANYTHING I COULD DO, I WOULD.
BUT RIGHT NOW, MY ENTIRE TEAM IS WORKING AROUND THE CLOCK TO SUPPORT THE PHOENIX RECOVERY EFFORTS.
EVEN IF THEY COMPLETED THE REPORT, AND ALL I HAD TO DO WAS BEND OVER AND PICK IT UP, I COULDN'T. WE'RE THAT FAR UNDERWATER.
I COULD FREE UP TWO ENGINEERS. MAYBE THEY COULD HELP DO SOME OF THE LEGWORK AROUND ESTIMATING THE REMEDIATION EFFORT?
THAT WOULD BE INCREDIBLY HELPFUL. PLEASE SEND WES AN EMAIL WITH A COUPLE OF BULLET POINTS ON EACH OF YOUR ENGINEERS.
WOW, IT'S LIBERATING TO STATE THAT MY TEAM IS ABSOLUTELY AT CAPACITY AND HAVE SOMEONE ACTUALLY BELIEVE ME.
ALSO, SOMETHING IS REALLY SCREWY IN THE WORLD WHEN I'M FINDING REASONS TO THANK DEVELOPMENT AND SECURITY ON THE SAME DAY.

CHAPTER 14 TUESDAY, SEPTEMBER 16

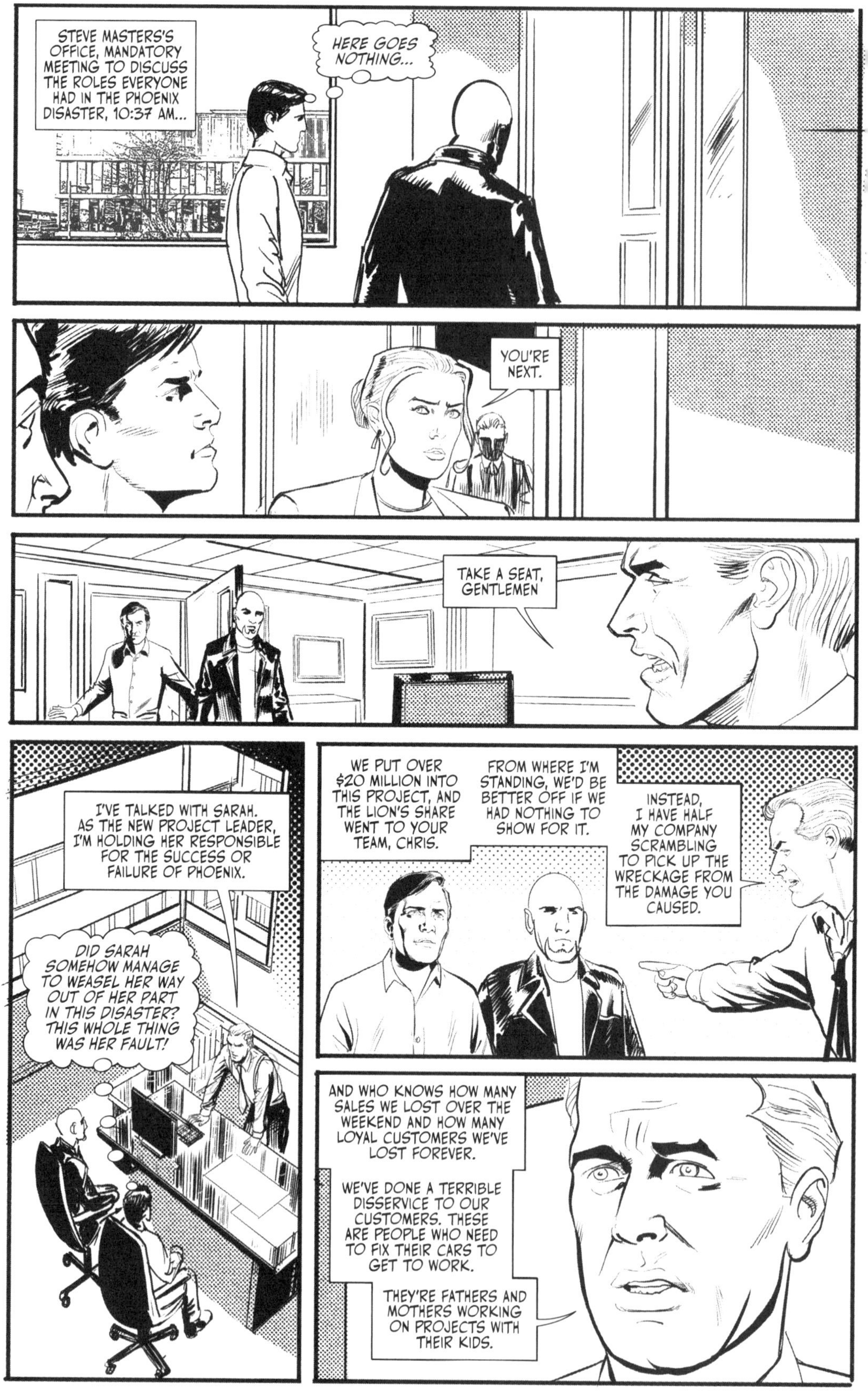
STEVE MASTERS'S OFFICE, MANDATORY MEETING TO DISCUSS THE ROLES EVERYONE HAD IN THE PHOENIX DISASTER, 10:37 AM...
HERE GOES NOTHING...
YOU'RE NEXT.
TAKE A SEAT, GENTLEMEN
I'VE TALKED WITH SARAH. AS THE NEW PROJECT LEADER, I'M HOLDING HER RESPONSIBLE FOR THE SUCCESS OR FAILURE OF PHOENIX.
DID SARAH SOMEHOW MANAGE TO WEASEL HER WAY OUT OF HER PART IN THIS DISASTER? THIS WHOLE THING WAS HER FAULT!
WE PUT OVER $20 MILLION INTO THIS PROJECT, AND THE LION'S SHARE WENT TO YOUR TEAM, CHRIS.
FROM WHERE I'M STANDING, WE'D BE BETTER OFF IF WE HAD NOTHING TO SHOW FOR IT.
INSTEAD, I HAVE HALF MY COMPANY SCRAMBLING TO PICK UP THE WRECKAGE FROM THE DAMAGE YOU CAUSED.
AND WHO KNOWS HOW MANY SALES WE LOST OVER THE WEEKEND AND HOW MANY LOYAL CUSTOMERS WE'VE LOST FOREVER.
WE'VE DONE A TERRIBLE DISSERVICE TO OUR CUSTOMERS. THESE ARE PEOPLE WHO NEED TO FIX THEIR CARS TO GET TO WORK.
THEY'RE FATHERS AND MOTHERS WORKING ON PROJECTS WITH THEIR KIDS.

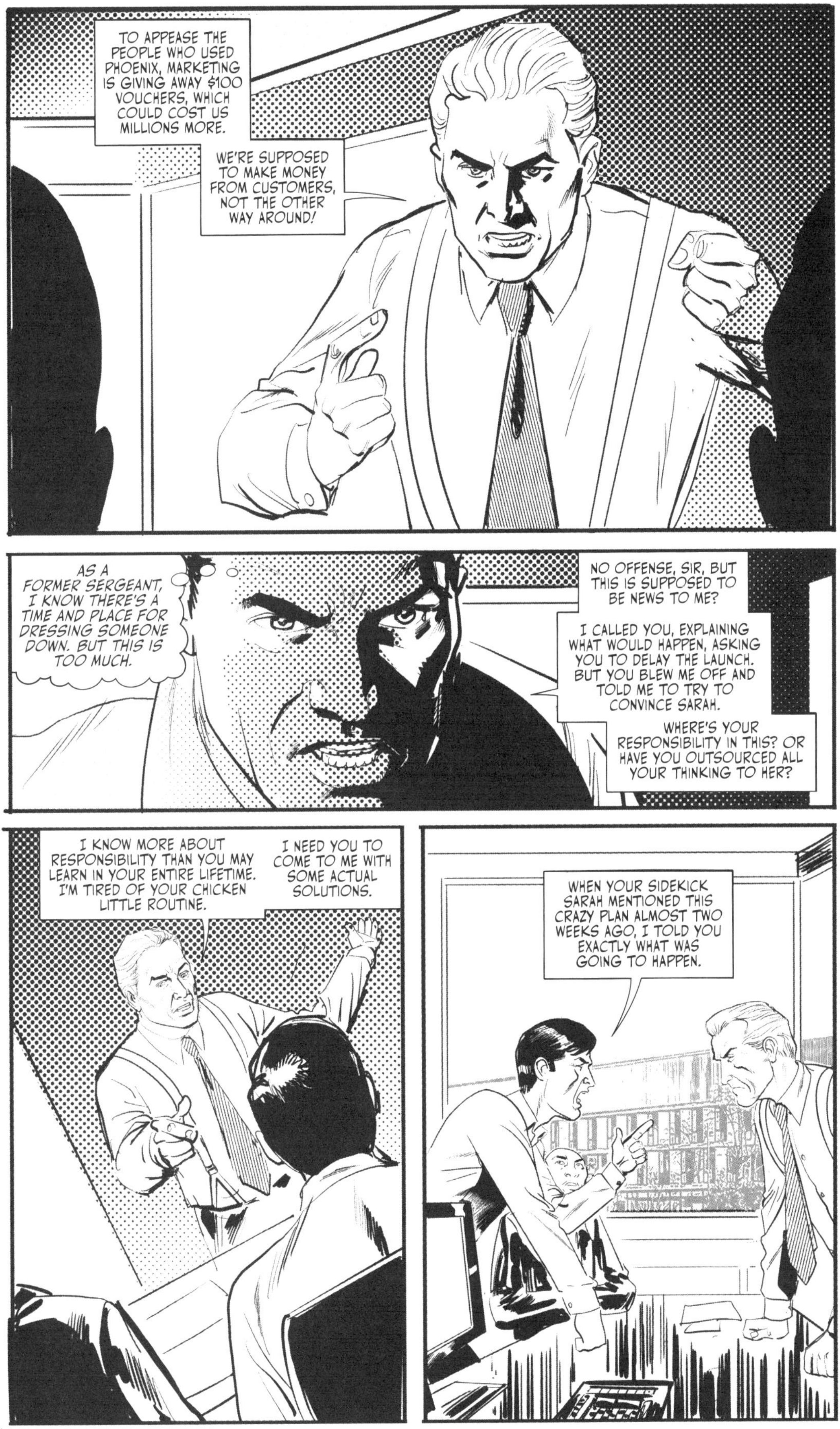
TO APPEASE THE PEOPLE WHO USED PHOENIX, MARKETING IS GIVING AWAY $100 VOUCHERS, WHICH COULD COST US MILLIONS MORE.
WE'RE SUPPOSED TO MAKE MONEY FROM CUSTOMERS, NOT THE OTHER WAY AROUND!
AS A FORMER SERGEANT, I KNOW THERE'S A TIME AND PLACE FOR DRESSING SOMEONE DOWN. BUT THIS IS TOO MUCH.
NO OFFENSE, SIR, BUT THIS IS SUPPOSED TO BE NEWS TO ME?
I CALLED YOU, EXPLAINING WHAT WOULD HAPPEN, ASKING YOU TO DELAY THE LAUNCH. BUT YOU BLEW ME OFF AND TOLD ME TO TRY TO CONVINCE SARAH.
WHERE'S YOUR RESPONSIBILITY IN THIS? OR HAVE YOU OUTSOURCED ALL YOUR THINKING TO HER?
I KNOW MORE ABOUT RESPONSIBILITY THAN YOU MAY LEARN IN YOUR ENTIRE LIFETIME. I'M TIRED OF YOUR CHICKEN LITTLE ROUTINE.
I NEED YOU TO COME TO ME WITH SOME ACTUAL SOLUTIONS.
WHEN YOUR SIDEKICK SARAH MENTIONED THIS CRAZY PLAN ALMOST TWO WEEKS AGO, I TOLD YOU EXACTLY WHAT WAS GOING TO HAPPEN.

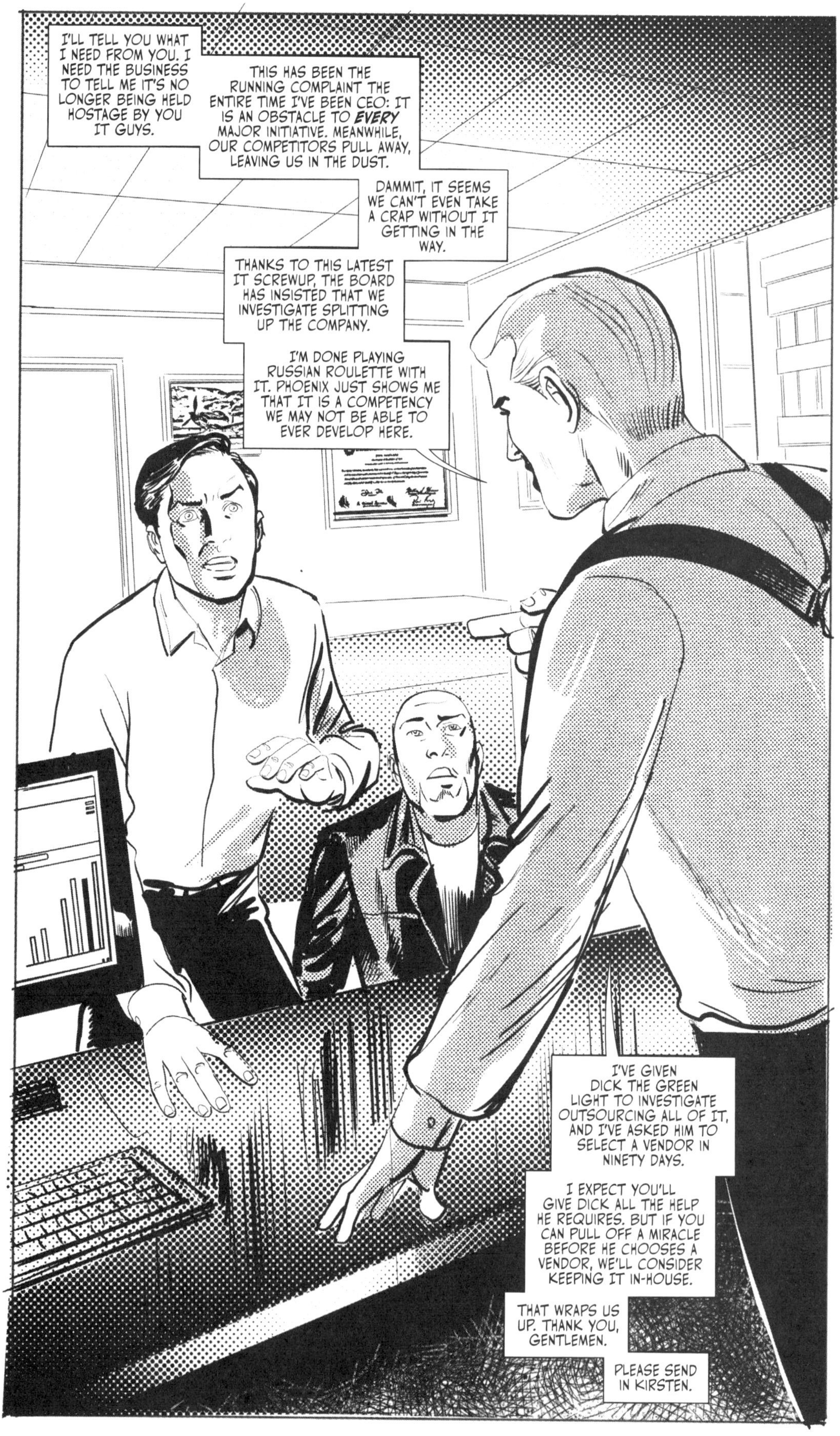
I'LL TELL YOU WHAT I NEED FROM YOU. I NEED THE BUSINESS TO TELL ME IT'S NO LONGER BEING HELD HOSTAGE BY YOU IT GUYS.
THIS HAS BEEN THE RUNNING COMPLAINT THE ENTIRE TIME I'VE BEEN CEO: IT IS AN OBSTACLE TO ***EVERY*** MAJOR INITIATIVE. MEANWHILE, OUR COMPETITORS PULL AWAY, LEAVING US IN THE DUST.
DAMMIT, IT SEEMS WE CAN'T EVEN TAKE A CRAP WITHOUT IT GETTING IN THE WAY.
THANKS TO THIS LATEST IT SCREWUP, THE BOARD HAS INSISTED THAT WE INVESTIGATE SPLITTING UP THE COMPANY.
I'M DONE PLAYING RUSSIAN ROULETTE WITH IT. PHOENIX JUST SHOWS ME THAT IT IS A COMPETENCY WE MAY NOT BE ABLE TO EVER DEVELOP HERE.
I'VE GIVEN DICK THE GREEN LIGHT TO INVESTIGATE OUTSOURCING ALL OF IT, AND I'VE ASKED HIM TO SELECT A VENDOR IN NINETY DAYS.
I EXPECT YOU'LL GIVE DICK ALL THE HELP HE REQUIRES. BUT IF YOU CAN PULL OFF A MIRACLE BEFORE HE CHOOSES A VENDOR, WE'LL CONSIDER KEEPING IT IN-HOUSE.
THAT WRAPS US UP. THANK YOU, GENTLEMEN.
PLEASE SEND IN KIRSTEN.

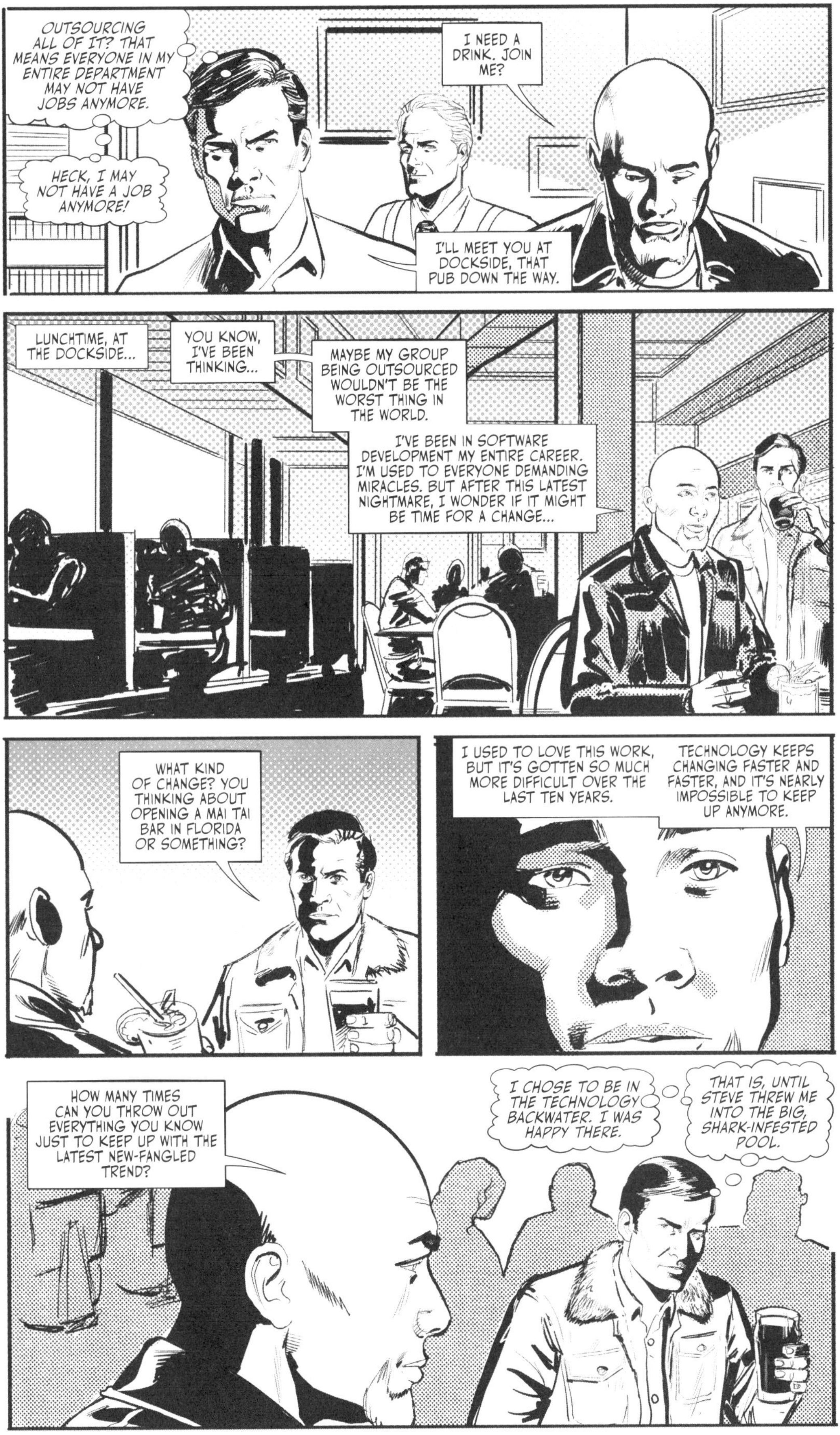
OUTSOURCING ALL OF IT? THAT MEANS EVERYONE IN MY ENTIRE DEPARTMENT MAY NOT HAVE JOBS ANYMORE.
HECK, I MAY NOT HAVE A JOB ANYMORE!
I NEED A DRINK. JOIN ME?
I'LL MEET YOU AT DOCKSIDE, THAT PUB DOWN THE WAY.
LUNCHTIME, AT THE DOCKSIDE...
YOU KNOW, I'VE BEEN THINKING...
MAYBE MY GROUP BEING OUTSOURCED WOULDN'T BE THE WORST THING IN THE WORLD.
I'VE BEEN IN SOFTWARE DEVELOPMENT MY ENTIRE CAREER. I'M USED TO EVERYONE DEMANDING MIRACLES. BUT AFTER THIS LATEST NIGHTMARE, I WONDER IF IT MIGHT BE TIME FOR A CHANGE...
WHAT KIND OF CHANGE? YOU THINKING ABOUT OPENING A MAI TAI BAR IN FLORIDA OR SOMETHING?
I USED TO LOVE THIS WORK, BUT IT'S GOTTEN SO MUCH MORE DIFFICULT OVER THE LAST TEN YEARS.
TECHNOLOGY KEEPS CHANGING FASTER AND FASTER, AND IT'S NEARLY IMPOSSIBLE TO KEEP UP ANYMORE.
HOW MANY TIMES CAN YOU THROW OUT EVERYTHING YOU KNOW JUST TO KEEP UP WITH THE LATEST NEW-FANGLED TREND?
I CHOSE TO BE IN THE TECHNOLOGY BACKWATER. I WAS HAPPY THERE.
THAT IS, UNTIL STEVE THREW ME INTO THE BIG, SHARK-INFESTED POOL.

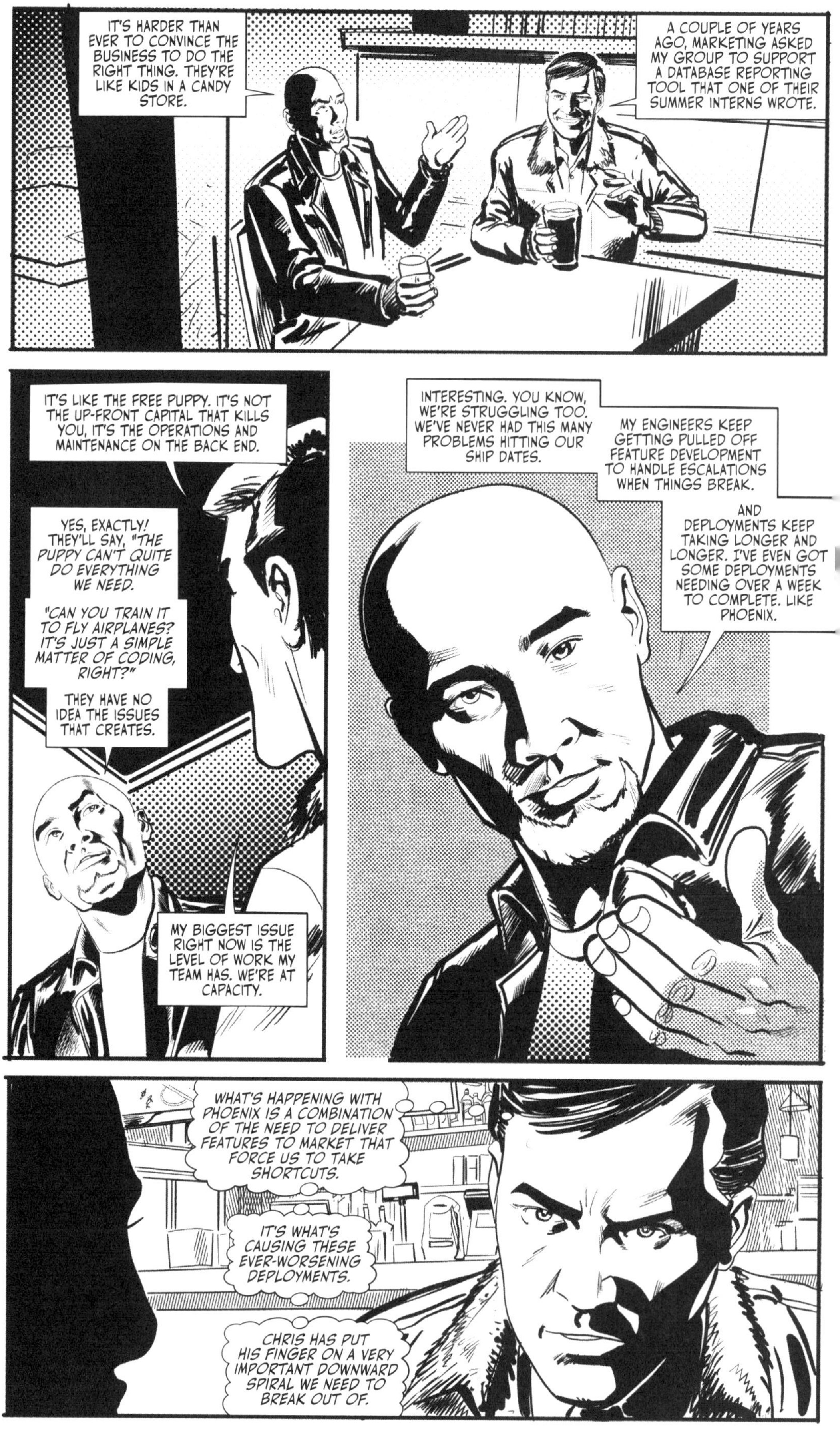
IT'S HARDER THAN EVER TO CONVINCE THE BUSINESS TO DO THE RIGHT THING. THEY'RE LIKE KIDS IN A CANDY STORE.
A COUPLE OF YEARS AGO, MARKETING ASKED MY GROUP TO SUPPORT A DATABASE REPORTING TOOL THAT ONE OF THEIR SUMMER INTERNS WROTE.
IT'S LIKE THE FREE PUPPY. IT'S NOT THE UP-FRONT CAPITAL THAT KILLS YOU, IT'S THE OPERATIONS AND MAINTENANCE ON THE BACK END.
YES, EXACTLY! THEY'LL SAY, "THE PUPPY CAN'T QUITE DO EVERYTHING WE NEED.
"CAN YOU TRAIN IT TO FLY AIRPLANES? IT'S JUST A SIMPLE MATTER OF CODING, RIGHT?"
THEY HAVE NO IDEA THE ISSUES THAT CREATES.
MY BIGGEST ISSUE RIGHT NOW IS THE LEVEL OF WORK MY TEAM HAS. WE'RE AT CAPACITY.
INTERESTING. YOU KNOW, WE'RE STRUGGLING TOO. WE'VE NEVER HAD THIS MANY PROBLEMS HITTING OUR SHIP DATES.
MY ENGINEERS KEEP GETTING PULLED OFF FEATURE DEVELOPMENT TO HANDLE ESCALATIONS WHEN THINGS BREAK.
AND DEPLOYMENTS KEEP TAKING LONGER AND LONGER. I'VE EVEN GOT SOME DEPLOYMENTS NEEDING OVER A WEEK TO COMPLETE. LIKE PHOENIX.
WHAT'S HAPPENING WITH PHOENIX IS A COMBINATION OF THE NEED TO DELIVER FEATURES TO MARKET THAT FORCE US TO TAKE SHORTCUTS.
IT'S WHAT'S CAUSING THESE EVER-WORSENING DEPLOYMENTS.
CHRIS HAS PUT HIS FINGER ON A VERY IMPORTANT DOWNWARD SPIRAL WE NEED TO BREAK OUT OF.

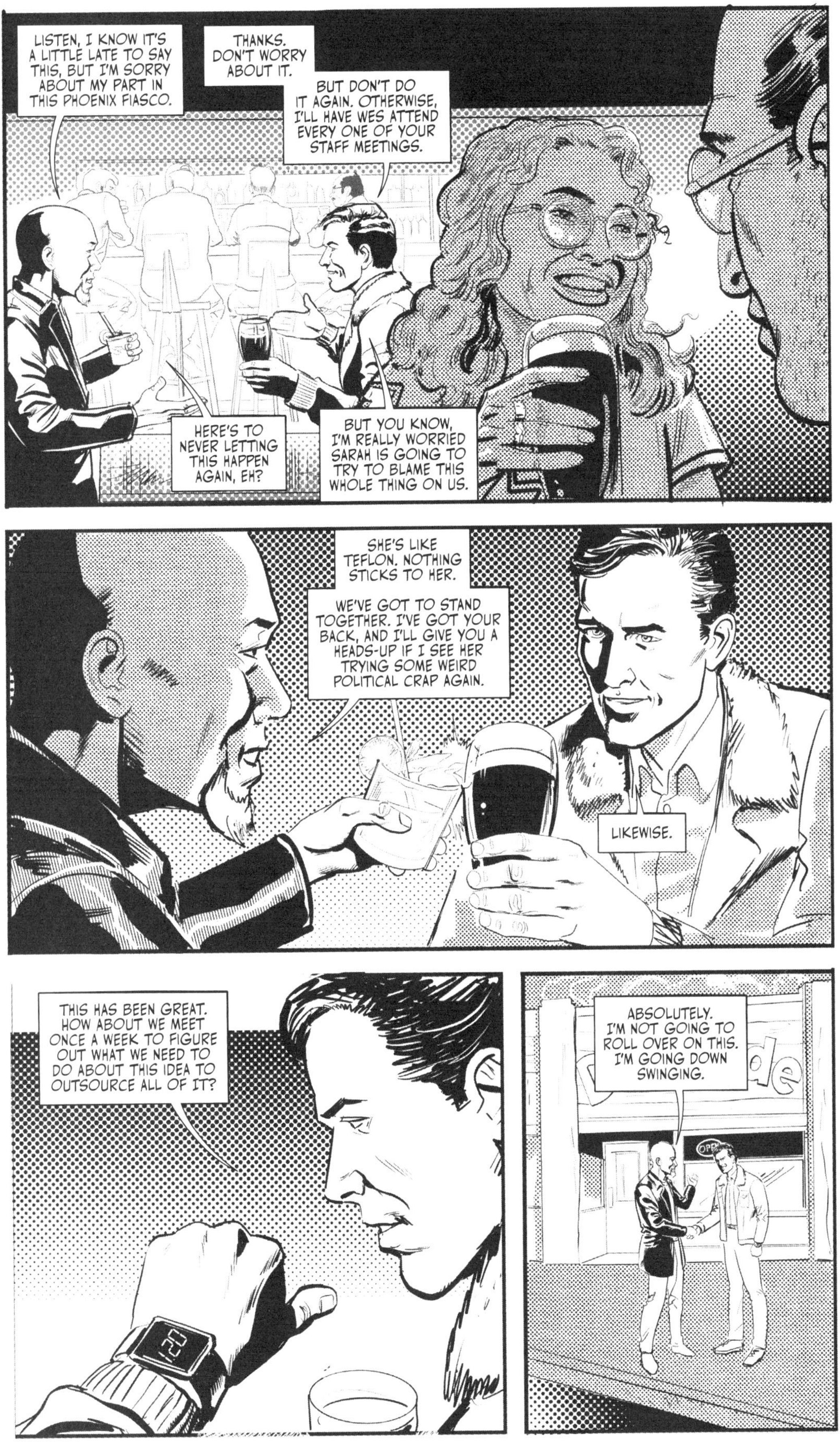
LISTEN, I KNOW IT'S A LITTLE LATE TO SAY THIS, BUT I'M SORRY ABOUT MY PART IN THIS PHOENIX FIASCO.
THANKS. DON'T WORRY ABOUT IT.
BUT DON'T DO IT AGAIN. OTHERWISE, I'LL HAVE WES ATTEND EVERY ONE OF YOUR STAFF MEETINGS.
HERE'S TO NEVER LETTING THIS HAPPEN AGAIN, EH?
BUT YOU KNOW, I'M REALLY WORRIED SARAH IS GOING TO TRY TO BLAME THIS WHOLE THING ON US.
SHE'S LIKE TEFLON. NOTHING STICKS TO HER.
WE'VE GOT TO STAND TOGETHER. I'VE GOT YOUR BACK, AND I'LL GIVE YOU A HEADS-UP IF I SEE HER TRYING SOME WEIRD POLITICAL CRAP AGAIN.
LIKEWISE.
THIS HAS BEEN GREAT. HOW ABOUT WE MEET ONCE A WEEK TO FIGURE OUT WHAT WE NEED TO DO ABOUT THIS IDEA TO OUTSOURCE ALL OF IT?
ABSOLUTELY. I'M NOT GOING TO ROLL OVER ON THIS. I'M GOING DOWN SWINGING.

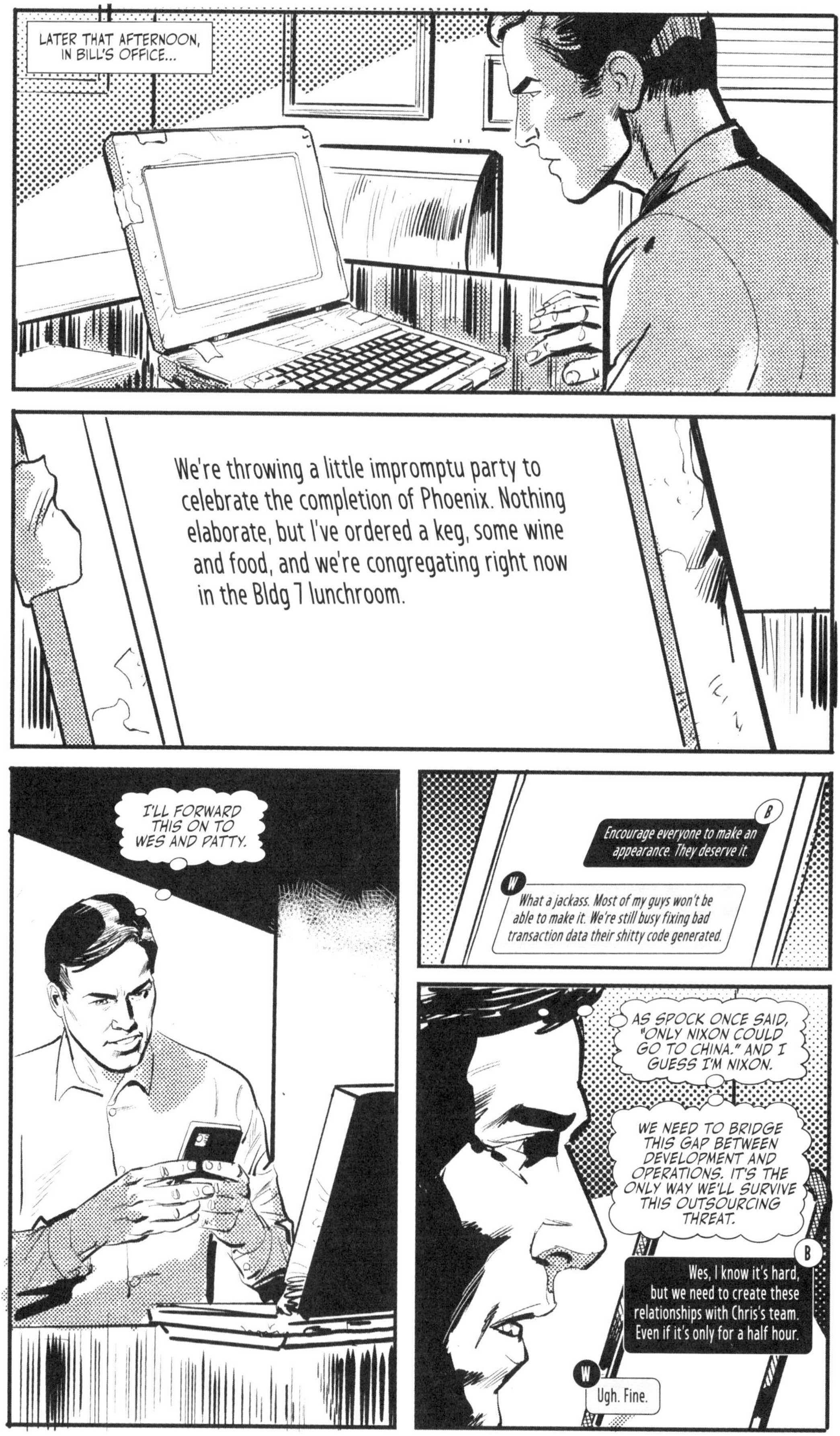

LATER THAT AFTERNOON, IN BILL'S OFFICE...
We're throwing a little impromptu party to celebrate the completion of Phoenix. Nothing elaborate, but I've ordered a keg, some wine and food, and we're congregating right now in the Bldg 7 lunchroom.
I'LL FORWARD THIS ON TO WES AND PATTY.
B
Encourage everyone to make an appearance. They deserve it.
W
What a jackass. Most of my guys won't be able to make it. We're still busy fixing bad transaction data their shitty code generated.
AS SPOCK ONCE SAID, "ONLY NIXON COULD GO TO CHINA." AND I GUESS I'M NIXON.
WE NEED TO BRIDGE THIS GAP BETWEEN DEVELOPMENT AND OPERATIONS. IT'S THE ONLY WAY WE'LL SURVIVE THIS OUTSOURCING THREAT.
B
Wes, I know it's hard, but we need to create these relationships with Chris's team. Even if it's only for a half hour.
W
Ugh. Fine.

CHAPTER 15 WEDNESDAY, SEPTEMBER 17

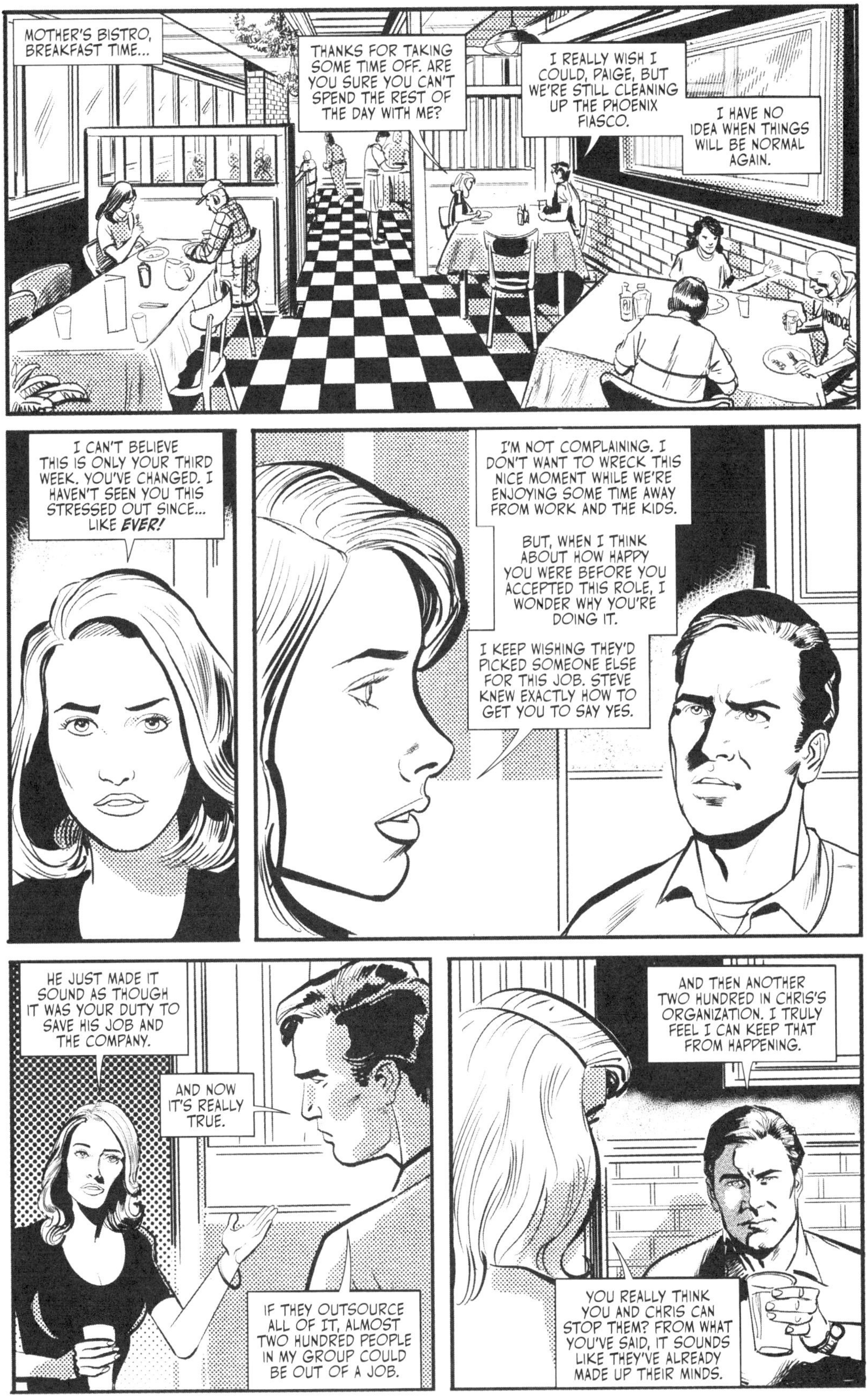

MOTHER'S BISTRO, BREAKFAST TIME...
THANKS FOR TAKING SOME TIME OFF. ARE YOU SURE YOU CAN'T SPEND THE REST OF THE DAY WITH ME?
I REALLY WISH I COULD, PAIGE, BUT WE'RE STILL CLEANING UP THE PHOENIX FIASCO.
I HAVE NO IDEA WHEN THINGS WILL BE NORMAL AGAIN.
I CAN'T BELIEVE THIS IS ONLY YOUR THIRD WEEK. YOU'VE CHANGED. I HAVEN'T SEEN YOU THIS STRESSED OUT SINCE... LIKE *EVER!*
I'M NOT COMPLAINING. I DON'T WANT TO WRECK THIS NICE MOMENT WHILE WE'RE ENJOYING SOME TIME AWAY FROM WORK AND THE KIDS.
BUT, WHEN I THINK ABOUT HOW HAPPY YOU WERE BEFORE YOU ACCEPTED THIS ROLE, I WONDER WHY YOU'RE DOING IT.
I KEEP WISHING THEY'D PICKED SOMEONE ELSE FOR THIS JOB. STEVE KNEW EXACTLY HOW TO GET YOU TO SAY YES.
HE JUST MADE IT SOUND AS THOUGH IT WAS YOUR DUTY TO SAVE HIS JOB AND THE COMPANY.
AND NOW IT'S REALLY TRUE.
IF THEY OUTSOURCE ALL OF IT, ALMOST TWO HUNDRED PEOPLE IN MY GROUP COULD BE OUT OF A JOB.
AND THEN ANOTHER TWO HUNDRED IN CHRIS'S ORGANIZATION. I TRULY FEEL I CAN KEEP THAT FROM HAPPENING.
YOU REALLY THINK YOU AND CHRIS CAN STOP THEM? FROM WHAT YOU'VE SAID, IT SOUNDS LIKE THEY'VE ALREADY MADE UP THEIR MINDS.

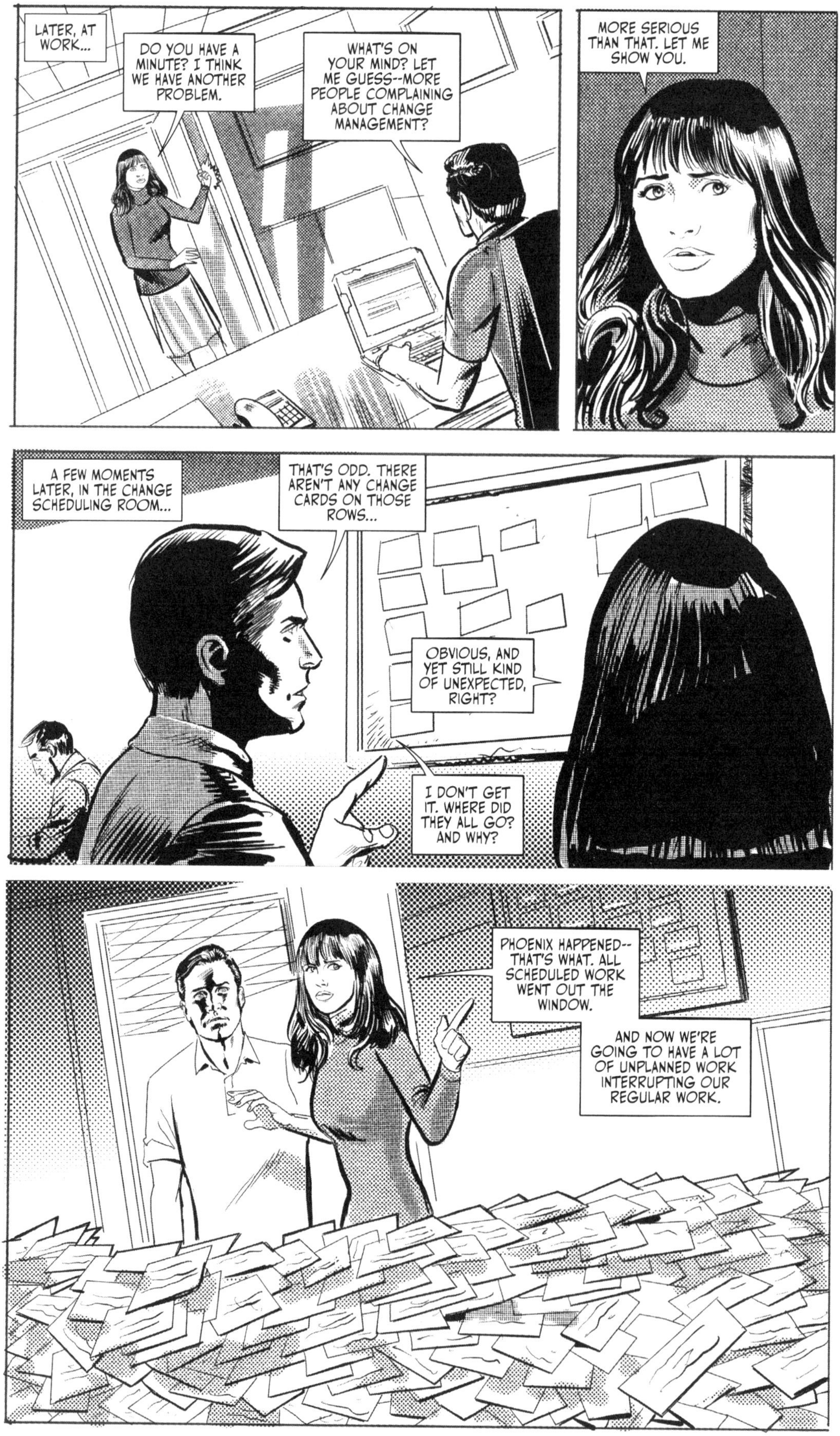
LATER, AT WORK...
DO YOU HAVE A MINUTE? I THINK WE HAVE ANOTHER PROBLEM.
WHAT'S ON YOUR MIND? LET ME GUESS--MORE PEOPLE COMPLAINING ABOUT CHANGE MANAGEMENT?
MORE SERIOUS THAN THAT. LET ME SHOW YOU.
A FEW MOMENTS LATER, IN THE CHANGE SCHEDULING ROOM...
THAT'S ODD. THERE AREN'T ANY CHANGE CARDS ON THOSE ROWS...
OBVIOUS, AND YET STILL KIND OF UNEXPECTED, RIGHT?
I DON'T GET IT. WHERE DID THEY ALL GO? AND WHY?
PHOENIX HAPPENED--THAT'S WHAT. ALL SCHEDULED WORK WENT OUT THE WINDOW.
AND NOW WE'RE GOING TO HAVE A LOT OF UNPLANNED WORK INTERRUPTING OUR REGULAR WORK.

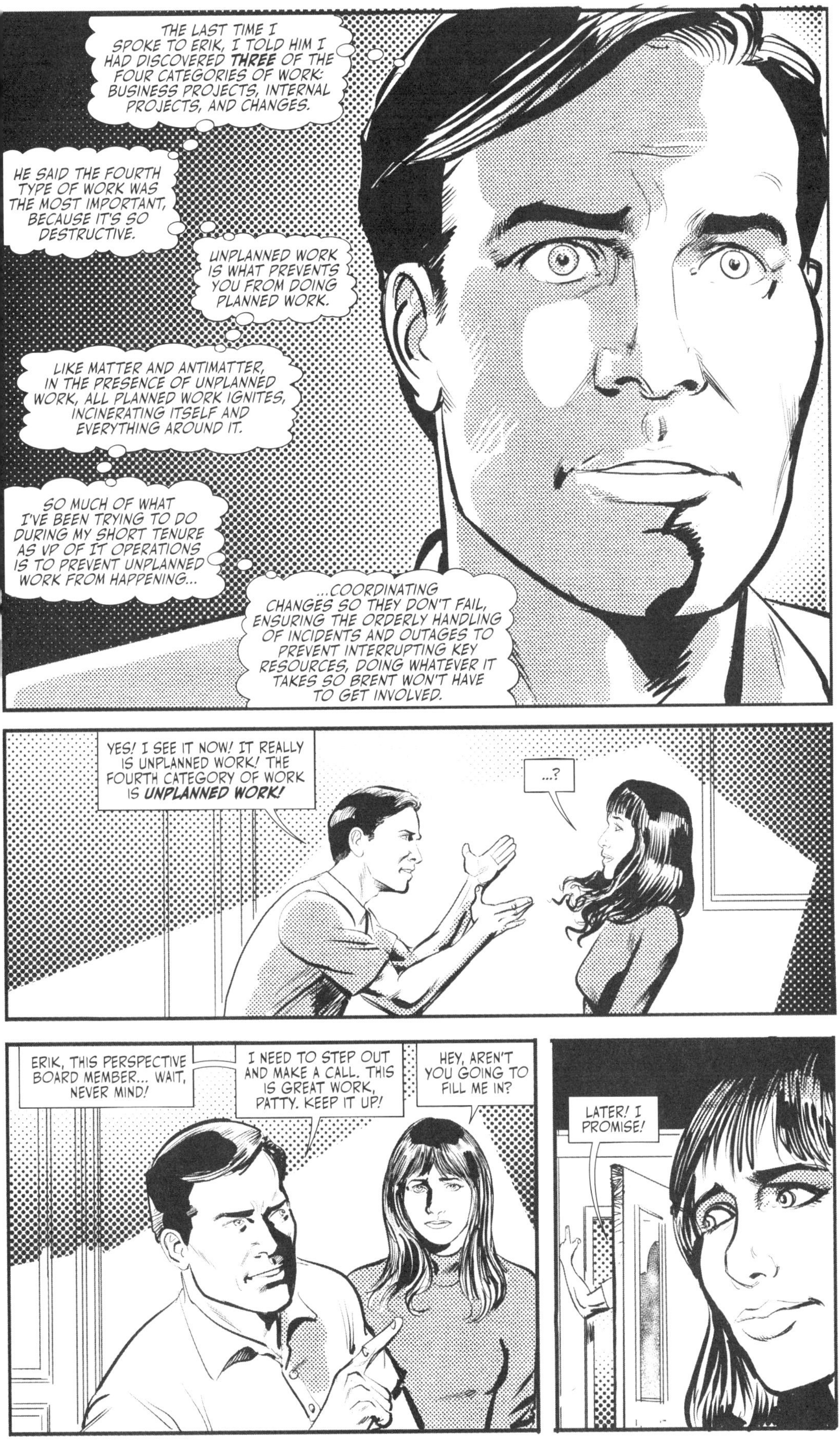
THE LAST TIME I SPOKE TO ERIK, I TOLD HIM I HAD DISCOVERED THREE OF THE FOUR CATEGORIES OF WORK: BUSINESS PROJECTS, INTERNAL PROJECTS, AND CHANGES.
HE SAID THE FOURTH TYPE OF WORK WAS THE MOST IMPORTANT, BECAUSE IT'S SO DESTRUCTIVE.
UNPLANNED WORK IS WHAT PREVENTS YOU FROM DOING PLANNED WORK.
LIKE MATTER AND ANTIMATTER, IN THE PRESENCE OF UNPLANNED WORK, ALL PLANNED WORK IGNITES, INCINERATING ITSELF AND EVERYTHING AROUND IT.
SO MUCH OF WHAT I'VE BEEN TRYING TO DO DURING MY SHORT TENURE AS VP OF IT OPERATIONS IS TO PREVENT UNPLANNED WORK FROM HAPPENING...
...COORDINATING CHANGES SO THEY DON'T FAIL, ENSURING THE ORDERLY HANDLING OF INCIDENTS AND OUTAGES TO PREVENT INTERRUPTING KEY RESOURCES, DOING WHATEVER IT TAKES SO BRENT WON'T HAVE TO GET INVOLVED.
YES! I SEE IT NOW! IT REALLY IS UNPLANNED WORK! THE FOURTH CATEGORY OF WORK IS UNPLANNED WORK!
...?
ERIK, THIS PERSPECTIVE BOARD MEMBER... WAIT, NEVER MIND!
I NEED TO STEP OUT AND MAKE A CALL. THIS IS GREAT WORK, PATTY. KEEP IT UP!
HEY, AREN'T YOU GOING TO FILL ME IN?
LATER! I PROMISE!

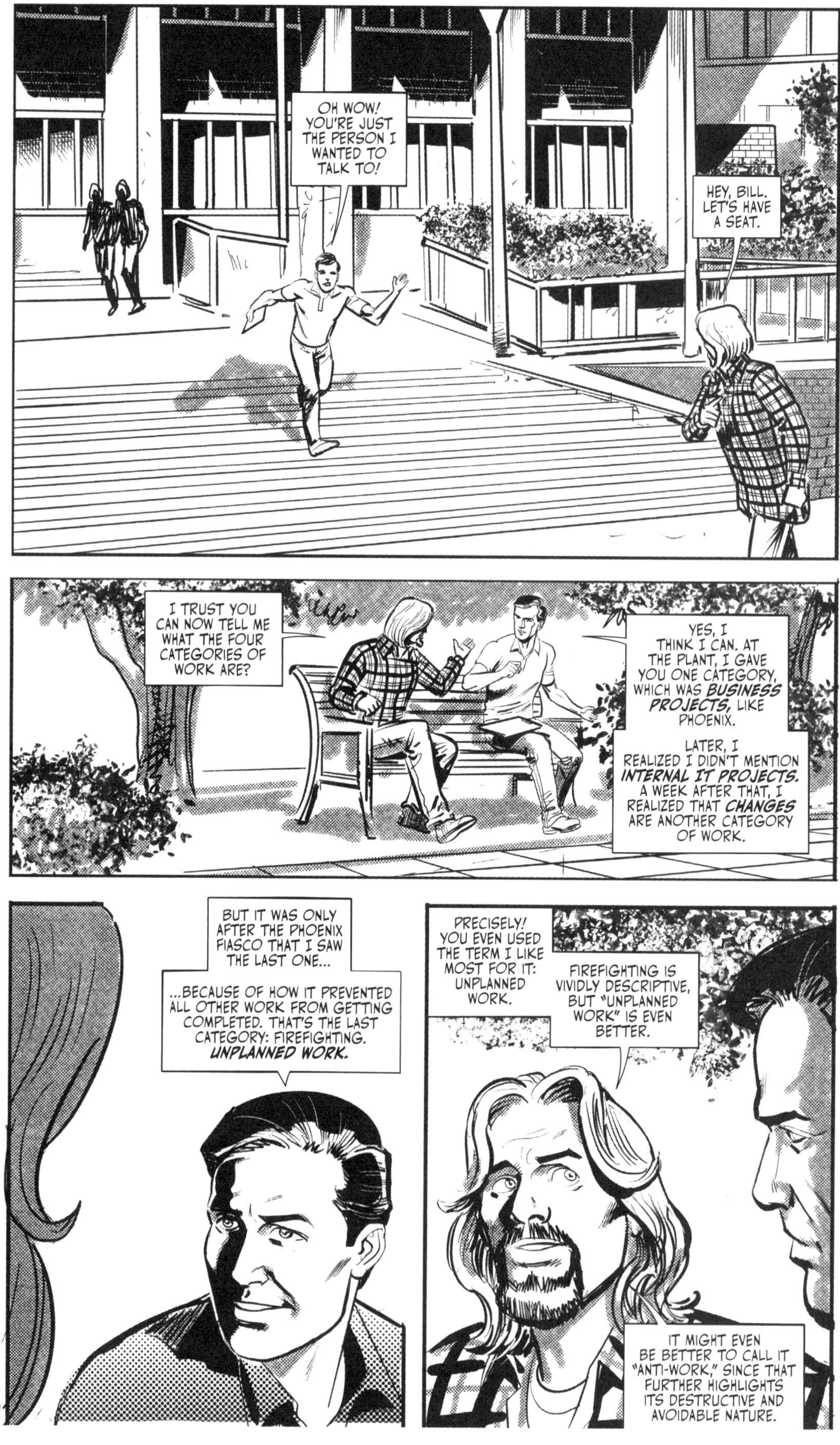

OH WOW! YOU'RE JUST THE PERSON I WANTED TO TALK TO!
HEY, BILL. LET'S HAVE A SEAT.
I TRUST YOU CAN NOW TELL ME WHAT THE FOUR CATEGORIES OF WORK ARE?
YES, I THINK I CAN. AT THE PLANT, I GAVE YOU ONE CATEGORY, WHICH WAS ***BUSINESS PROJECTS,*** LIKE PHOENIX.
LATER, I REALIZED I DIDN'T MENTION ***INTERNAL IT PROJECTS.*** A WEEK AFTER THAT, I REALIZED THAT ***CHANGES*** ARE ANOTHER CATEGORY OF WORK.
BUT IT WAS ONLY AFTER THE PHOENIX FIASCO THAT I SAW THE LAST ONE...
...BECAUSE OF HOW IT PREVENTED ALL OTHER WORK FROM GETTING COMPLETED. THAT'S THE LAST CATEGORY: FIREFIGHTING. ***UNPLANNED WORK.***
PRECISELY! YOU EVEN USED THE TERM I LIKE MOST FOR IT: UNPLANNED WORK.
FIREFIGHTING IS VIVIDLY DESCRIPTIVE, BUT "UNPLANNED WORK" IS EVEN BETTER.
IT MIGHT EVEN BE BETTER TO CALL IT "ANTI-WORK," SINCE THAT FURTHER HIGHLIGHTS ITS DESTRUCTIVE AND AVOIDABLE NATURE.

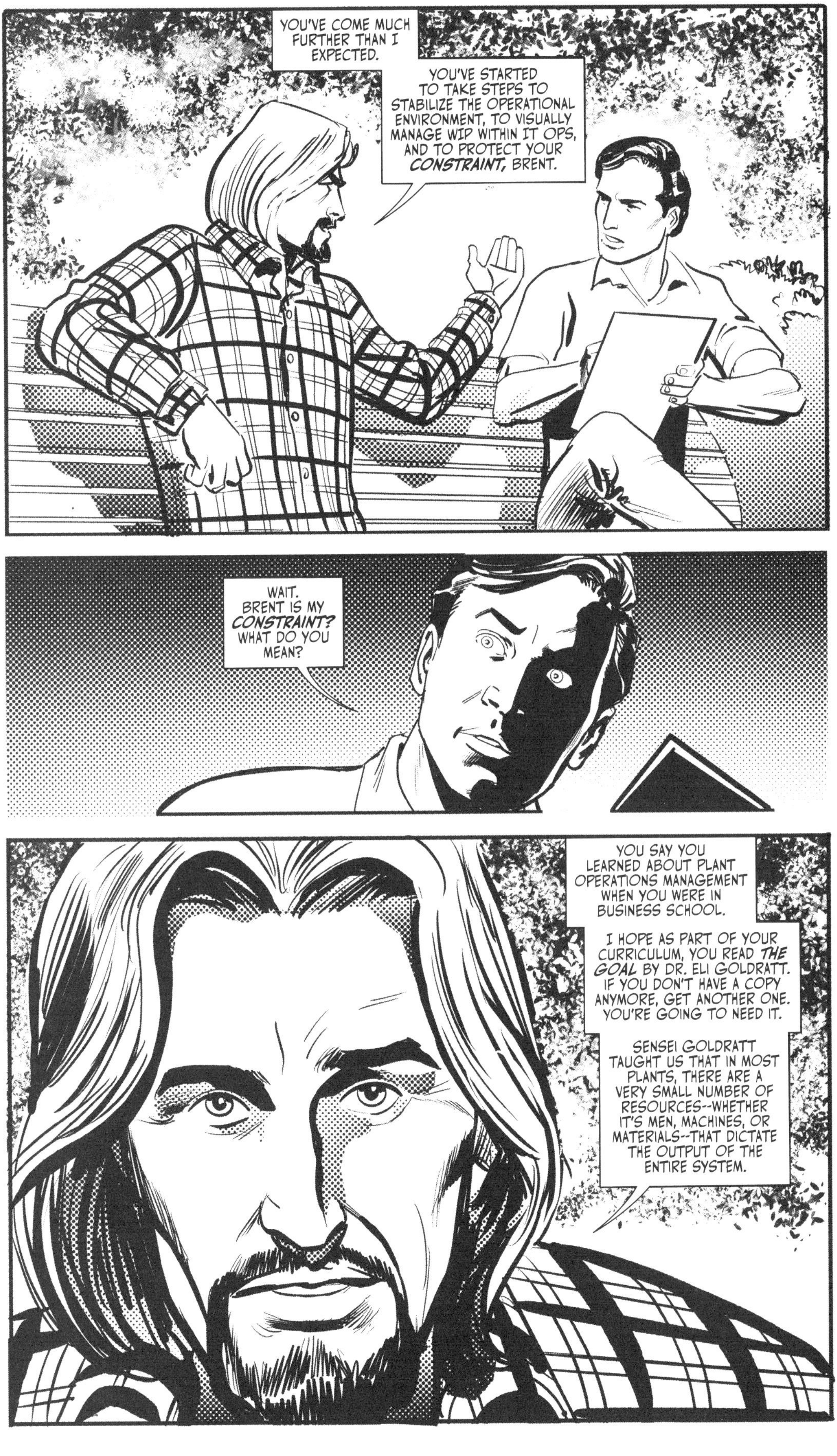
YOU'VE COME MUCH FURTHER THAN I EXPECTED.
YOU'VE STARTED TO TAKE STEPS TO STABILIZE THE OPERATIONAL ENVIRONMENT, TO VISUALLY MANAGE WIP WITHIN IT OPS, AND TO PROTECT YOUR ***CONSTRAINT,*** BRENT.
WAIT. BRENT IS MY ***CONSTRAINT?*** WHAT DO YOU MEAN?
YOU SAY YOU LEARNED ABOUT PLANT OPERATIONS MANAGEMENT WHEN YOU WERE IN BUSINESS SCHOOL.
I HOPE AS PART OF YOUR CURRICULUM, YOU READ ***THE GOAL*** BY DR. ELI GOLDRATT. IF YOU DON'T HAVE A COPY ANYMORE, GET ANOTHER ONE. YOU'RE GOING TO NEED IT.
SENSEI GOLDRATT TAUGHT US THAT IN MOST PLANTS, THERE ARE A VERY SMALL NUMBER OF RESOURCES--WHETHER IT'S MEN, MACHINES, OR MATERIALS--THAT DICTATE THE OUTPUT OF THE ENTIRE SYSTEM.

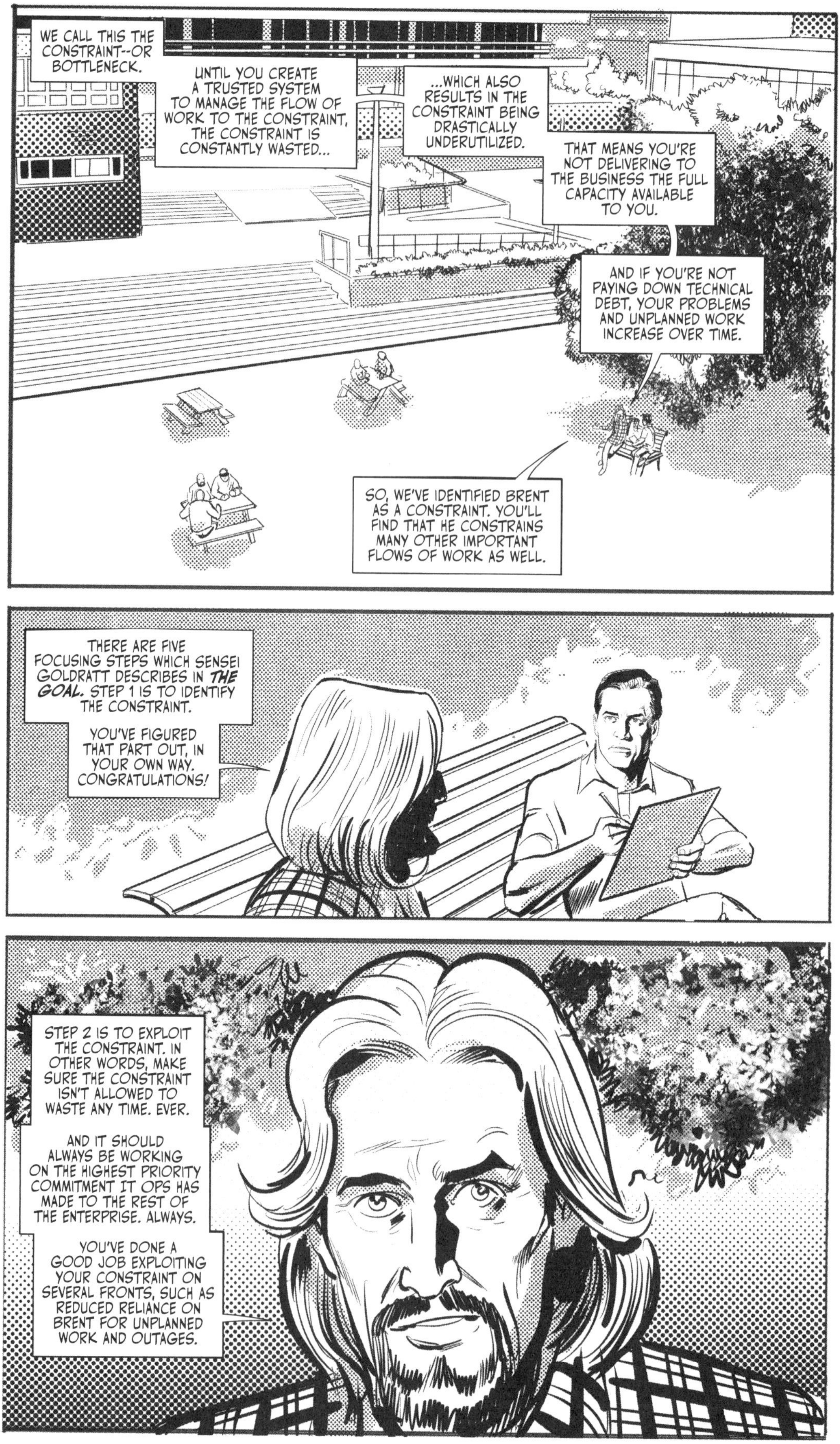
WE CALL THIS THE CONSTRAINT--OR BOTTLENECK.
UNTIL YOU CREATE A TRUSTED SYSTEM TO MANAGE THE FLOW OF WORK TO THE CONSTRAINT, THE CONSTRAINT IS CONSTANTLY WASTED...
...WHICH ALSO RESULTS IN THE CONSTRAINT BEING DRASTICALLY UNDERUTILIZED.
THAT MEANS YOU'RE NOT DELIVERING TO THE BUSINESS THE FULL CAPACITY AVAILABLE TO YOU.
AND IF YOU'RE NOT PAYING DOWN TECHNICAL DEBT, YOUR PROBLEMS AND UNPLANNED WORK INCREASE OVER TIME.
SO, WE'VE IDENTIFIED BRENT AS A CONSTRAINT. YOU'LL FIND THAT HE CONSTRAINS MANY OTHER IMPORTANT FLOWS OF WORK AS WELL.
THERE ARE FIVE FOCUSING STEPS WHICH SENSEI GOLDRATT DESCRIBES IN ***THE GOAL***. STEP 1 IS TO IDENTIFY THE CONSTRAINT.
YOU'VE FIGURED THAT PART OUT, IN YOUR OWN WAY. CONGRATULATIONS!
STEP 2 IS TO EXPLOIT THE CONSTRAINT. IN OTHER WORDS, MAKE SURE THE CONSTRAINT ISN'T ALLOWED TO WASTE ANY TIME. EVER.
AND IT SHOULD ALWAYS BE WORKING ON THE HIGHEST PRIORITY COMMITMENT IT OPS HAS MADE TO THE REST OF THE ENTERPRISE. ALWAYS.
YOU'VE DONE A GOOD JOB EXPLOITING YOUR CONSTRAINT ON SEVERAL FRONTS, SUCH AS REDUCED RELIANCE ON BRENT FOR UNPLANNED WORK AND OUTAGES.

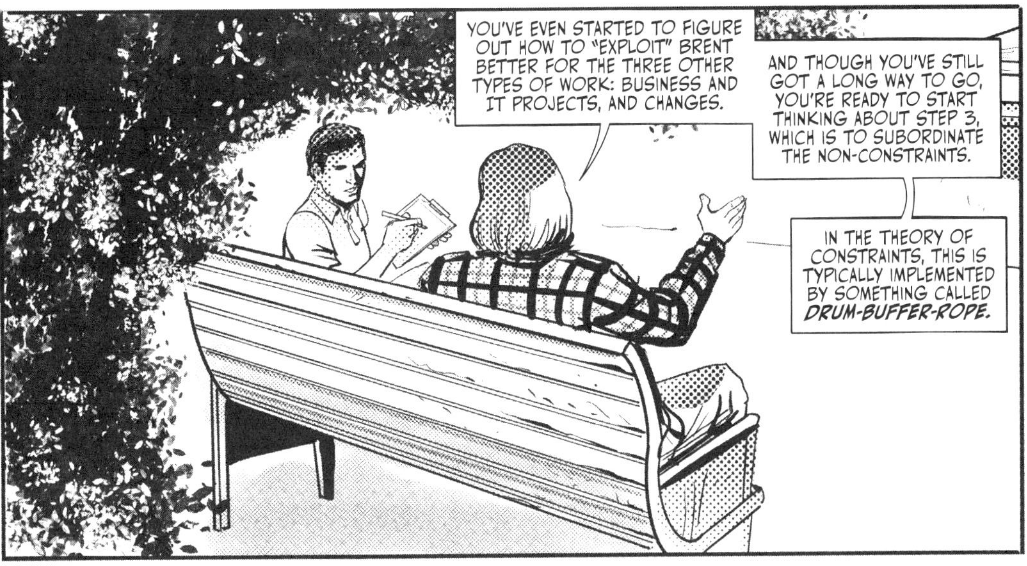
YOU'VE EVEN STARTED TO FIGURE OUT HOW TO "EXPLOIT" BRENT BETTER FOR THE THREE OTHER TYPES OF WORK: BUSINESS AND IT PROJECTS, AND CHANGES.
AND THOUGH YOU'VE STILL GOT A LONG WAY TO GO, YOU'RE READY TO START THINKING ABOUT STEP 3, WHICH IS TO SUBORDINATE THE NON-CONSTRAINTS.
IN THE THEORY OF CONSTRAINTS, THIS IS TYPICALLY IMPLEMENTED BY SOMETHING CALLED ***DRUM-BUFFER-ROPE.***

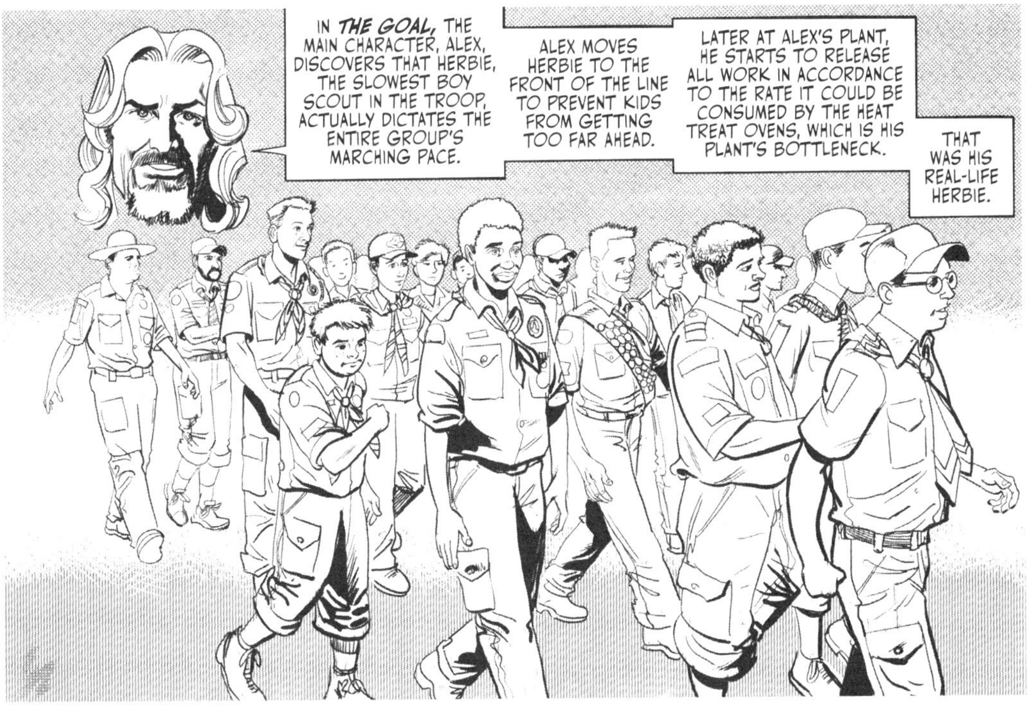
IN ***THE GOAL,*** THE MAIN CHARACTER, ALEX, DISCOVERS THAT HERBIE, THE SLOWEST BOY SCOUT IN THE TROOP, ACTUALLY DICTATES THE ENTIRE GROUP'S MARCHING PACE.
ALEX MOVES HERBIE TO THE FRONT OF THE LINE TO PREVENT KIDS FROM GETTING TOO FAR AHEAD.
LATER AT ALEX'S PLANT, HE STARTS TO RELEASE ALL WORK IN ACCORDANCE TO THE RATE IT COULD BE CONSUMED BY THE HEAT TREAT OVENS, WHICH IS HIS PLANT'S BOTTLENECK.
THAT WAS HIS REAL-LIFE HERBIE.

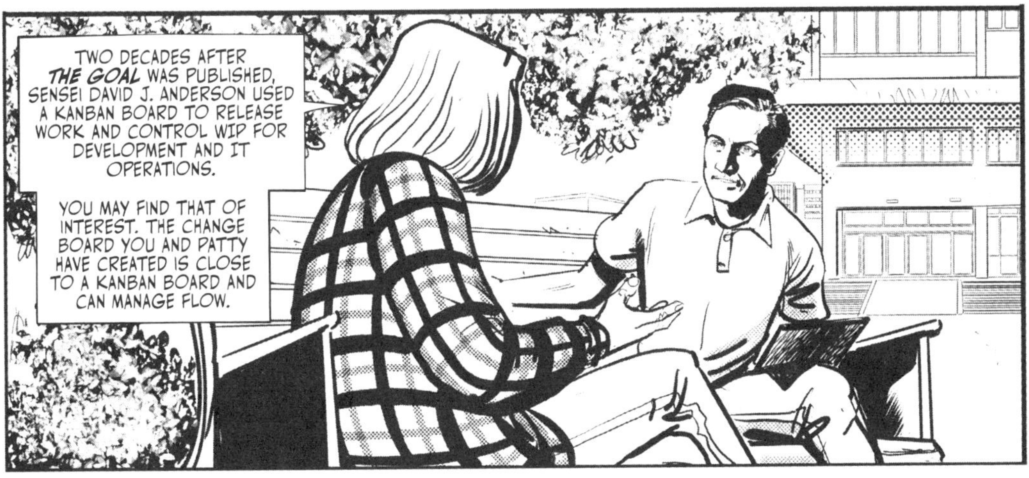
TWO DECADES AFTER ***THE GOAL*** WAS PUBLISHED, SENSEI DAVID J. ANDERSON USED A KANBAN BOARD TO RELEASE WORK AND CONTROL WIP FOR DEVELOPMENT AND IT OPERATIONS.
YOU MAY FIND THAT OF INTEREST. THE CHANGE BOARD YOU AND PATTY HAVE CREATED IS CLOSE TO A KANBAN BOARD AND CAN MANAGE FLOW.

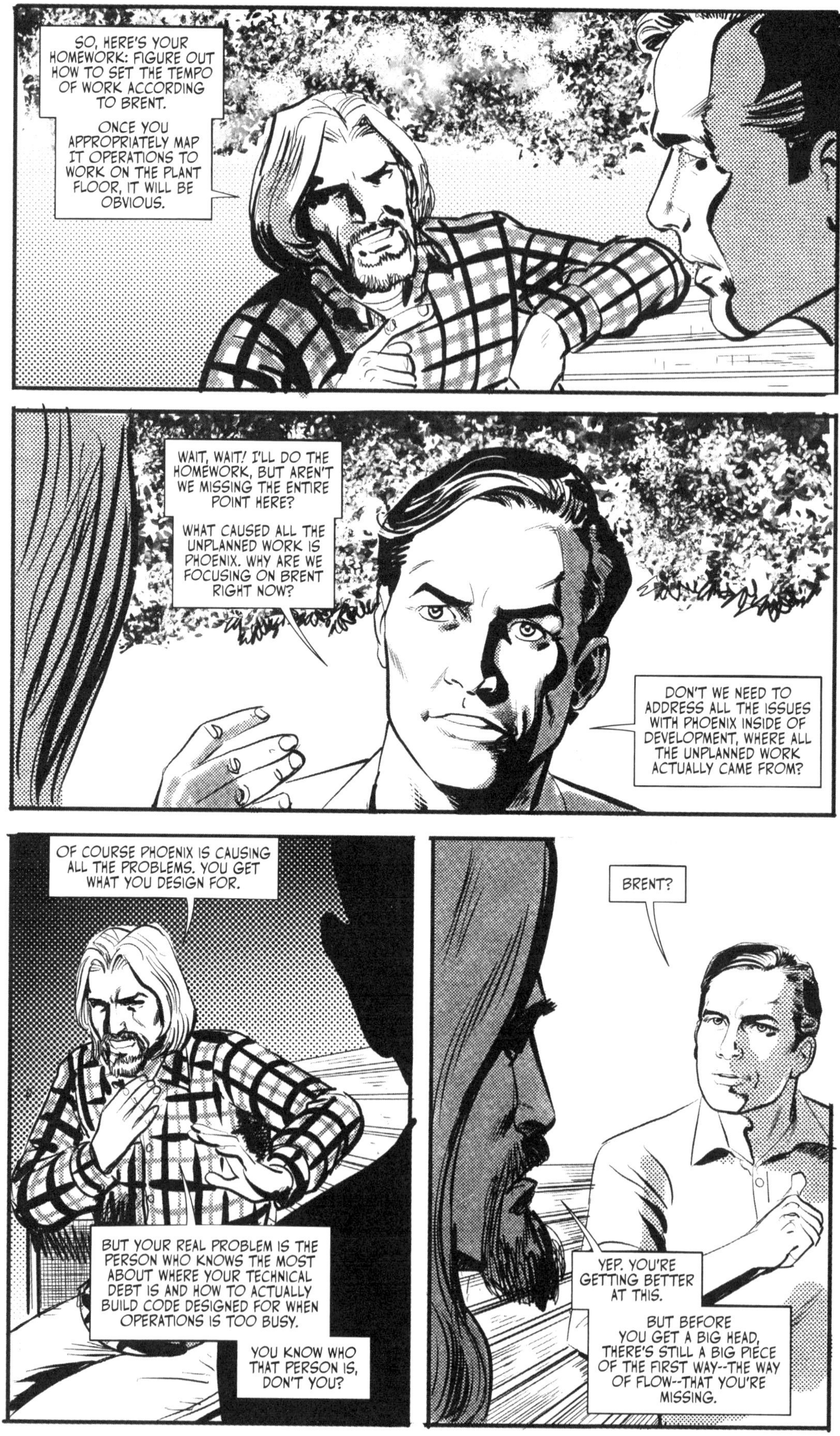
SO, HERE'S YOUR HOMEWORK: FIGURE OUT HOW TO SET THE TEMPO OF WORK ACCORDING TO BRENT.
ONCE YOU APPROPRIATELY MAP IT OPERATIONS TO WORK ON THE PLANT FLOOR, IT WILL BE OBVIOUS.
WAIT, WAIT! I'LL DO THE HOMEWORK, BUT AREN'T WE MISSING THE ENTIRE POINT HERE?
WHAT CAUSED ALL THE UNPLANNED WORK IS PHOENIX. WHY ARE WE FOCUSING ON BRENT RIGHT NOW?
DON'T WE NEED TO ADDRESS ALL THE ISSUES WITH PHOENIX INSIDE OF DEVELOPMENT, WHERE ALL THE UNPLANNED WORK ACTUALLY CAME FROM?
OF COURSE PHOENIX IS CAUSING ALL THE PROBLEMS. YOU GET WHAT YOU DESIGN FOR.
BUT YOUR REAL PROBLEM IS THE PERSON WHO KNOWS THE MOST ABOUT WHERE YOUR TECHNICAL DEBT IS AND HOW TO ACTUALLY BUILD CODE DESIGNED FOR WHEN OPERATIONS IS TOO BUSY.
YOU KNOW WHO THAT PERSON IS, DON'T YOU?
BRENT?
YEP. YOU'RE GETTING BETTER AT THIS.
BUT BEFORE YOU GET A BIG HEAD, THERE'S STILL A BIG PIECE OF THE FIRST WAY--THE WAY OF FLOW--THAT YOU'RE MISSING.

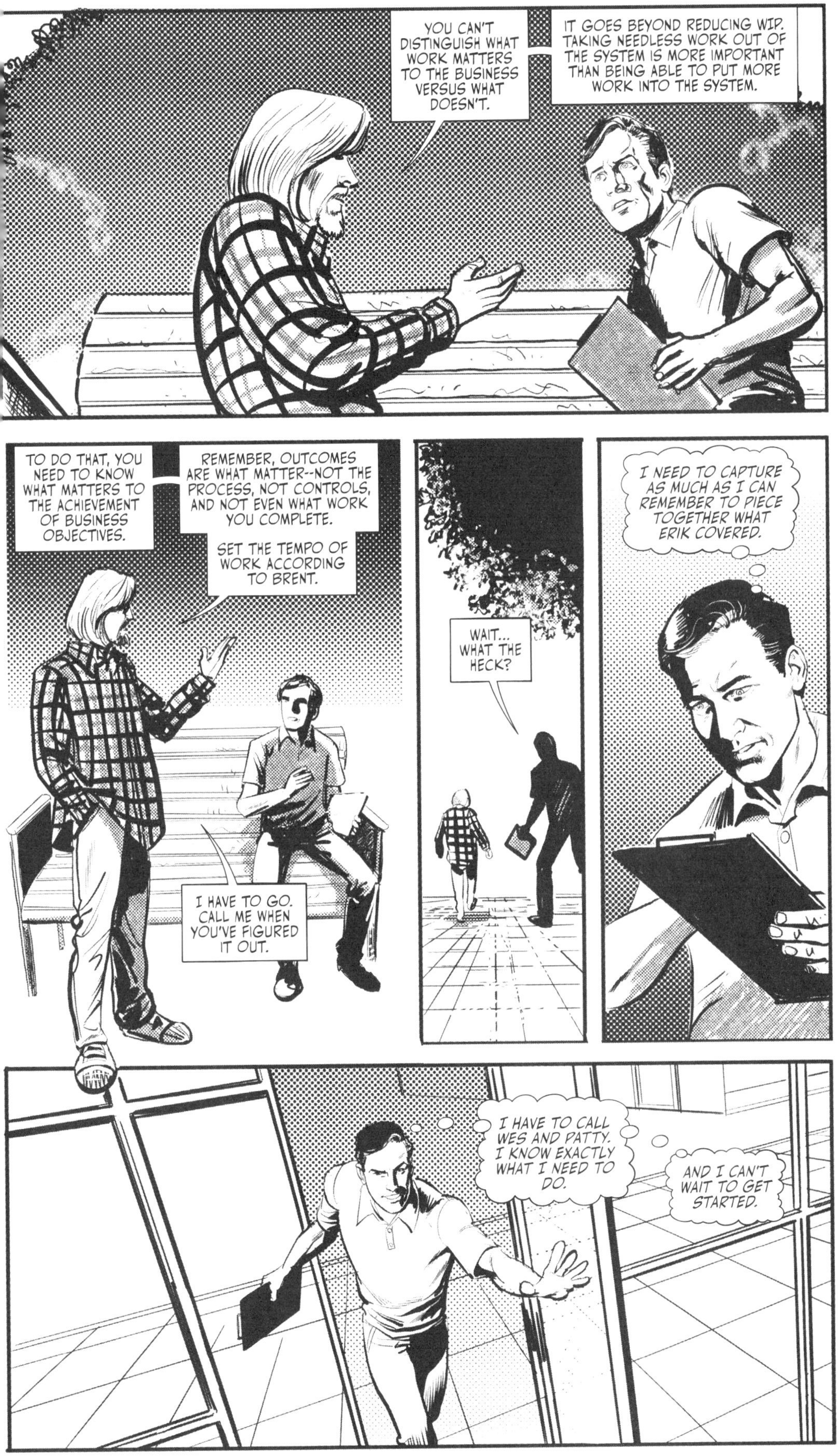
YOU CAN'T DISTINGUISH WHAT WORK MATTERS TO THE BUSINESS VERSUS WHAT DOESN'T.
IT GOES BEYOND REDUCING WIP. TAKING NEEDLESS WORK OUT OF THE SYSTEM IS MORE IMPORTANT THAN BEING ABLE TO PUT MORE WORK INTO THE SYSTEM.
TO DO THAT, YOU NEED TO KNOW WHAT MATTERS TO THE ACHIEVEMENT OF BUSINESS OBJECTIVES.
REMEMBER, OUTCOMES ARE WHAT MATTER--NOT THE PROCESS, NOT CONTROLS, AND NOT EVEN WHAT WORK YOU COMPLETE.
SET THE TEMPO OF WORK ACCORDING TO BRENT.
I HAVE TO GO. CALL ME WHEN YOU'VE FIGURED IT OUT.
WAIT... WHAT THE HECK?
I NEED TO CAPTURE AS MUCH AS I CAN REMEMBER TO PIECE TOGETHER WHAT ERIK COVERED.
I HAVE TO CALL WES AND PATTY. I KNOW EXACTLY WHAT I NEED TO DO.
AND I CAN'T WAIT TO GET STARTED.

CHAPTER 16 THURSDAY, SEPTEMBER 18

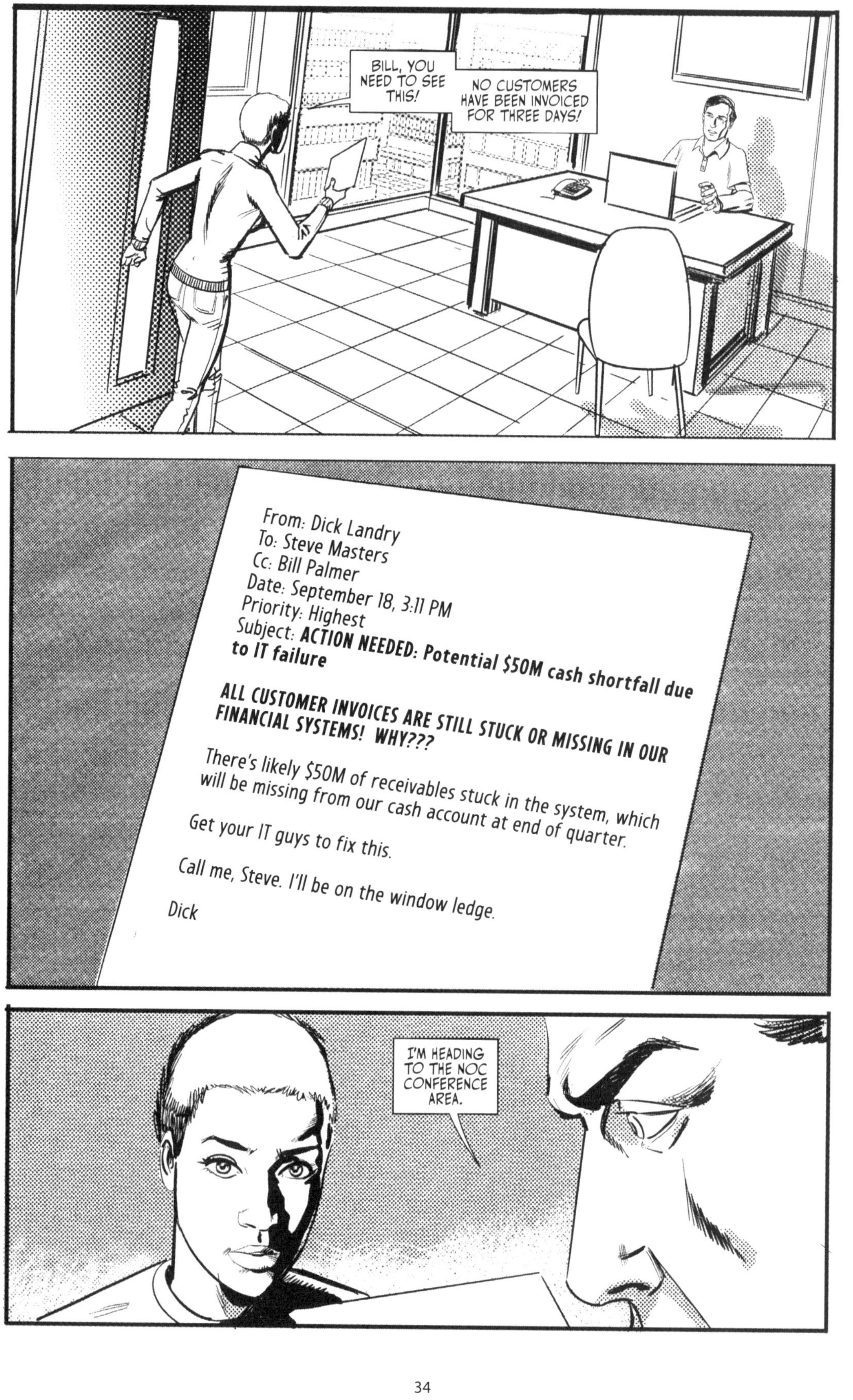
BILL, YOU NEED TO SEE THIS!
NO CUSTOMERS HAVE BEEN INVOICED FOR THREE DAYS!
From: Dick Landry
To: Steve Masters
Cc: Bill Palmer
Date: September 18, 3:11 PM
Priority: Highest
Subject: **ACTION NEEDED: Potential $50M cash shortfall due to IT failure**
ALL CUSTOMER INVOICES ARE STILL STUCK OR MISSING IN OUR FINANCIAL SYSTEMS! WHY???
There's likely $50M of receivables stuck in the system, which will be missing from our cash account at end of quarter.
Get your IT guys to fix this.
Call me, Steve. I'll be on the window ledge.
Dick
I'M HEADING TO THE NOC CONFERENCE AREA.

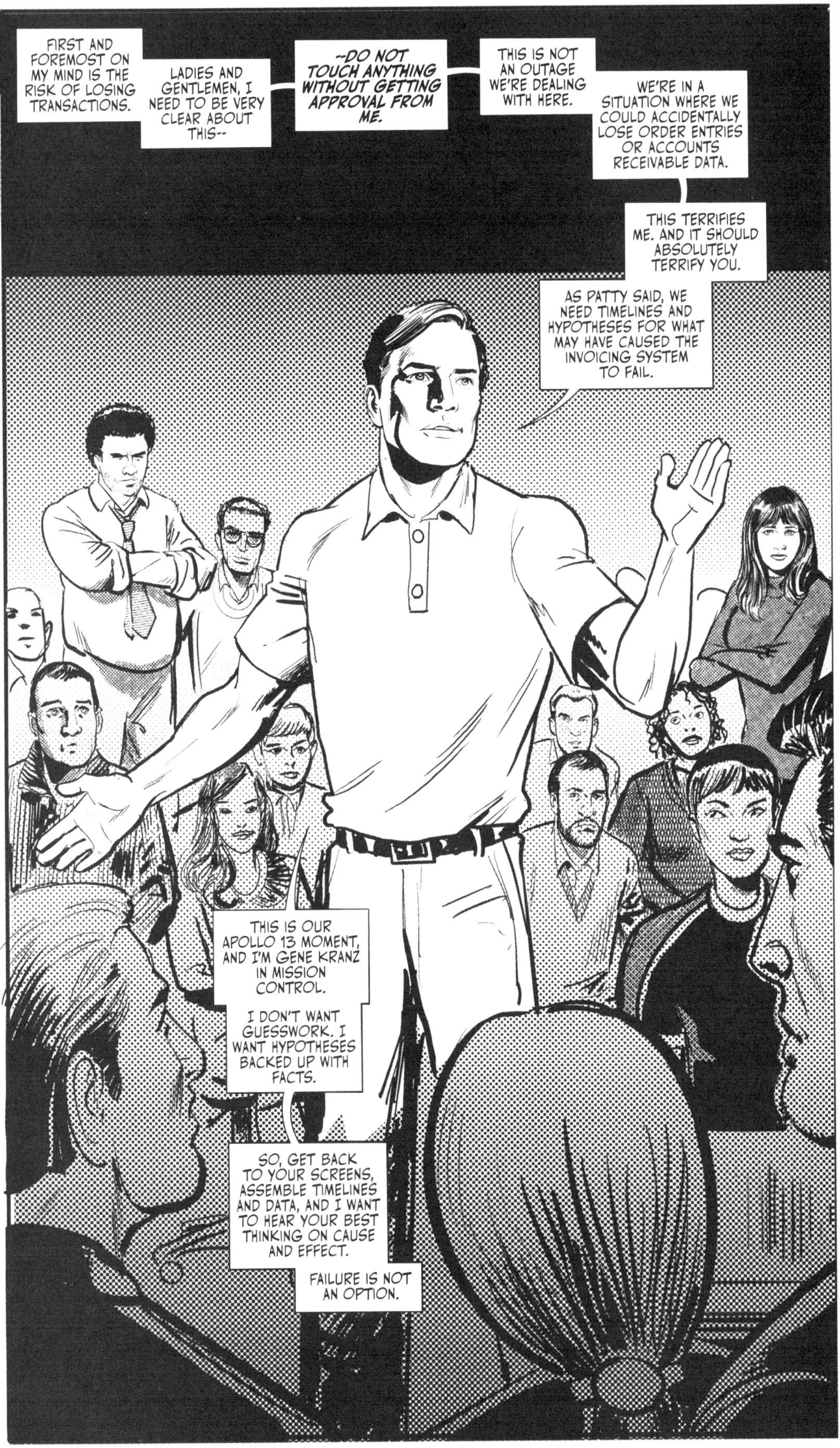
FIRST AND FOREMOST ON MY MIND IS THE RISK OF LOSING TRANSACTIONS.
LADIES AND GENTLEMEN, I NEED TO BE VERY CLEAR ABOUT THIS--
--DO NOT TOUCH ANYTHING WITHOUT GETTING APPROVAL FROM ME.
THIS IS NOT AN OUTAGE WE'RE DEALING WITH HERE.
WE'RE IN A SITUATION WHERE WE COULD ACCIDENTALLY LOSE ORDER ENTRIES OR ACCOUNTS RECEIVABLE DATA.
THIS TERRIFIES ME. AND IT SHOULD ABSOLUTELY TERRIFY YOU.
AS PATTY SAID, WE NEED TIMELINES AND HYPOTHESES FOR WHAT MAY HAVE CAUSED THE INVOICING SYSTEM TO FAIL.
THIS IS OUR APOLLO 13 MOMENT, AND I'M GENE KRANZ IN MISSION CONTROL.
I DON'T WANT GUESSWORK. I WANT HYPOTHESES BACKED UP WITH FACTS.
SO, GET BACK TO YOUR SCREENS, ASSEMBLE TIMELINES AND DATA, AND I WANT TO HEAR YOUR BEST THINKING ON CAUSE AND EFFECT.
FAILURE IS NOT AN OPTION.

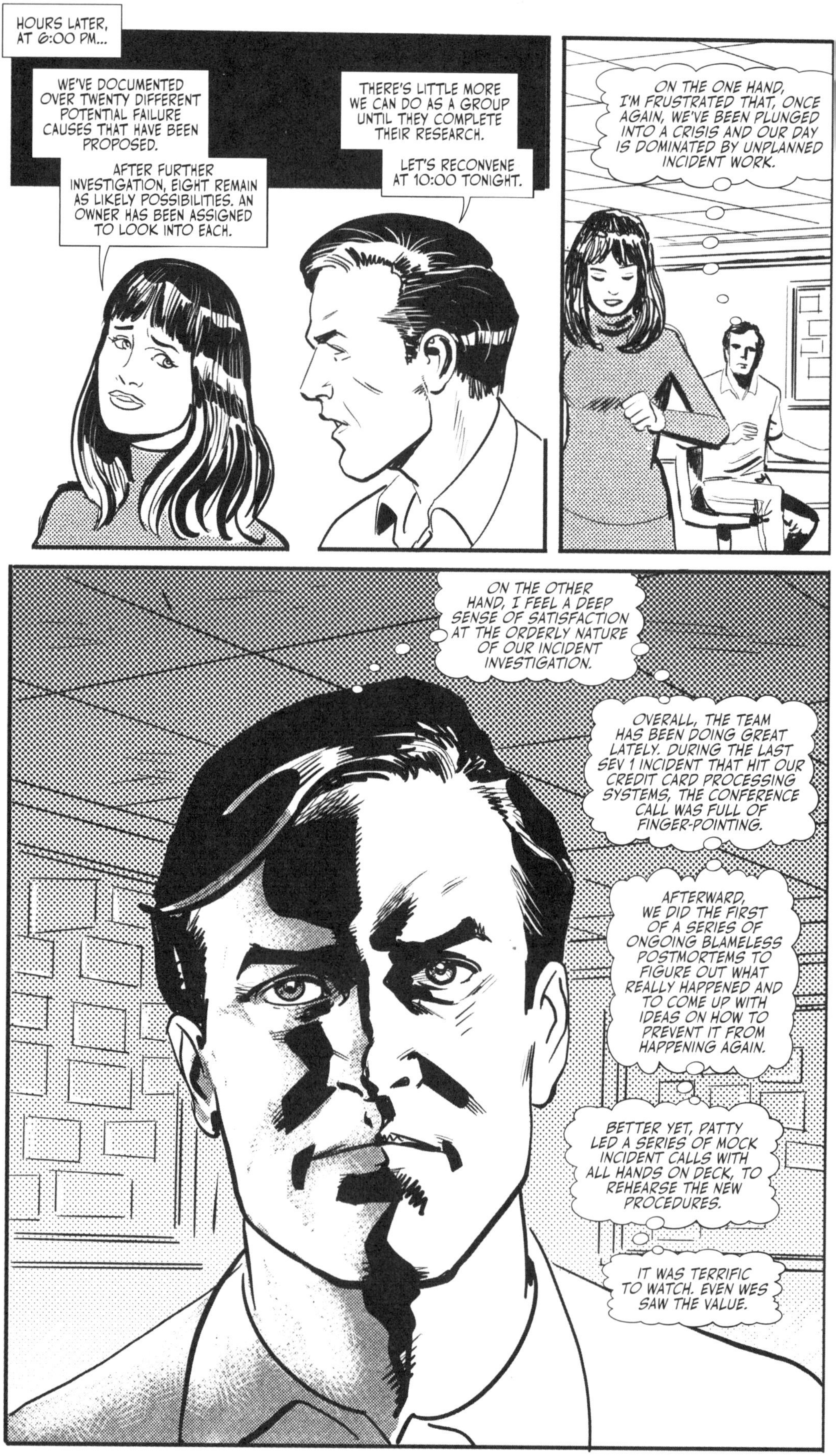
HOURS LATER, AT 6:00 PM...
WE'VE DOCUMENTED OVER TWENTY DIFFERENT POTENTIAL FAILURE CAUSES THAT HAVE BEEN PROPOSED.
AFTER FURTHER INVESTIGATION, EIGHT REMAIN AS LIKELY POSSIBILITIES. AN OWNER HAS BEEN ASSIGNED TO LOOK INTO EACH.
THERE'S LITTLE MORE WE CAN DO AS A GROUP UNTIL THEY COMPLETE THEIR RESEARCH.
LET'S RECONVENE AT 10:00 TONIGHT.
ON THE ONE HAND, I'M FRUSTRATED THAT, ONCE AGAIN, WE'VE BEEN PLUNGED INTO A CRISIS AND OUR DAY IS DOMINATED BY UNPLANNED INCIDENT WORK.
ON THE OTHER HAND, I FEEL A DEEP SENSE OF SATISFACTION AT THE ORDERLY NATURE OF OUR INCIDENT INVESTIGATION.
OVERALL, THE TEAM HAS BEEN DOING GREAT LATELY. DURING THE LAST SEV 1 INCIDENT THAT HIT OUR CREDIT CARD PROCESSING SYSTEMS, THE CONFERENCE CALL WAS FULL OF FINGER-POINTING.
AFTERWARD, WE DID THE FIRST OF A SERIES OF ONGOING BLAMELESS POSTMORTEMS TO FIGURE OUT WHAT REALLY HAPPENED AND TO COME UP WITH IDEAS ON HOW TO PREVENT IT FROM HAPPENING AGAIN.
BETTER YET, PATTY LED A SERIES OF MOCK INCIDENT CALLS WITH ALL HANDS ON DECK, TO REHEARSE THE NEW PROCEDURES.
IT WAS TERRIFIC TO WATCH. EVEN WES SAW THE VALUE.

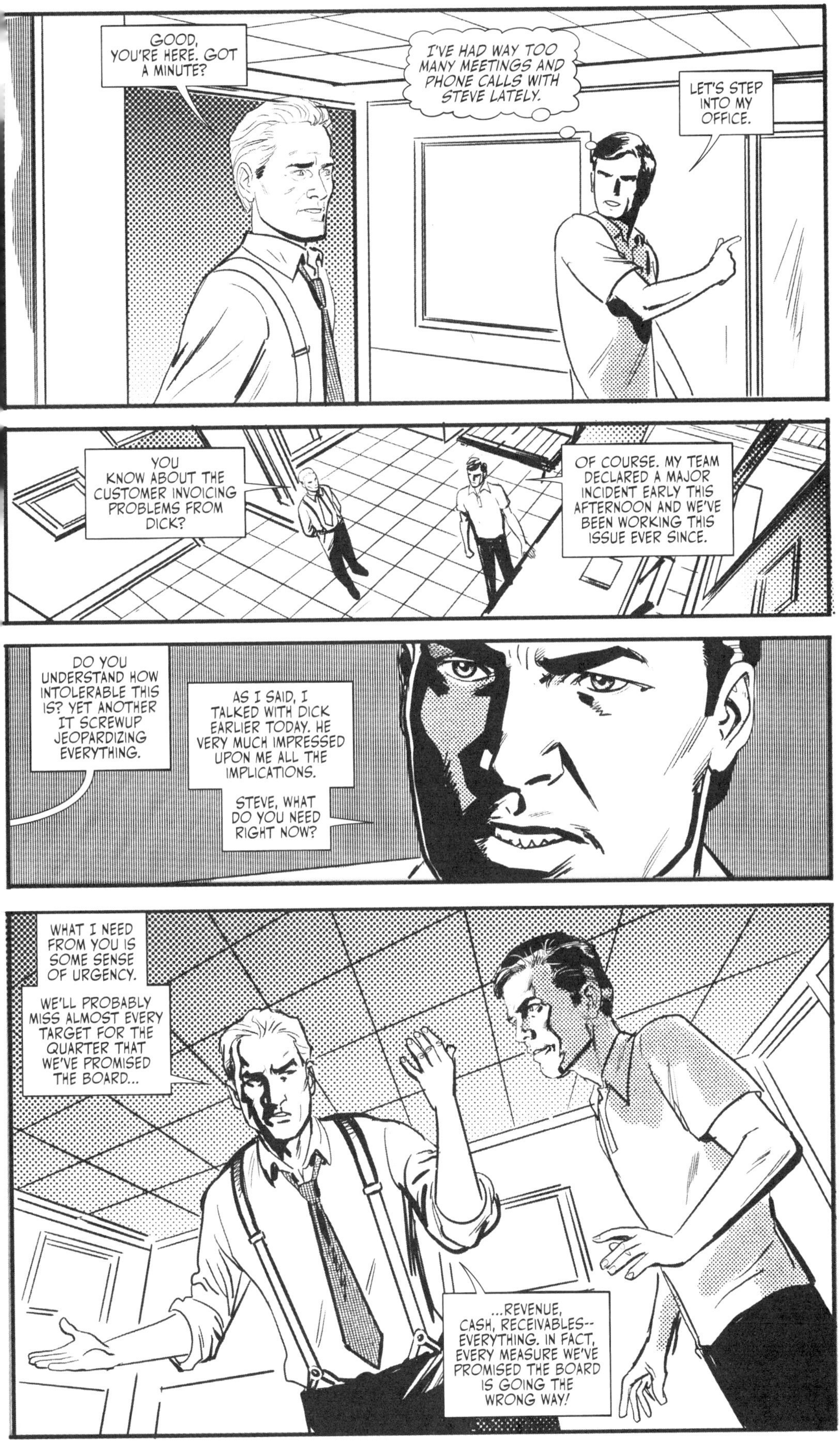
GOOD, YOU'RE HERE. GOT A MINUTE?
I'VE HAD WAY TOO MANY MEETINGS AND PHONE CALLS WITH STEVE LATELY.
LET'S STEP INTO MY OFFICE.
YOU KNOW ABOUT THE CUSTOMER INVOICING PROBLEMS FROM DICK?
OF COURSE. MY TEAM DECLARED A MAJOR INCIDENT EARLY THIS AFTERNOON AND WE'VE BEEN WORKING THIS ISSUE EVER SINCE.
DO YOU UNDERSTAND HOW INTOLERABLE THIS IS? YET ANOTHER IT SCREWUP JEOPARDIZING EVERYTHING.
AS I SAID, I TALKED WITH DICK EARLIER TODAY. HE VERY MUCH IMPRESSED UPON ME ALL THE IMPLICATIONS.
STEVE, WHAT DO YOU NEED RIGHT NOW?
WHAT I NEED FROM YOU IS SOME SENSE OF URGENCY.
WE'LL PROBABLY MISS ALMOST EVERY TARGET FOR THE QUARTER THAT WE'VE PROMISED THE BOARD...
...REVENUE, CASH, RECEIVABLES--EVERYTHING. IN FACT, EVERY MEASURE WE'VE PROMISED THE BOARD IS GOING THE WRONG WAY!

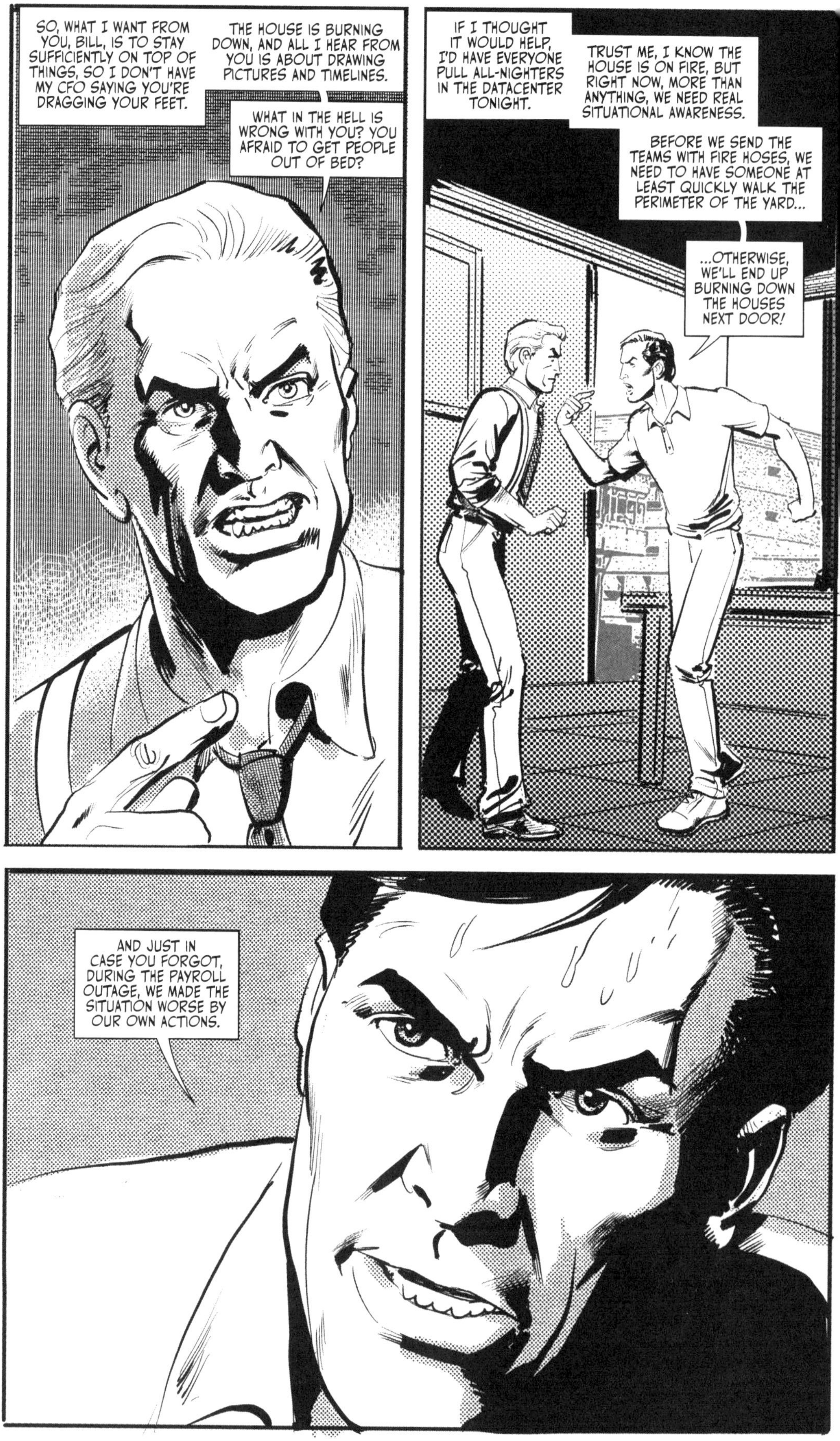
SO, WHAT I WANT FROM YOU, BILL, IS TO STAY SUFFICIENTLY ON TOP OF THINGS, SO I DON'T HAVE MY CFO SAYING YOU'RE DRAGGING YOUR FEET.
THE HOUSE IS BURNING DOWN, AND ALL I HEAR FROM YOU IS ABOUT DRAWING PICTURES AND TIMELINES.
WHAT IN THE HELL IS WRONG WITH YOU? YOU AFRAID TO GET PEOPLE OUT OF BED?
IF I THOUGHT IT WOULD HELP, I'D HAVE EVERYONE PULL ALL-NIGHTERS IN THE DATACENTER TONIGHT.
TRUST ME, I KNOW THE HOUSE IS ON FIRE, BUT RIGHT NOW, MORE THAN ANYTHING, WE NEED REAL SITUATIONAL AWARENESS.
BEFORE WE SEND THE TEAMS WITH FIRE HOSES, WE NEED TO HAVE SOMEONE AT LEAST QUICKLY WALK THE PERIMETER OF THE YARD...
...OTHERWISE, WE'LL END UP BURNING DOWN THE HOUSES NEXT DOOR!
AND JUST IN CASE YOU FORGOT, DURING THE PAYROLL OUTAGE, WE MADE THE SITUATION WORSE BY OUR OWN ACTIONS.

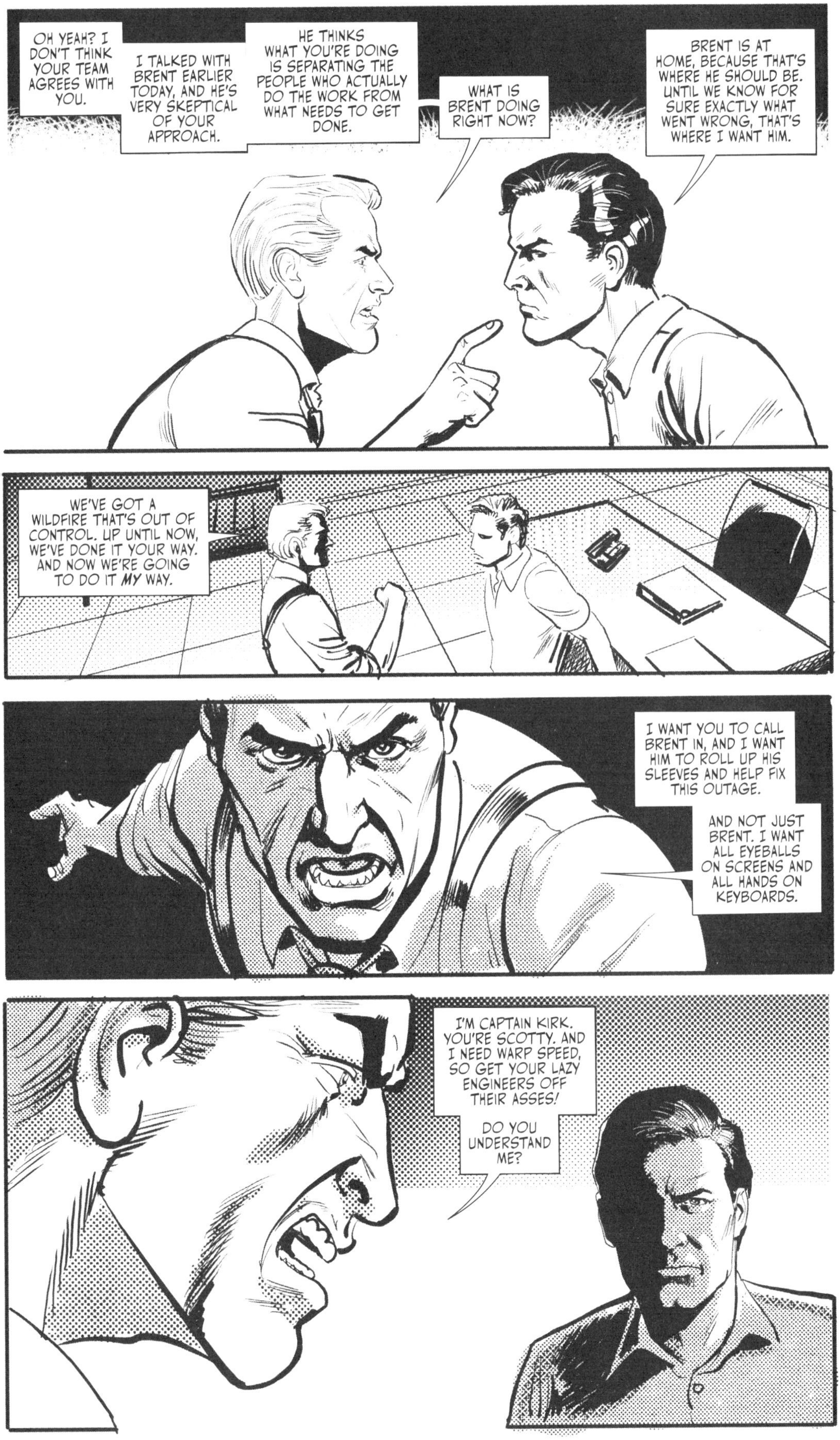
OH YEAH? I DON'T THINK YOUR TEAM AGREES WITH YOU.
I TALKED WITH BRENT EARLIER TODAY, AND HE'S VERY SKEPTICAL OF YOUR APPROACH.
HE THINKS WHAT YOU'RE DOING IS SEPARATING THE PEOPLE WHO ACTUALLY DO THE WORK FROM WHAT NEEDS TO GET DONE.
WHAT IS BRENT DOING RIGHT NOW?
BRENT IS AT HOME, BECAUSE THAT'S WHERE HE SHOULD BE. UNTIL WE KNOW FOR SURE EXACTLY WHAT WENT WRONG, THAT'S WHERE I WANT HIM.
WE'VE GOT A WILDFIRE THAT'S OUT OF CONTROL. UP UNTIL NOW, WE'VE DONE IT YOUR WAY. AND NOW WE'RE GOING TO DO IT *MY* WAY.
I WANT YOU TO CALL BRENT IN, AND I WANT HIM TO ROLL UP HIS SLEEVES AND HELP FIX THIS OUTAGE.
AND NOT JUST BRENT. I WANT ALL EYEBALLS ON SCREENS AND ALL HANDS ON KEYBOARDS.
I'M CAPTAIN KIRK. YOU'RE SCOTTY. AND I NEED WARP SPEED, SO GET YOUR LAZY ENGINEERS OFF THEIR ASSES!
DO YOU UNDERSTAND ME?

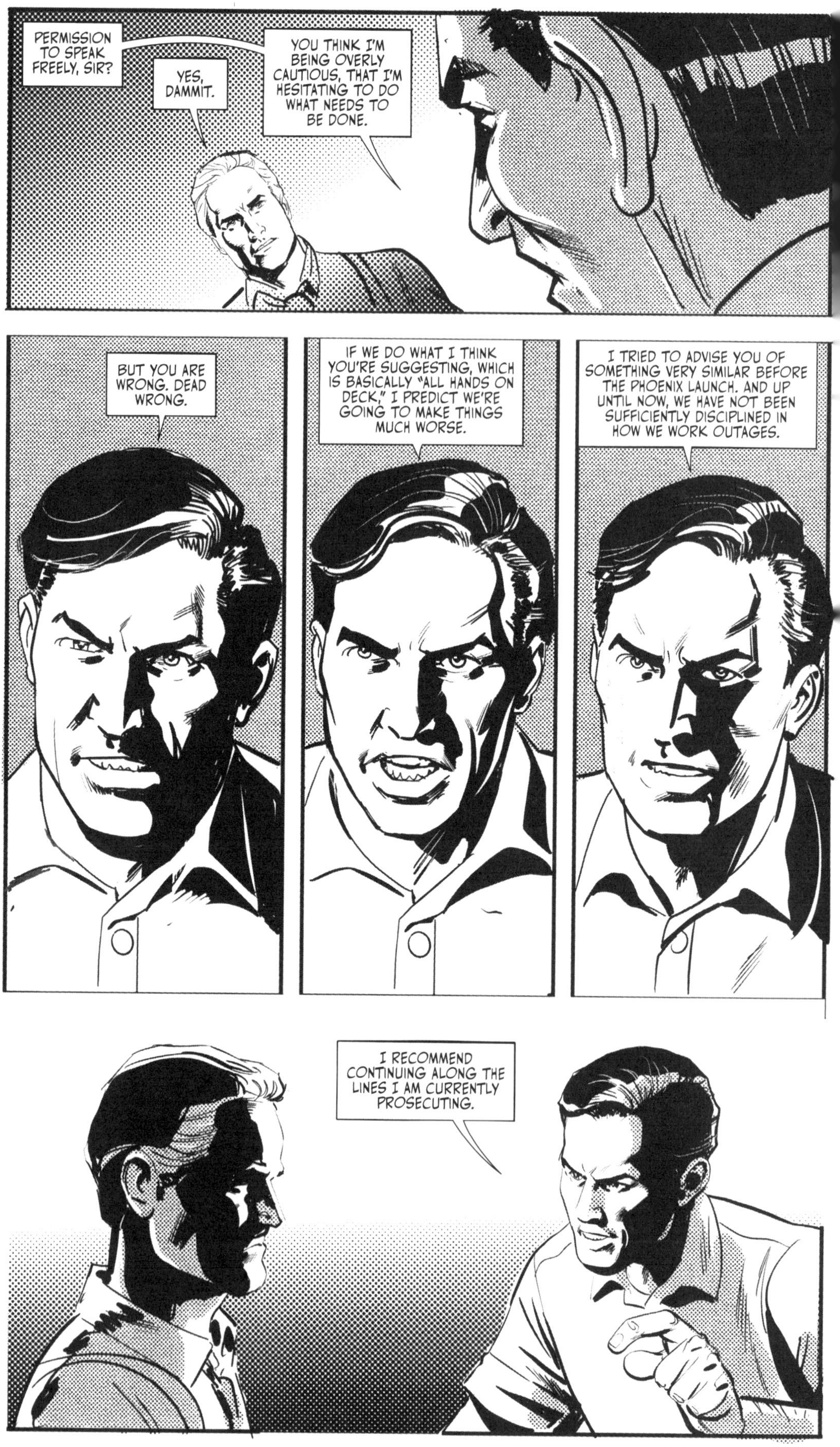
PERMISSION TO SPEAK FREELY, SIR?
YES, DAMMIT.
YOU THINK I'M BEING OVERLY CAUTIOUS, THAT I'M HESITATING TO DO WHAT NEEDS TO BE DONE.
BUT YOU ARE WRONG. DEAD WRONG.
IF WE DO WHAT I THINK YOU'RE SUGGESTING, WHICH IS BASICALLY "ALL HANDS ON DECK," I PREDICT WE'RE GOING TO MAKE THINGS MUCH WORSE.
I TRIED TO ADVISE YOU OF SOMETHING VERY SIMILAR BEFORE THE PHOENIX LAUNCH. AND UP UNTIL NOW, WE HAVE NOT BEEN SUFFICIENTLY DISCIPLINED IN HOW WE WORK OUTAGES.
I RECOMMEND CONTINUING ALONG THE LINES I AM CURRENTLY PROSECUTING.

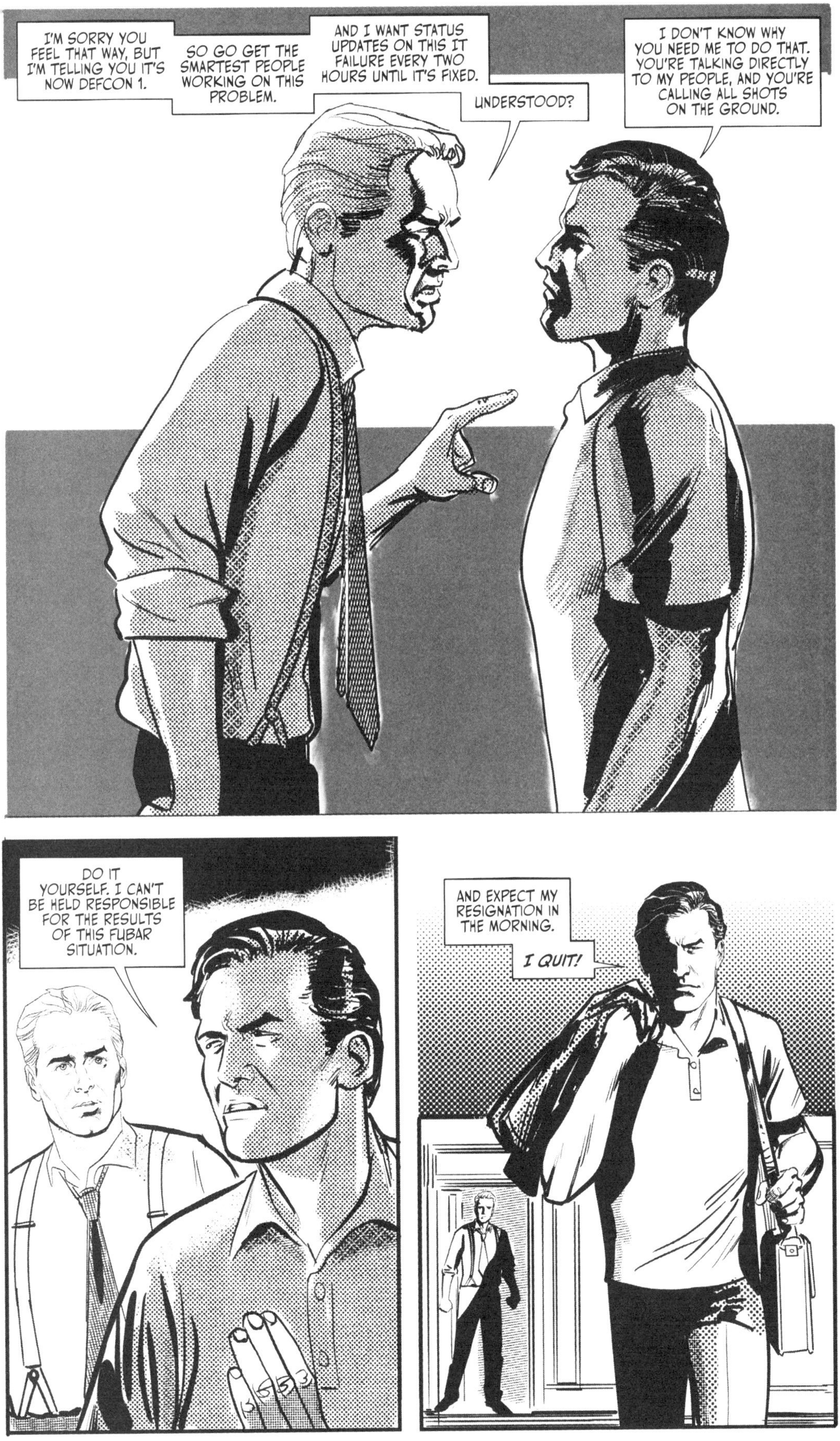
I'M SORRY YOU FEEL THAT WAY, BUT I'M TELLING YOU IT'S NOW DEFCON 1.
SO GO GET THE SMARTEST PEOPLE WORKING ON THIS PROBLEM.
AND I WANT STATUS UPDATES ON THIS IT FAILURE EVERY TWO HOURS UNTIL IT'S FIXED.
UNDERSTOOD?
I DON'T KNOW WHY YOU NEED ME TO DO THAT. YOU'RE TALKING DIRECTLY TO MY PEOPLE, AND YOU'RE CALLING ALL SHOTS ON THE GROUND.
DO IT YOURSELF. I CAN'T BE HELD RESPONSIBLE FOR THE RESULTS OF THIS FUBAR SITUATION.
AND EXPECT MY RESIGNATION IN THE MORNING.
I QUIT!

CHAPTER 17 MONDAY, SEPTEMBER 22

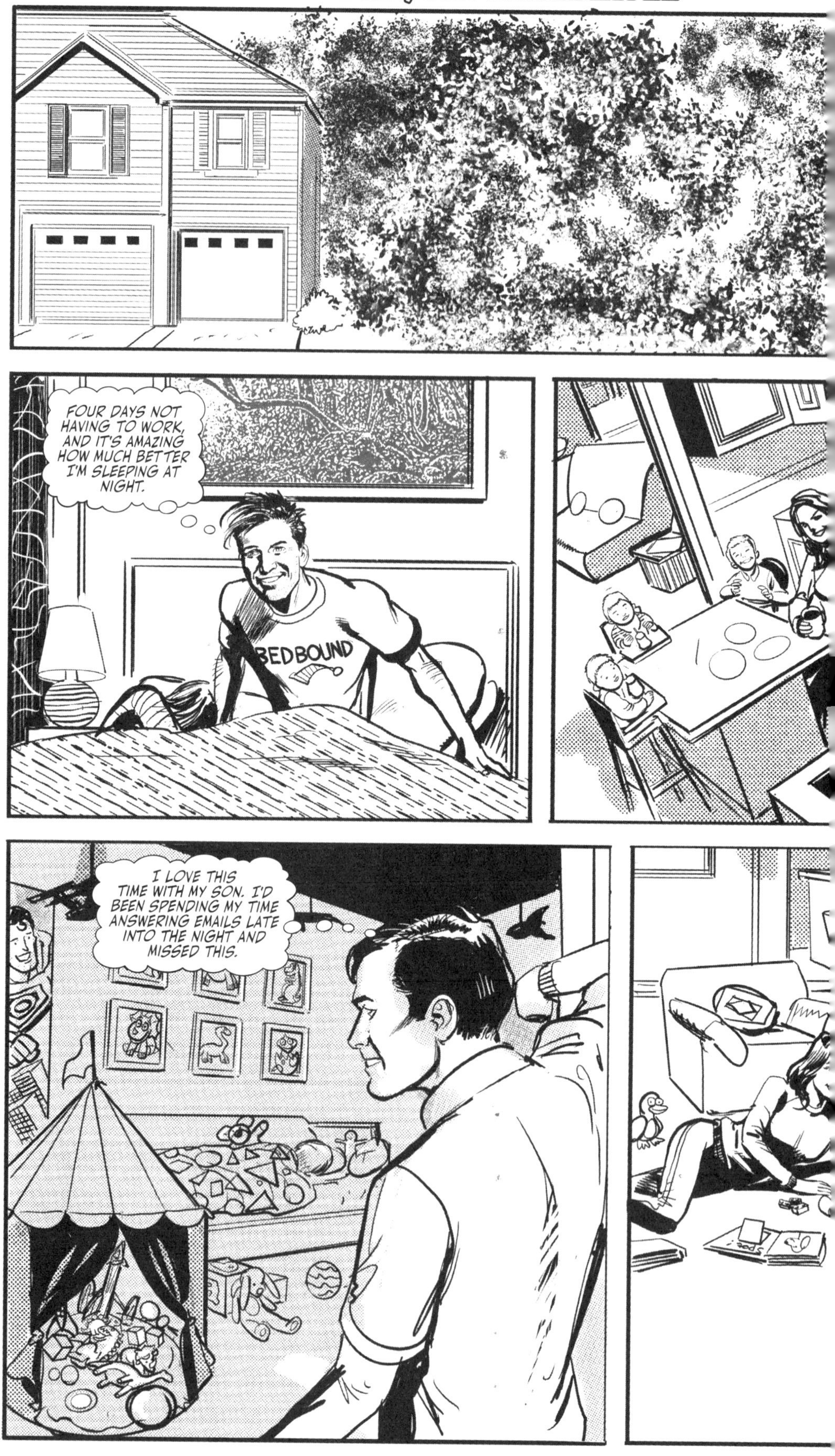
FOUR DAYS NOT HAVING TO WORK, AND IT'S AMAZING HOW MUCH BETTER I'M SLEEPING AT NIGHT.
BEDBOUND
I LOVE THIS TIME WITH MY SON. I'D BEEN SPENDING MY TIME ANSWERING EMAILS LATE INTO THE NIGHT AND MISSED THIS.

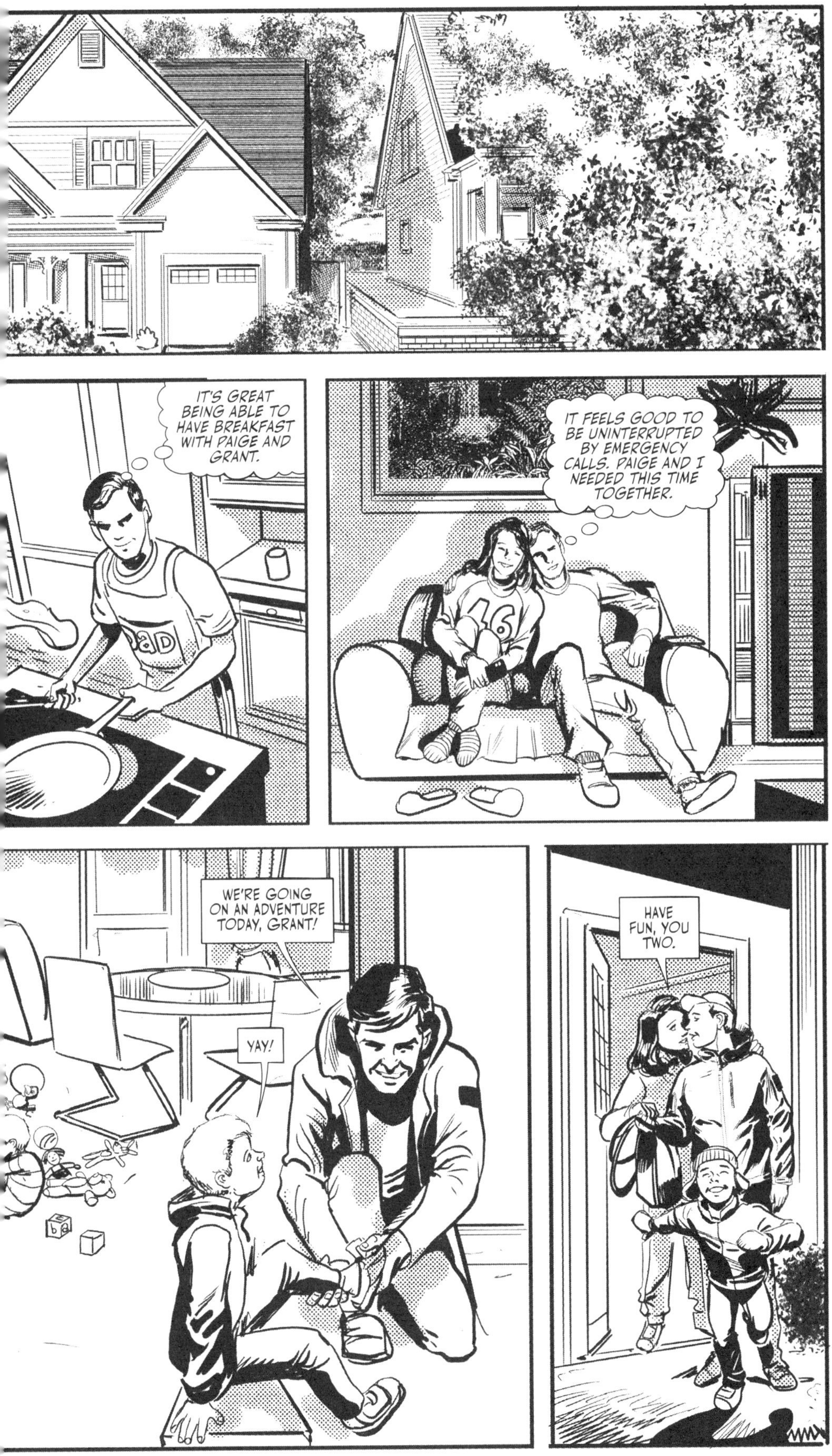
IT'S GREAT BEING ABLE TO HAVE BREAKFAST WITH PAIGE AND GRANT.
BAD
IT FEELS GOOD TO BE UNINTERRUPTED BY EMERGENCY CALLS. PAIGE AND I NEEDED THIS TIME TOGETHER.
46
WE'RE GOING ON AN ADVENTURE TODAY, GRANT!
YAY!
HAVE FUN, YOU TWO.

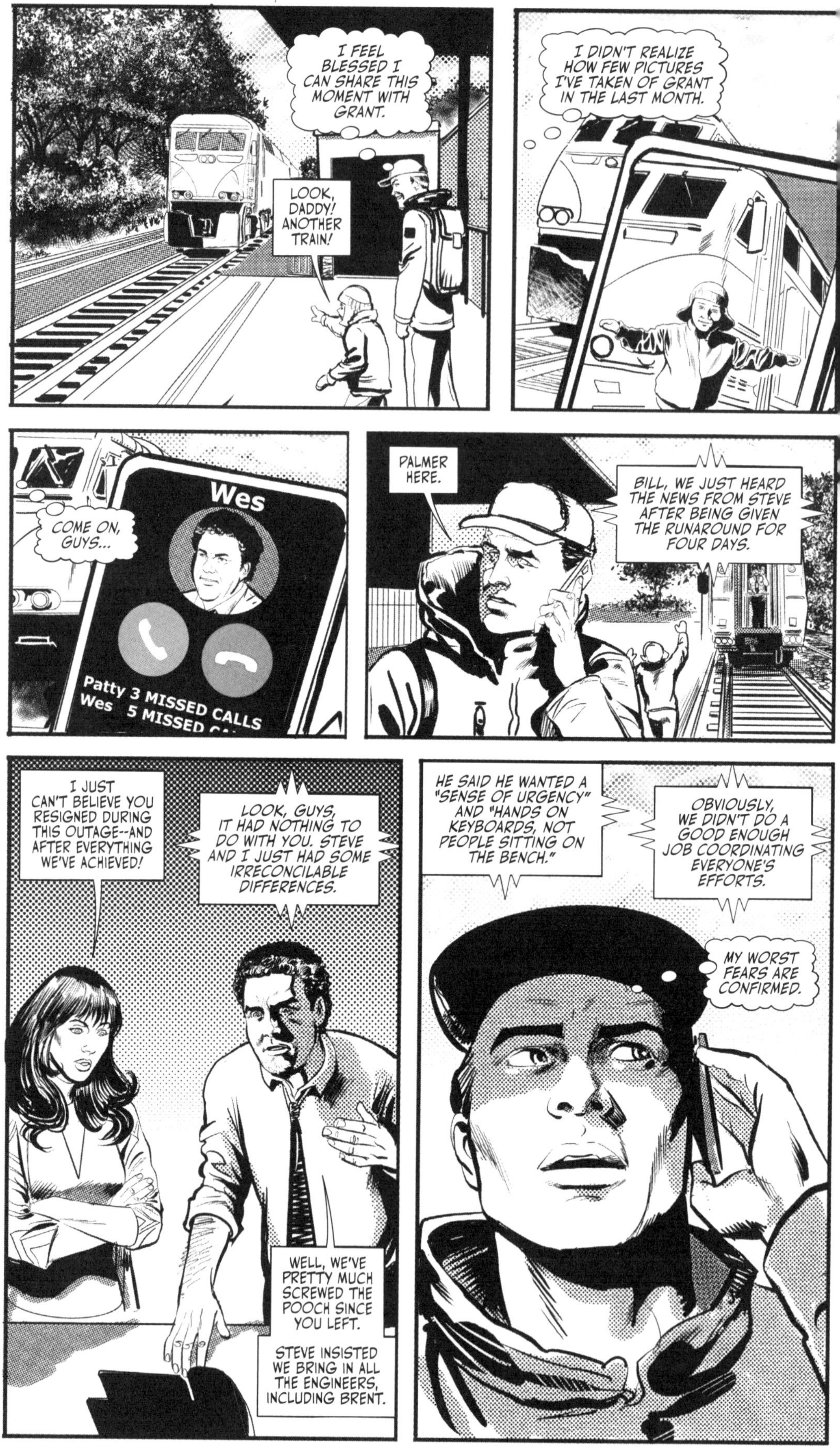
I FEEL BLESSED I CAN SHARE THIS MOMENT WITH GRANT.
LOOK, DADDY! ANOTHER TRAIN!
I DIDN'T REALIZE HOW FEW PICTURES I'VE TAKEN OF GRANT IN THE LAST MONTH.
COME ON, GUYS...
Wes
Patty 3 MISSED CALLS
Wes 5 MISSED
PALMER HERE.
BILL, WE JUST HEARD THE NEWS FROM STEVE AFTER BEING GIVEN THE RUNAROUND FOR FOUR DAYS.
I JUST CAN'T BELIEVE YOU RESIGNED DURING THIS OUTAGE--AND AFTER EVERYTHING WE'VE ACHIEVED!
LOOK, GUYS, IT HAD NOTHING TO DO WITH YOU. STEVE AND I JUST HAD SOME IRRECONCILABLE DIFFERENCES.
WELL, WE'VE PRETTY MUCH SCREWED THE POOCH SINCE YOU LEFT.
STEVE INSISTED WE BRING IN ALL THE ENGINEERS, INCLUDING BRENT.
HE SAID HE WANTED A "SENSE OF URGENCY" AND "HANDS ON KEYBOARDS, NOT PEOPLE SITTING ON THE BENCH."
OBVIOUSLY, WE DIDN'T DO A GOOD ENOUGH JOB COORDINATING EVERYONE'S EFFORTS.
MY WORST FEARS ARE CONFIRMED.

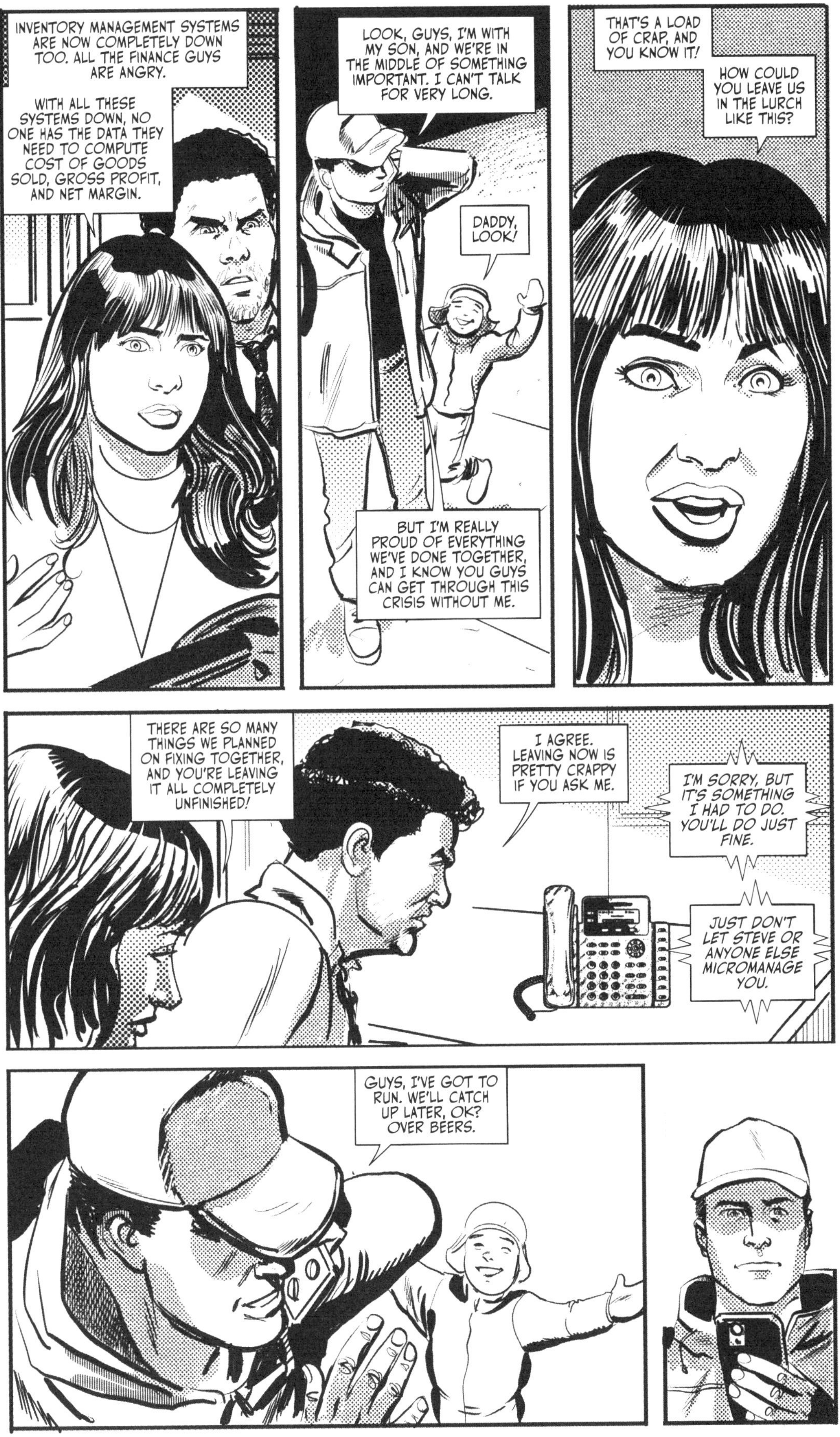
INVENTORY MANAGEMENT SYSTEMS ARE NOW COMPLETELY DOWN TOO. ALL THE FINANCE GUYS ARE ANGRY.
WITH ALL THESE SYSTEMS DOWN, NO ONE HAS THE DATA THEY NEED TO COMPUTE COST OF GOODS SOLD, GROSS PROFIT, AND NET MARGIN.
LOOK, GUYS, I'M WITH MY SON, AND WE'RE IN THE MIDDLE OF SOMETHING IMPORTANT. I CAN'T TALK FOR VERY LONG.
DADDY, LOOK!
BUT I'M REALLY PROUD OF EVERYTHING WE'VE DONE TOGETHER, AND I KNOW YOU GUYS CAN GET THROUGH THIS CRISIS WITHOUT ME.
THAT'S A LOAD OF CRAP, AND YOU KNOW IT!
HOW COULD YOU LEAVE US IN THE LURCH LIKE THIS?
THERE ARE SO MANY THINGS WE PLANNED ON FIXING TOGETHER, AND YOU'RE LEAVING IT ALL COMPLETELY UNFINISHED!
I AGREE. LEAVING NOW IS PRETTY CRAPPY IF YOU ASK ME.
I'M SORRY, BUT IT'S SOMETHING I HAD TO DO. YOU'LL DO JUST FINE.
JUST DON'T LET STEVE OR ANYONE ELSE MICROMANAGE YOU.
GUYS, I'VE GOT TO RUN. WE'LL CATCH UP LATER, OK? OVER BEERS.

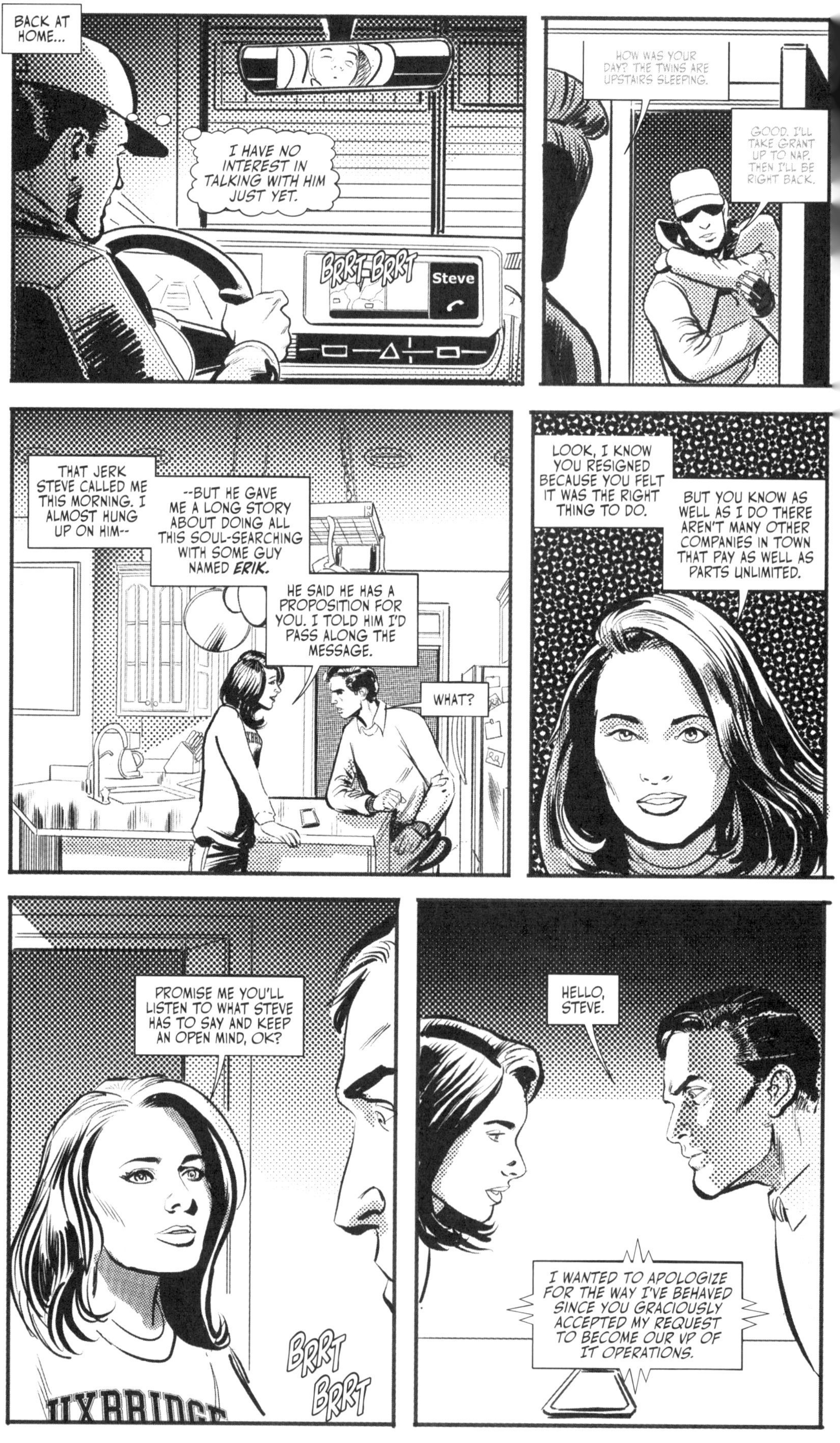
BACK AT HOME...
I HAVE NO INTEREST IN TALKING WITH HIM JUST YET.
BRRT-BRRT
Steve
HOW WAS YOUR DAY? THE TWINS ARE UPSTAIRS SLEEPING.
GOOD. I'LL TAKE GRANT UP TO NAP. THEN I'LL BE RIGHT BACK.
THAT JERK STEVE CALLED ME THIS MORNING. I ALMOST HUNG UP ON HIM--
--BUT HE GAVE ME A LONG STORY ABOUT DOING ALL THIS SOUL-SEARCHING WITH SOME GUY NAMED ERIK.
HE SAID HE HAS A PROPOSITION FOR YOU. I TOLD HIM I'D PASS ALONG THE MESSAGE.
WHAT?
LOOK, I KNOW YOU RESIGNED BECAUSE YOU FELT IT WAS THE RIGHT THING TO DO.
BUT YOU KNOW AS WELL AS I DO THERE AREN'T MANY OTHER COMPANIES IN TOWN THAT PAY AS WELL AS PARTS UNLIMITED.
PROMISE ME YOU'LL LISTEN TO WHAT STEVE HAS TO SAY AND KEEP AN OPEN MIND, OK?
BRRT BRRT
HELLO, STEVE.
I WANTED TO APOLOGIZE FOR THE WAY I'VE BEHAVED SINCE YOU GRACIOUSLY ACCEPTED MY REQUEST TO BECOME OUR VP OF IT OPERATIONS.

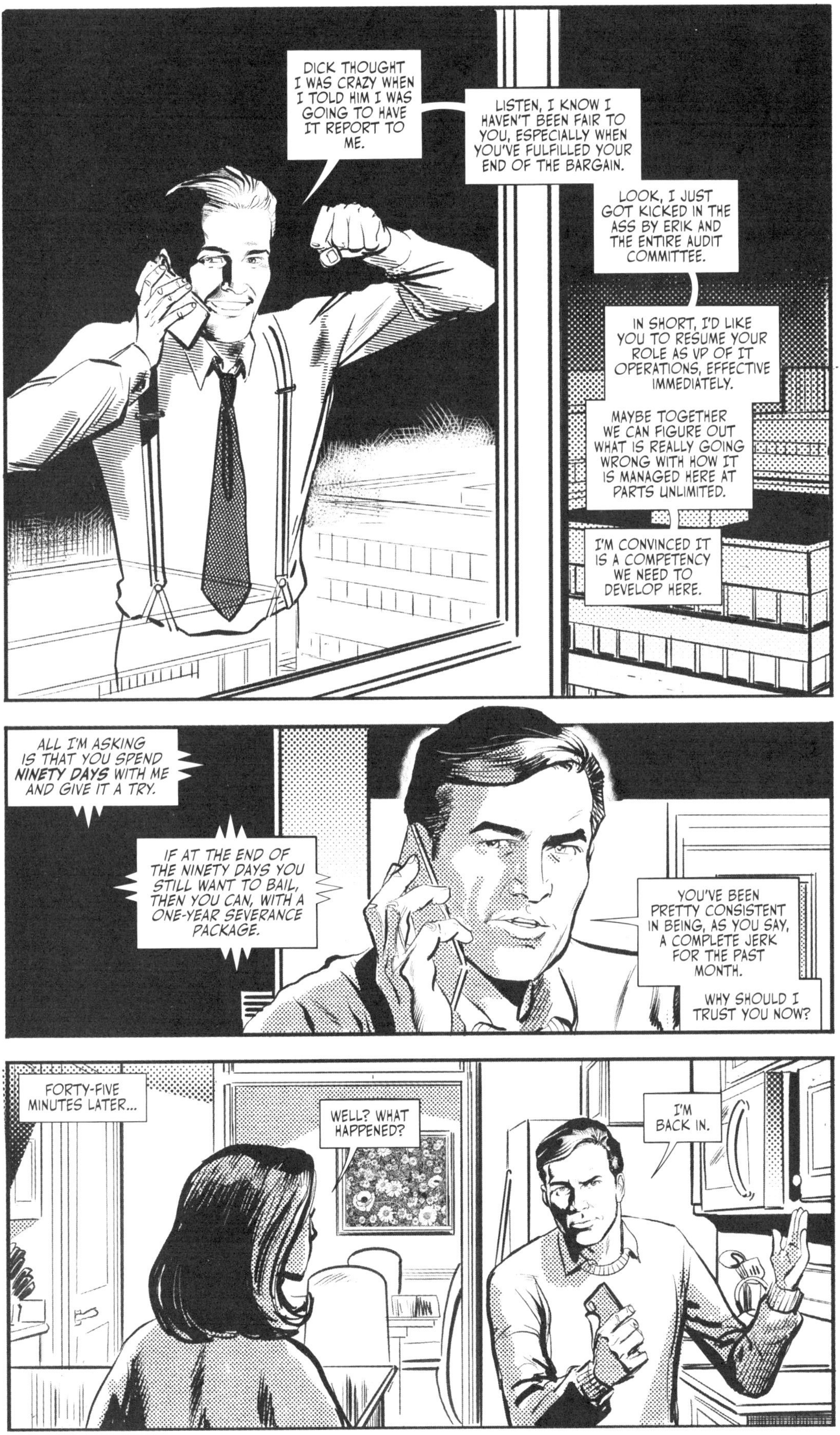

DICK THOUGHT I WAS CRAZY WHEN I TOLD HIM I WAS GOING TO HAVE IT REPORT TO ME.
LISTEN, I KNOW I HAVEN'T BEEN FAIR TO YOU, ESPECIALLY WHEN YOU'VE FULFILLED YOUR END OF THE BARGAIN.
LOOK, I JUST GOT KICKED IN THE ASS BY ERIK AND THE ENTIRE AUDIT COMMITTEE.
IN SHORT, I'D LIKE YOU TO RESUME YOUR ROLE AS VP OF IT OPERATIONS, EFFECTIVE IMMEDIATELY.
MAYBE TOGETHER WE CAN FIGURE OUT WHAT IS REALLY GOING WRONG WITH HOW IT IS MANAGED HERE AT PARTS UNLIMITED.
I'M CONVINCED IT IS A COMPETENCY WE NEED TO DEVELOP HERE.
ALL I'M ASKING IS THAT YOU SPEND NINETY DAYS WITH ME AND GIVE IT A TRY.
IF AT THE END OF THE NINETY DAYS YOU STILL WANT TO BAIL, THEN YOU CAN, WITH A ONE-YEAR SEVERANCE PACKAGE.
YOU'VE BEEN PRETTY CONSISTENT IN BEING, AS YOU SAY, A COMPLETE JERK FOR THE PAST MONTH.
WHY SHOULD I TRUST YOU NOW?
FORTY-FIVE MINUTES LATER...
WELL? WHAT HAPPENED?
I'M BACK IN.

CHAPTER 18 TUESDAY, SEPTEMBER 23

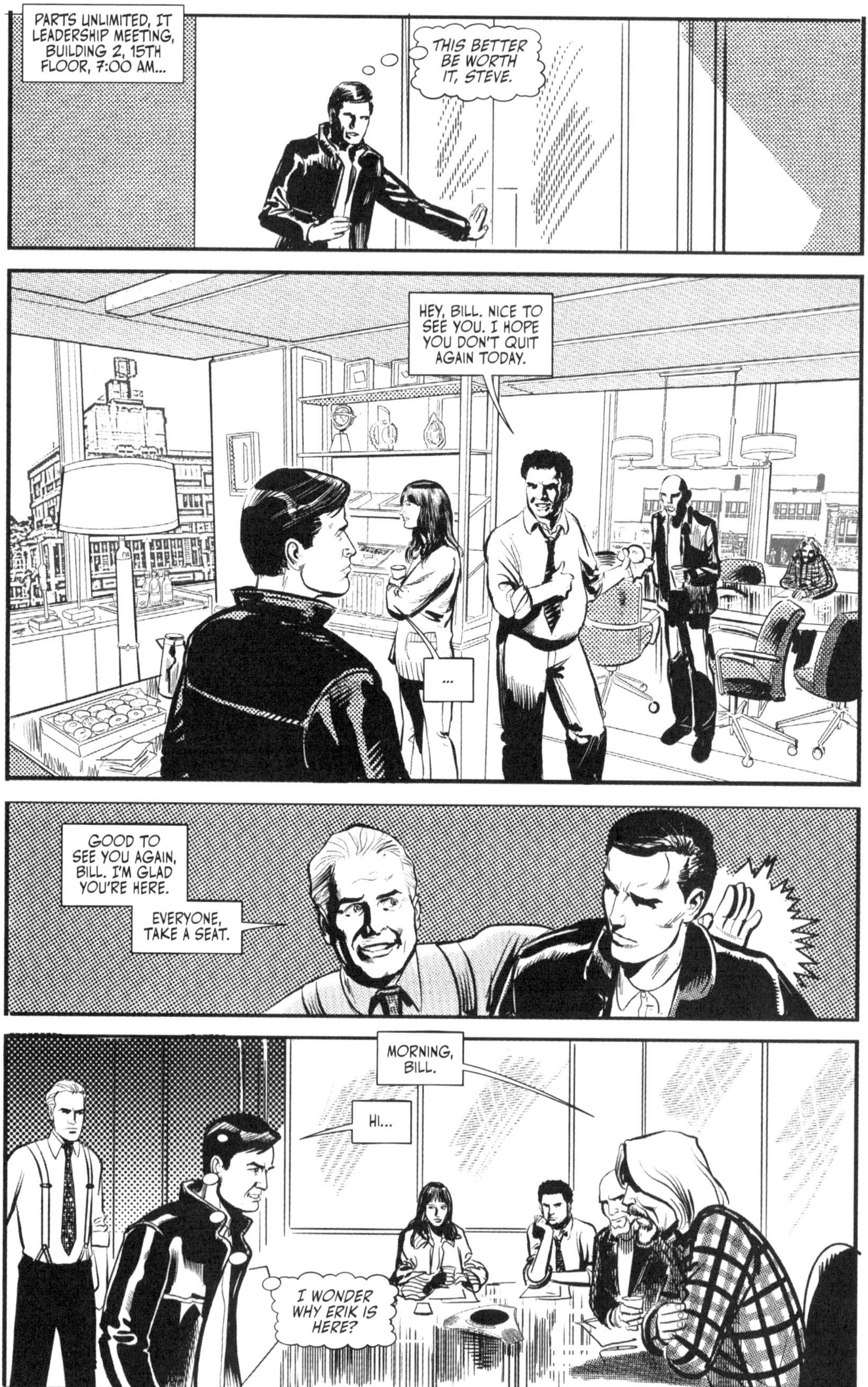

PARTS UNLIMITED, IT LEADERSHIP MEETING, BUILDING 2, 15TH FLOOR, 7:00 AM...
THIS BETTER BE WORTH IT, STEVE.
HEY, BILL. NICE TO SEE YOU. I HOPE YOU DON'T QUIT AGAIN TODAY.
...
GOOD TO SEE YOU AGAIN, BILL. I'M GLAD YOU'RE HERE.
EVERYONE, TAKE A SEAT.
MORNING, BILL.
HI...
I WONDER WHY ERIK IS HERE?

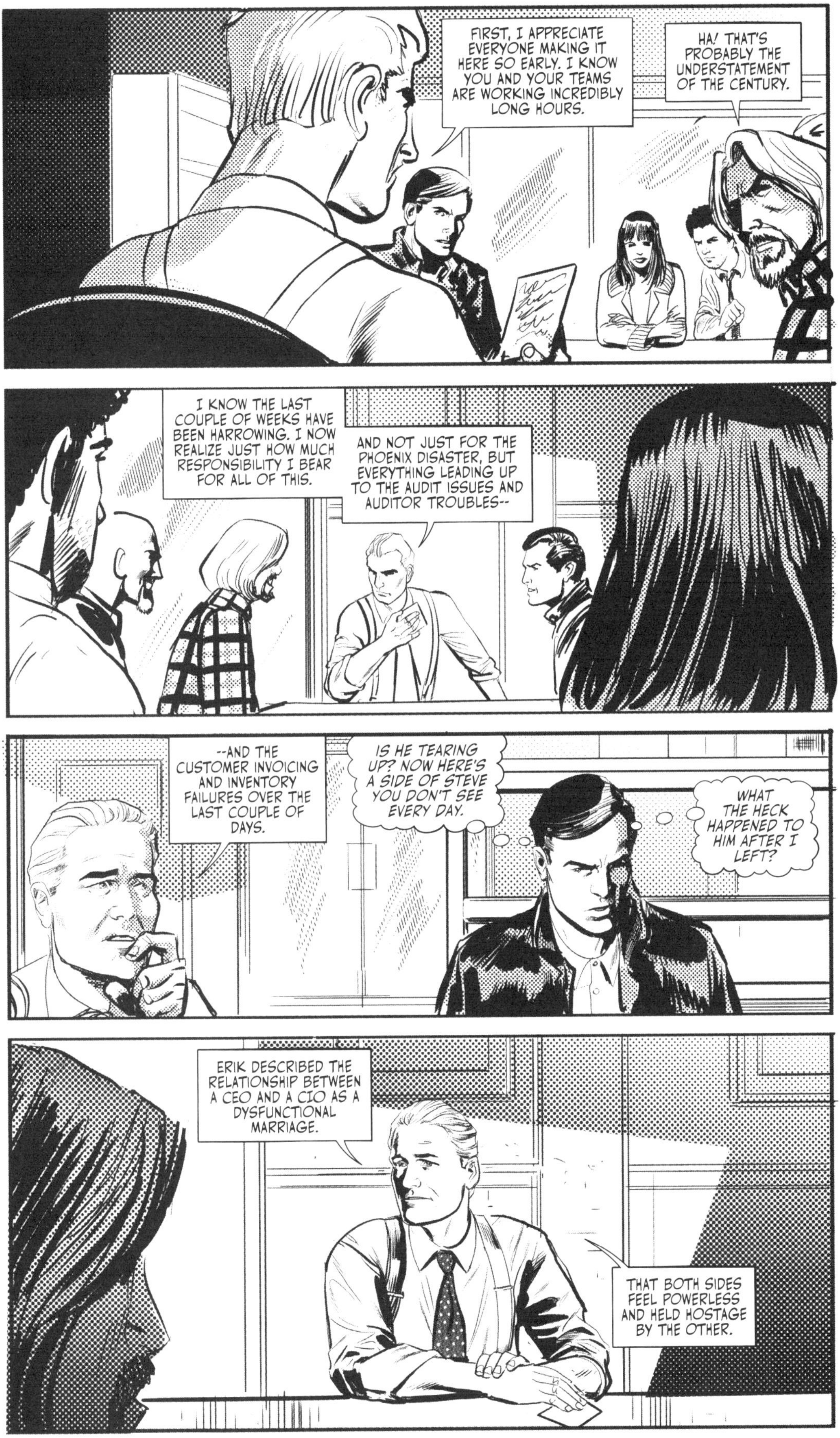
FIRST, I APPRECIATE EVERYONE MAKING IT HERE SO EARLY. I KNOW YOU AND YOUR TEAMS ARE WORKING INCREDIBLY LONG HOURS.
HA! THAT'S PROBABLY THE UNDERSTATEMENT OF THE CENTURY.
I KNOW THE LAST COUPLE OF WEEKS HAVE BEEN HARROWING. I NOW REALIZE JUST HOW MUCH RESPONSIBILITY I BEAR FOR ALL OF THIS.
AND NOT JUST FOR THE PHOENIX DISASTER, BUT EVERYTHING LEADING UP TO THE AUDIT ISSUES AND AUDITOR TROUBLES--
--AND THE CUSTOMER INVOICING AND INVENTORY FAILURES OVER THE LAST COUPLE OF DAYS.
IS HE TEARING UP? NOW HERE'S A SIDE OF STEVE YOU DON'T SEE EVERY DAY.
WHAT THE HECK HAPPENED TO HIM AFTER I LEFT?
ERIK DESCRIBED THE RELATIONSHIP BETWEEN A CEO AND A CIO AS A DYSFUNCTIONAL MARRIAGE.
THAT BOTH SIDES FEEL POWERLESS AND HELD HOSTAGE BY THE OTHER.

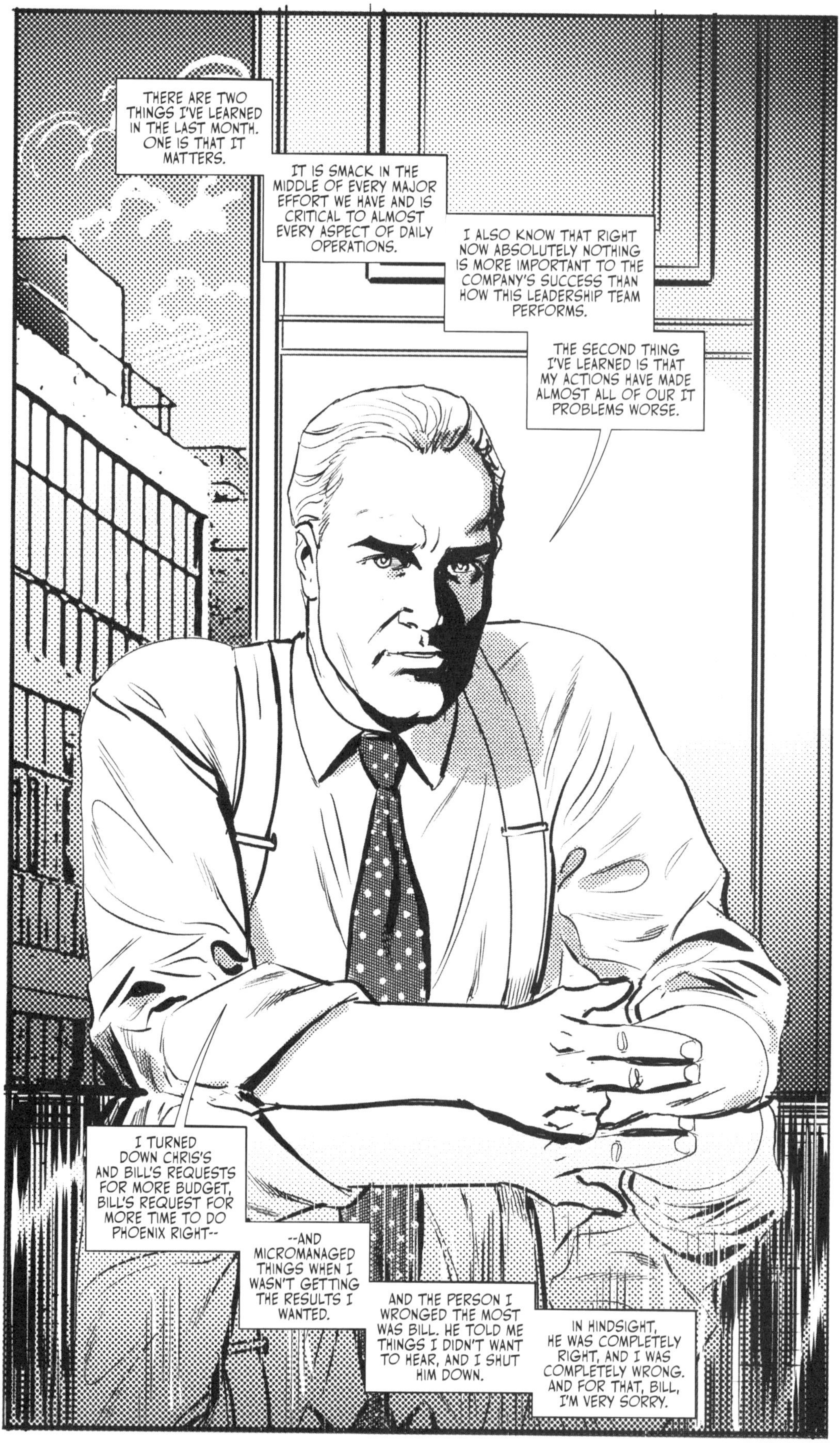
THERE ARE TWO THINGS I'VE LEARNED IN THE LAST MONTH. ONE IS THAT IT MATTERS.
IT IS SMACK IN THE MIDDLE OF EVERY MAJOR EFFORT WE HAVE AND IS CRITICAL TO ALMOST EVERY ASPECT OF DAILY OPERATIONS.
I ALSO KNOW THAT RIGHT NOW ABSOLUTELY NOTHING IS MORE IMPORTANT TO THE COMPANY'S SUCCESS THAN HOW THIS LEADERSHIP TEAM PERFORMS.
THE SECOND THING I'VE LEARNED IS THAT MY ACTIONS HAVE MADE ALMOST ALL OF OUR IT PROBLEMS WORSE.
I TURNED DOWN CHRIS'S AND BILL'S REQUESTS FOR MORE BUDGET, BILL'S REQUEST FOR MORE TIME TO DO PHOENIX RIGHT--
--AND MICROMANAGED THINGS WHEN I WASN'T GETTING THE RESULTS I WANTED.
AND THE PERSON I WRONGED THE MOST WAS BILL. HE TOLD ME THINGS I DIDN'T WANT TO HEAR, AND I SHUT HIM DOWN.
IN HINDSIGHT, HE WAS COMPLETELY RIGHT, AND I WAS COMPLETELY WRONG. AND FOR THAT, BILL, I'M VERY SORRY.

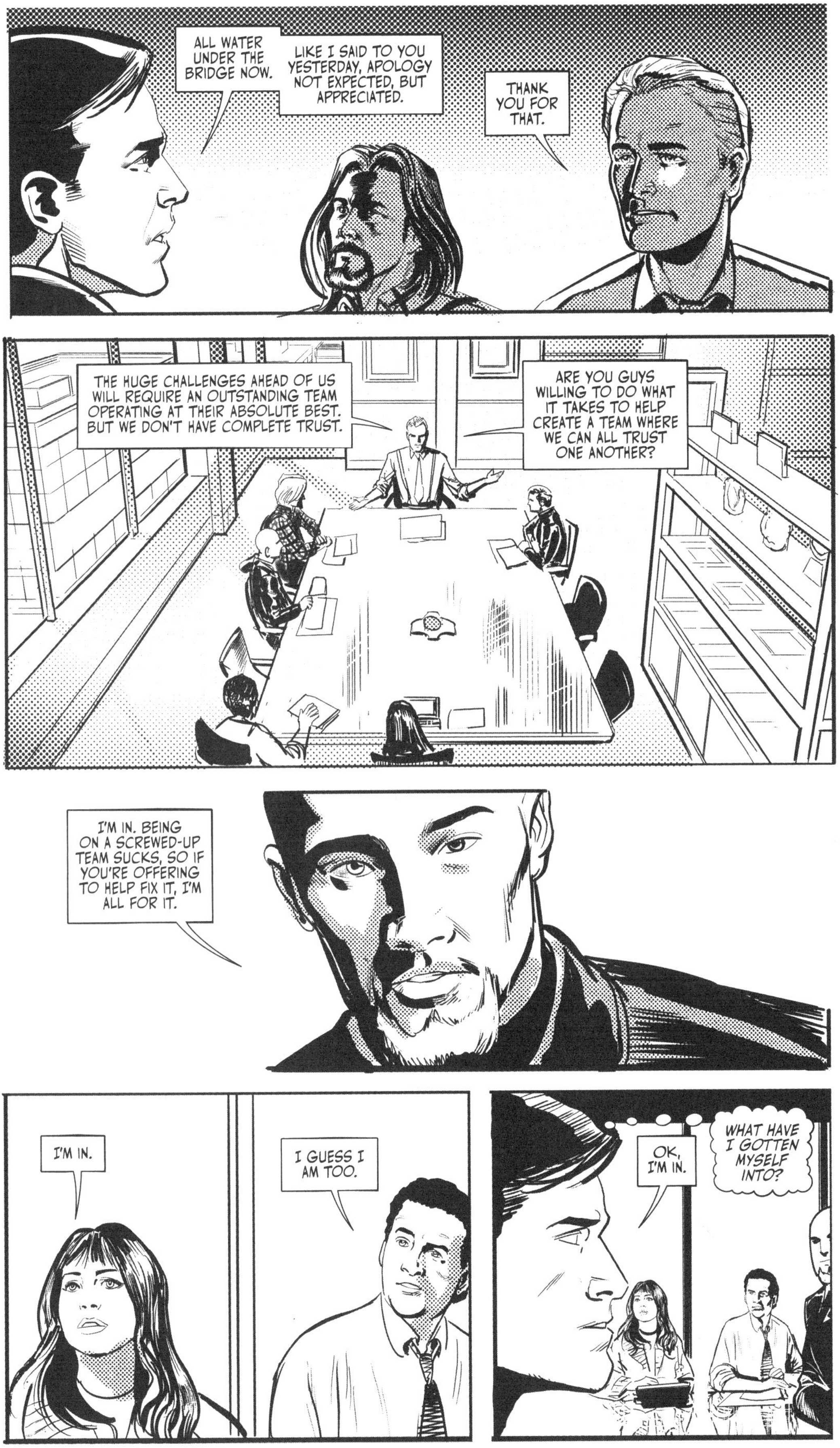
ALL WATER UNDER THE BRIDGE NOW.
LIKE I SAID TO YOU YESTERDAY, APOLOGY NOT EXPECTED, BUT APPRECIATED.
THANK YOU FOR THAT.
THE HUGE CHALLENGES AHEAD OF US WILL REQUIRE AN OUTSTANDING TEAM OPERATING AT THEIR ABSOLUTE BEST. BUT WE DON'T HAVE COMPLETE TRUST.
ARE YOU GUYS WILLING TO DO WHAT IT TAKES TO HELP CREATE A TEAM WHERE WE CAN ALL TRUST ONE ANOTHER?
I'M IN. BEING ON A SCREWED-UP TEAM SUCKS, SO IF YOU'RE OFFERING TO HELP FIX IT, I'M ALL FOR IT.
I'M IN.
I GUESS I AM TOO.
OK, I'M IN.
WHAT HAVE I GOTTEN MYSELF INTO?

CHAPTER 19 TUESDAY, SEPTEMBER 23

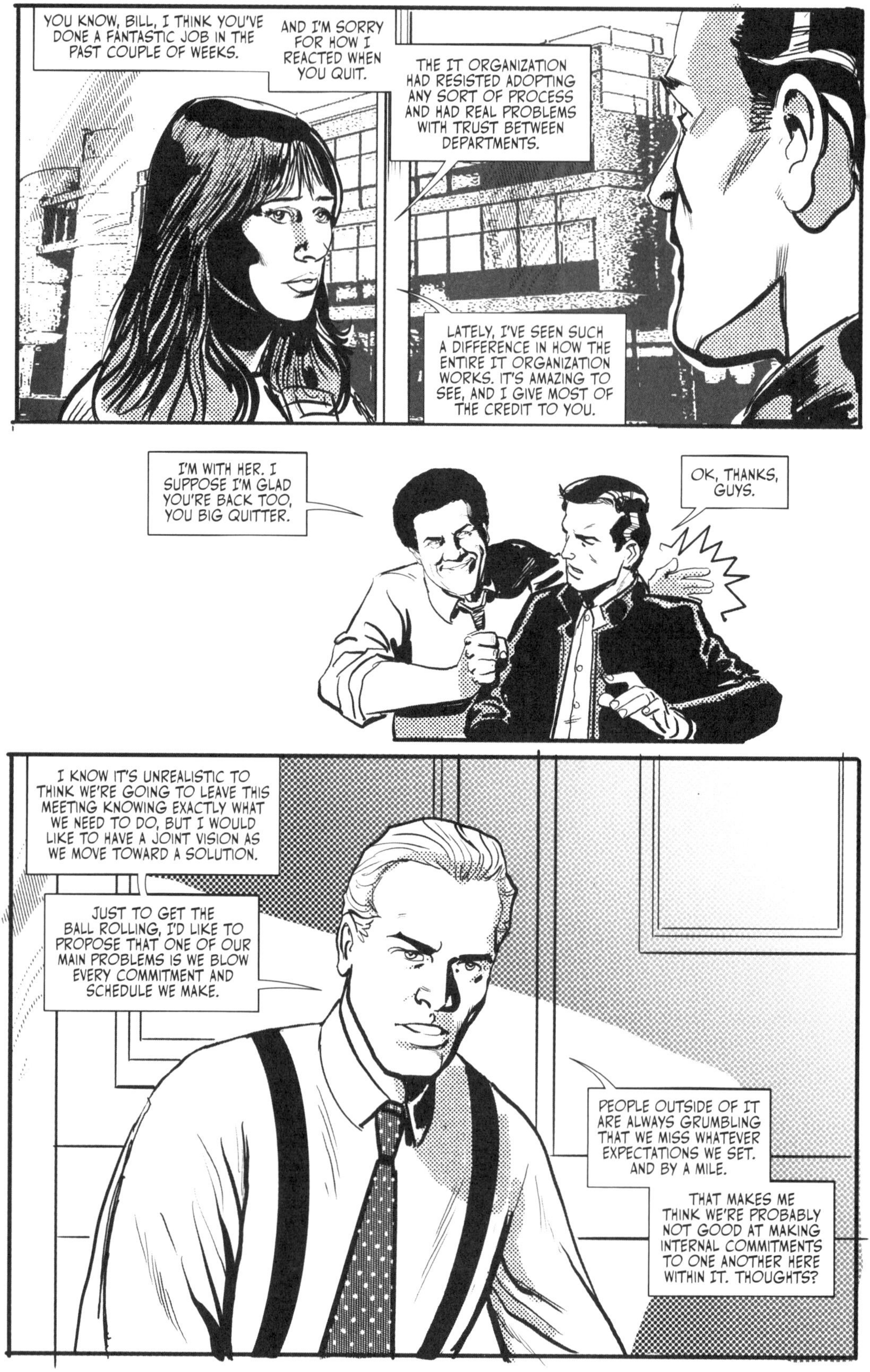

YOU KNOW, BILL, I THINK YOU'VE DONE A FANTASTIC JOB IN THE PAST COUPLE OF WEEKS.
AND I'M SORRY FOR HOW I REACTED WHEN YOU QUIT.
THE IT ORGANIZATION HAD RESISTED ADOPTING ANY SORT OF PROCESS AND HAD REAL PROBLEMS WITH TRUST BETWEEN DEPARTMENTS.
LATELY, I'VE SEEN SUCH A DIFFERENCE IN HOW THE ENTIRE IT ORGANIZATION WORKS. IT'S AMAZING TO SEE, AND I GIVE MOST OF THE CREDIT TO YOU.
I'M WITH HER. I SUPPOSE I'M GLAD YOU'RE BACK TOO, YOU BIG QUITTER.
OK, THANKS, GUYS.
I KNOW IT'S UNREALISTIC TO THINK WE'RE GOING TO LEAVE THIS MEETING KNOWING EXACTLY WHAT WE NEED TO DO, BUT I WOULD LIKE TO HAVE A JOINT VISION AS WE MOVE TOWARD A SOLUTION.
JUST TO GET THE BALL ROLLING, I'D LIKE TO PROPOSE THAT ONE OF OUR MAIN PROBLEMS IS WE BLOW EVERY COMMITMENT AND SCHEDULE WE MAKE.
PEOPLE OUTSIDE OF IT ARE ALWAYS GRUMBLING THAT WE MISS WHATEVER EXPECTATIONS WE SET. AND BY A MILE.
THAT MAKES ME THINK WE'RE PROBABLY NOT GOOD AT MAKING INTERNAL COMMITMENTS TO ONE ANOTHER HERE WITHIN IT. THOUGHTS?

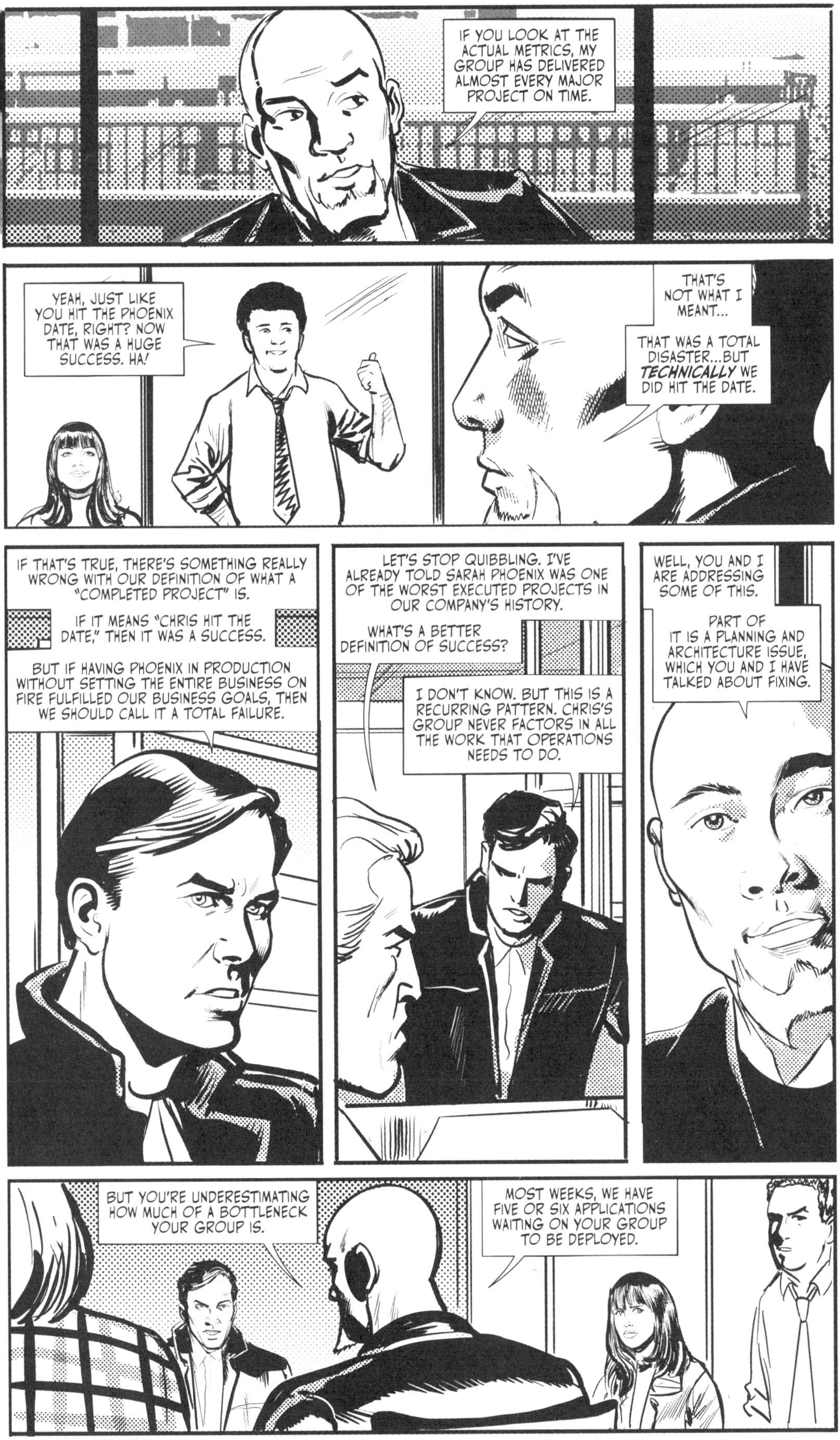
IF YOU LOOK AT THE ACTUAL METRICS, MY GROUP HAS DELIVERED ALMOST EVERY MAJOR PROJECT ON TIME.
YEAH, JUST LIKE YOU HIT THE PHOENIX DATE, RIGHT? NOW THAT WAS A HUGE SUCCESS. HA!
THAT'S NOT WHAT I MEANT...
THAT WAS A TOTAL DISASTER...BUT TECHNICALLY WE DID HIT THE DATE.
IF THAT'S TRUE, THERE'S SOMETHING REALLY WRONG WITH OUR DEFINITION OF WHAT A "COMPLETED PROJECT" IS.
IF IT MEANS "CHRIS HIT THE DATE," THEN IT WAS A SUCCESS.
BUT IF HAVING PHOENIX IN PRODUCTION WITHOUT SETTING THE ENTIRE BUSINESS ON FIRE FULFILLED OUR BUSINESS GOALS, THEN WE SHOULD CALL IT A TOTAL FAILURE.
LET'S STOP QUIBBLING. I'VE ALREADY TOLD SARAH PHOENIX WAS ONE OF THE WORST EXECUTED PROJECTS IN OUR COMPANY'S HISTORY.
WHAT'S A BETTER DEFINITION OF SUCCESS?
I DON'T KNOW. BUT THIS IS A RECURRING PATTERN. CHRIS'S GROUP NEVER FACTORS IN ALL THE WORK THAT OPERATIONS NEEDS TO DO.
WELL, YOU AND I ARE ADDRESSING SOME OF THIS.
PART OF IT IS A PLANNING AND ARCHITECTURE ISSUE, WHICH YOU AND I HAVE TALKED ABOUT FIXING.
BUT YOU'RE UNDERESTIMATING HOW MUCH OF A BOTTLENECK YOUR GROUP IS.
MOST WEEKS, WE HAVE FIVE OR SIX APPLICATIONS WAITING ON YOUR GROUP TO BE DEPLOYED.

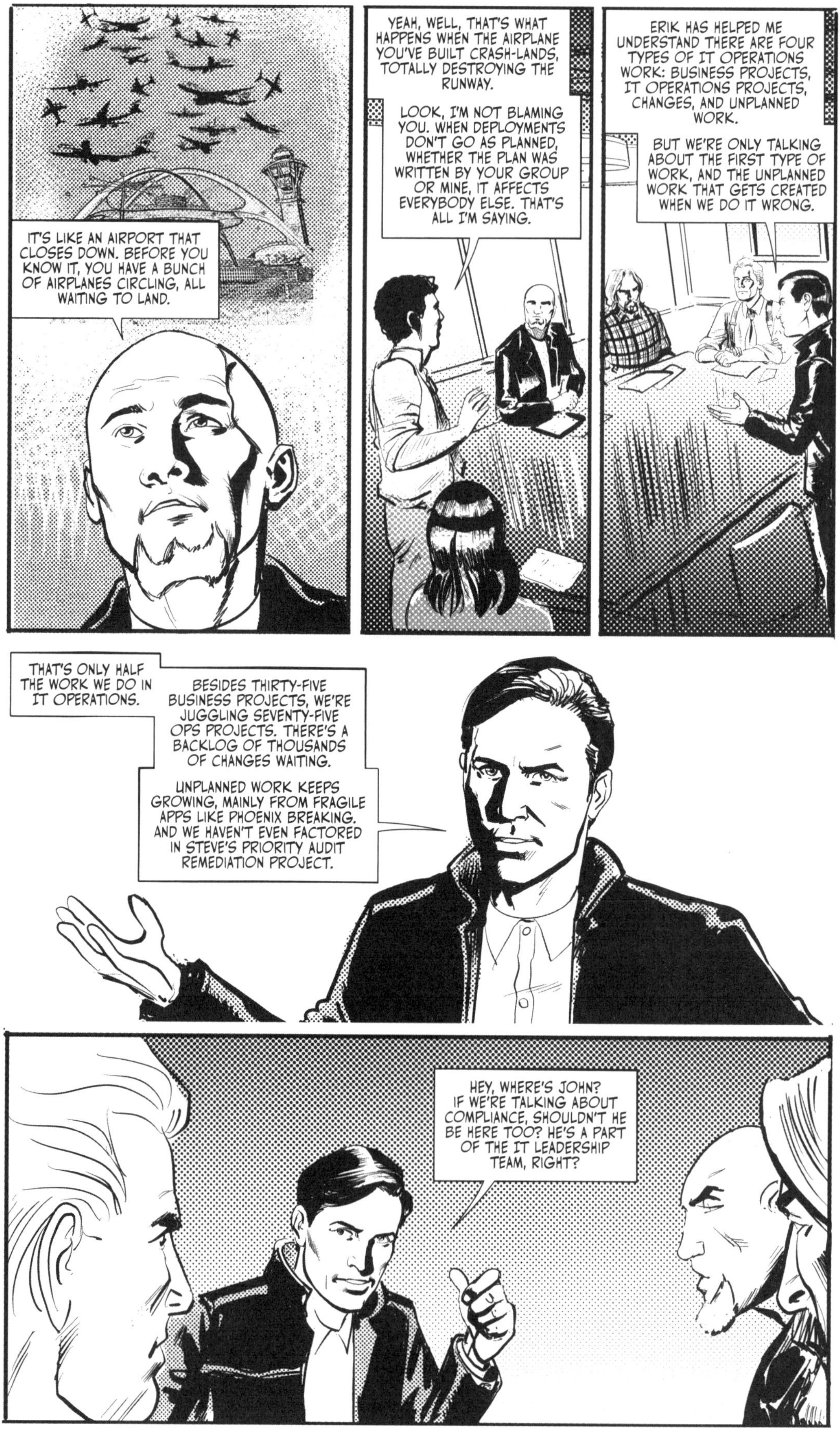

IT'S LIKE AN AIRPORT THAT CLOSES DOWN. BEFORE YOU KNOW IT, YOU HAVE A BUNCH OF AIRPLANES CIRCLING, ALL WAITING TO LAND.
YEAH, WELL, THAT'S WHAT HAPPENS WHEN THE AIRPLANE YOU'VE BUILT CRASH-LANDS, TOTALLY DESTROYING THE RUNWAY.
LOOK, I'M NOT BLAMING YOU. WHEN DEPLOYMENTS DON'T GO AS PLANNED, WHETHER THE PLAN WAS WRITTEN BY YOUR GROUP OR MINE, IT AFFECTS EVERYBODY ELSE. THAT'S ALL I'M SAYING.
ERIK HAS HELPED ME UNDERSTAND THERE ARE FOUR TYPES OF IT OPERATIONS WORK: BUSINESS PROJECTS, IT OPERATIONS PROJECTS, CHANGES, AND UNPLANNED WORK.
BUT WE'RE ONLY TALKING ABOUT THE FIRST TYPE OF WORK, AND THE UNPLANNED WORK THAT GETS CREATED WHEN WE DO IT WRONG.
THAT'S ONLY HALF THE WORK WE DO IN IT OPERATIONS.
BESIDES THIRTY-FIVE BUSINESS PROJECTS, WE'RE JUGGLING SEVENTY-FIVE OPS PROJECTS. THERE'S A BACKLOG OF THOUSANDS OF CHANGES WAITING.
UNPLANNED WORK KEEPS GROWING, MAINLY FROM FRAGILE APPS LIKE PHOENIX BREAKING. AND WE HAVEN'T EVEN FACTORED IN STEVE'S PRIORITY AUDIT REMEDIATION PROJECT.
HEY, WHERE'S JOHN? IF WE'RE TALKING ABOUT COMPLIANCE, SHOULDN'T HE BE HERE TOO? HE'S A PART OF THE IT LEADERSHIP TEAM, RIGHT?

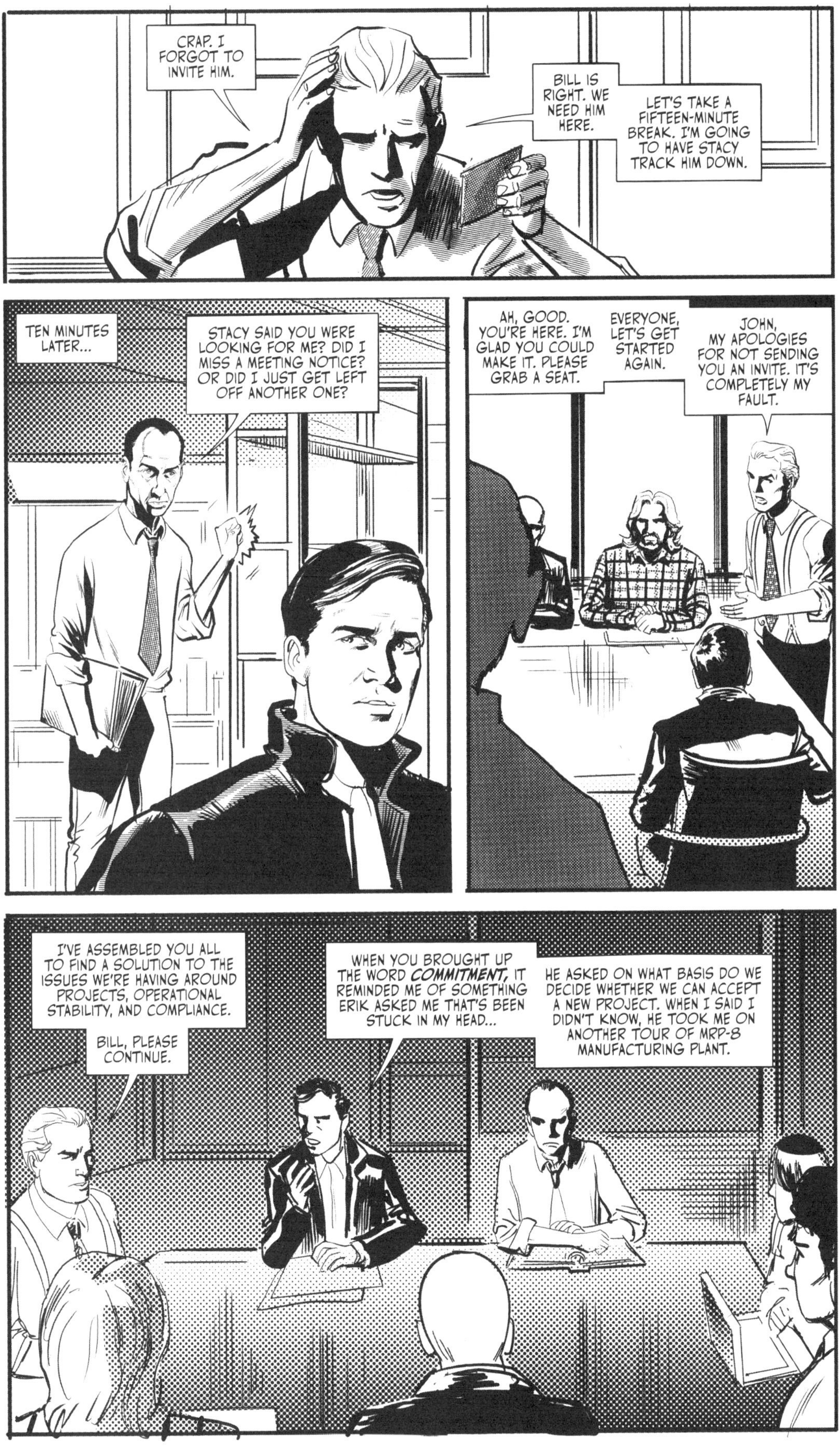
CRAP. I FORGOT TO INVITE HIM.
BILL IS RIGHT. WE NEED HIM HERE.
LET'S TAKE A FIFTEEN-MINUTE BREAK. I'M GOING TO HAVE STACY TRACK HIM DOWN.
TEN MINUTES LATER...
STACY SAID YOU WERE LOOKING FOR ME? DID I MISS A MEETING NOTICE? OR DID I JUST GET LEFT OFF ANOTHER ONE?
AH, GOOD. YOU'RE HERE. I'M GLAD YOU COULD MAKE IT. PLEASE GRAB A SEAT.
EVERYONE, LET'S GET STARTED AGAIN.
JOHN, MY APOLOGIES FOR NOT SENDING YOU AN INVITE. IT'S COMPLETELY MY FAULT.
I'VE ASSEMBLED YOU ALL TO FIND A SOLUTION TO THE ISSUES WE'RE HAVING AROUND PROJECTS, OPERATIONAL STABILITY, AND COMPLIANCE.
BILL, PLEASE CONTINUE.
WHEN YOU BROUGHT UP THE WORD ***COMMITMENT,*** IT REMINDED ME OF SOMETHING ERIK ASKED ME THAT'S BEEN STUCK IN MY HEAD...
HE ASKED ON WHAT BASIS DO WE DECIDE WHETHER WE CAN ACCEPT A NEW PROJECT. WHEN I SAID I DIDN'T KNOW, HE TOOK ME ON ANOTHER TOUR OF MRP-8 MANUFACTURING PLANT.

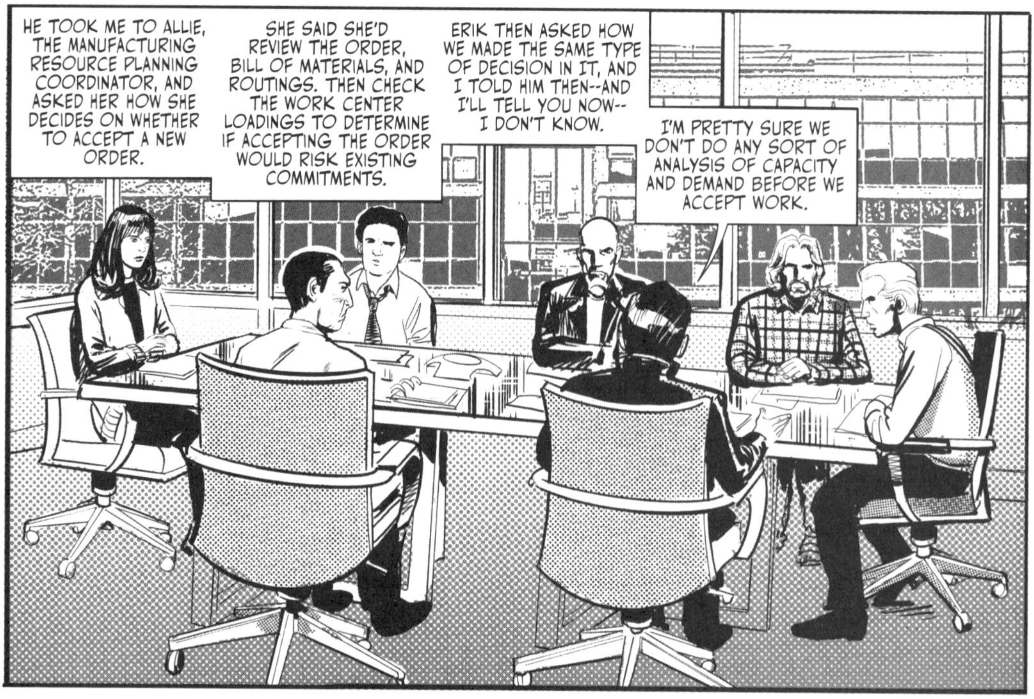
HE TOOK ME TO ALLIE, THE MANUFACTURING RESOURCE PLANNING COORDINATOR, AND ASKED HER HOW SHE DECIDES ON WHETHER TO ACCEPT A NEW ORDER.
SHE SAID SHE'D REVIEW THE ORDER, BILL OF MATERIALS, AND ROUTINGS. THEN CHECK THE WORK CENTER LOADINGS TO DETERMINE IF ACCEPTING THE ORDER WOULD RISK EXISTING COMMITMENTS.
ERIK THEN ASKED HOW WE MADE THE SAME TYPE OF DECISION IN IT, AND I TOLD HIM THEN--AND I'LL TELL YOU NOW-- I DON'T KNOW.
I'M PRETTY SURE WE DON'T DO ANY SORT OF ANALYSIS OF CAPACITY AND DEMAND BEFORE WE ACCEPT WORK.

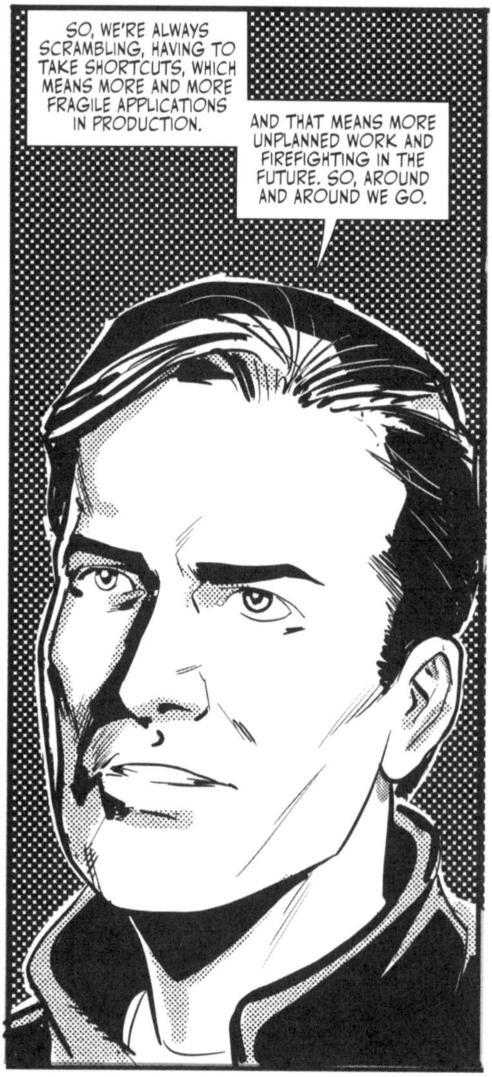
SO, WE'RE ALWAYS SCRAMBLING, HAVING TO TAKE SHORTCUTS, WHICH MEANS MORE AND MORE FRAGILE APPLICATIONS IN PRODUCTION.
AND THAT MEANS MORE UNPLANNED WORK AND FIREFIGHTING IN THE FUTURE. SO, AROUND AND AROUND WE GO.

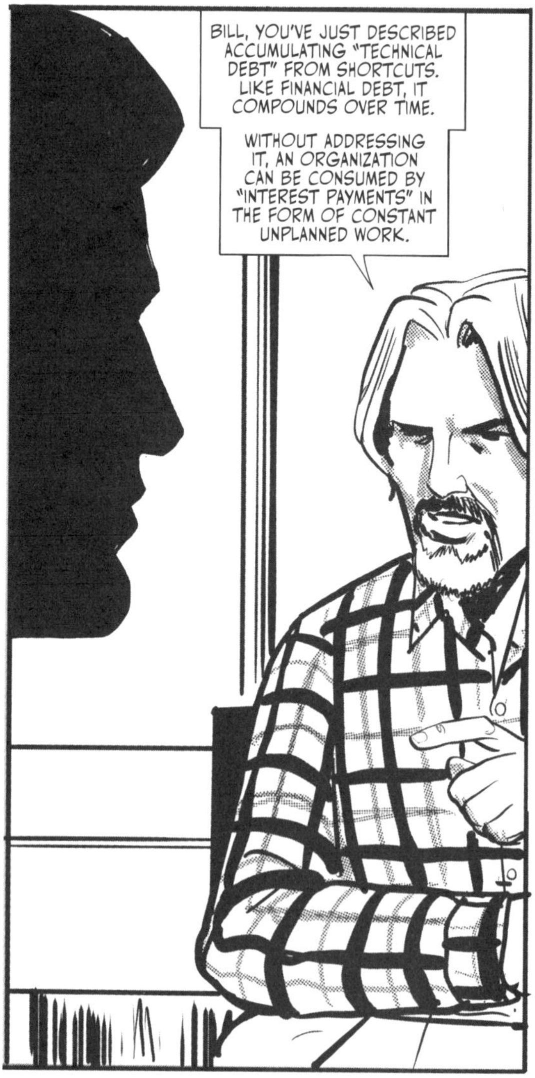
BILL, YOU'VE JUST DESCRIBED ACCUMULATING "TECHNICAL DEBT" FROM SHORTCUTS. LIKE FINANCIAL DEBT, IT COMPOUNDS OVER TIME.
WITHOUT ADDRESSING IT, AN ORGANIZATION CAN BE CONSUMED BY "INTEREST PAYMENTS" IN THE FORM OF CONSTANT UNPLANNED WORK.

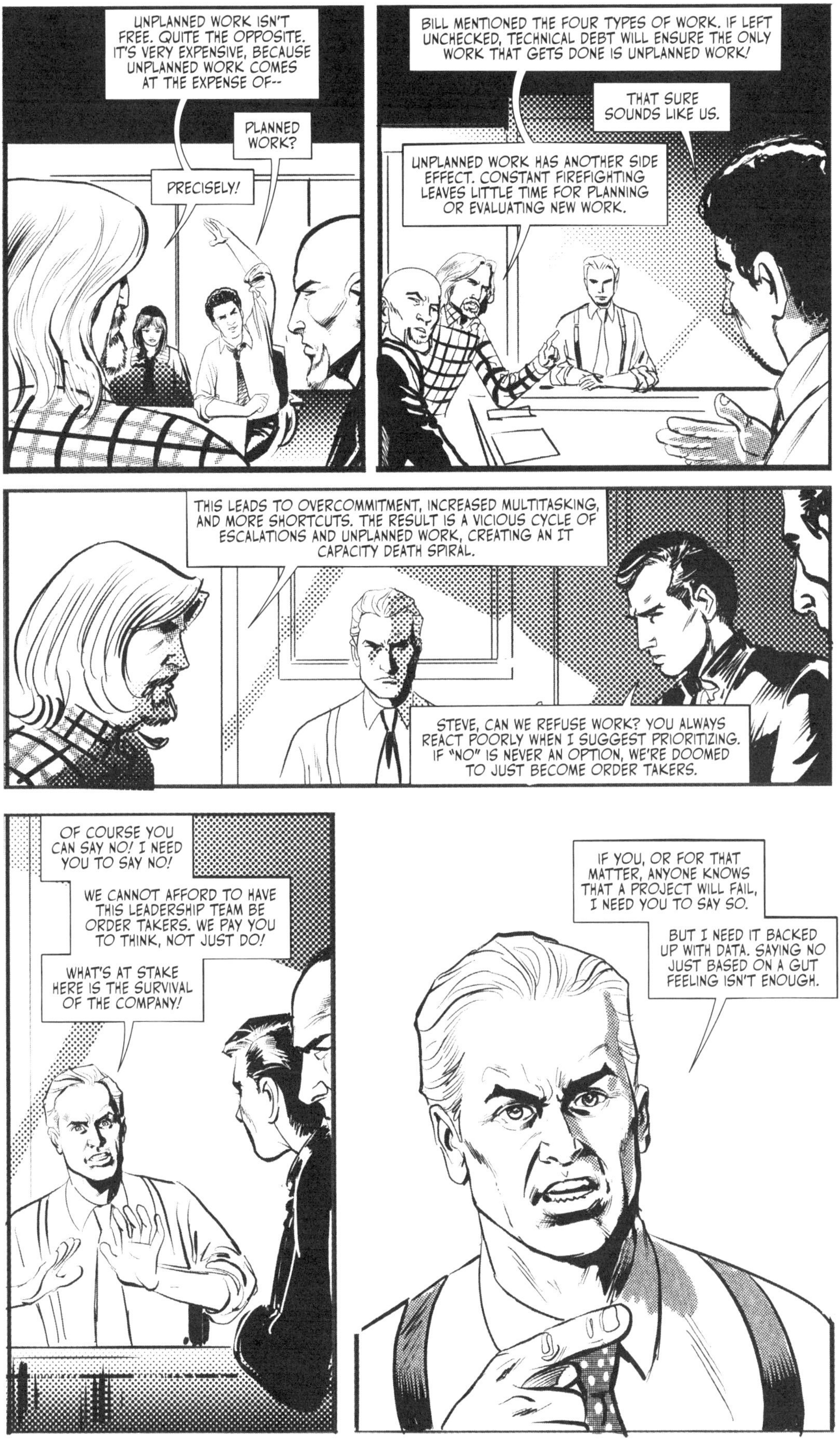

UNPLANNED WORK ISN'T FREE. QUITE THE OPPOSITE. IT'S VERY EXPENSIVE, BECAUSE UNPLANNED WORK COMES AT THE EXPENSE OF--
PLANNED WORK?
PRECISELY!
BILL MENTIONED THE FOUR TYPES OF WORK. IF LEFT UNCHECKED, TECHNICAL DEBT WILL ENSURE THE ONLY WORK THAT GETS DONE IS UNPLANNED WORK!
THAT SURE SOUNDS LIKE US.
UNPLANNED WORK HAS ANOTHER SIDE EFFECT. CONSTANT FIREFIGHTING LEAVES LITTLE TIME FOR PLANNING OR EVALUATING NEW WORK.
THIS LEADS TO OVERCOMMITMENT, INCREASED MULTITASKING, AND MORE SHORTCUTS. THE RESULT IS A VICIOUS CYCLE OF ESCALATIONS AND UNPLANNED WORK, CREATING AN IT CAPACITY DEATH SPIRAL.
STEVE, CAN WE REFUSE WORK? YOU ALWAYS REACT POORLY WHEN I SUGGEST PRIORITIZING. IF "NO" IS NEVER AN OPTION, WE'RE DOOMED TO JUST BECOME ORDER TAKERS.
OF COURSE YOU CAN SAY NO! I NEED YOU TO SAY NO!
WE CANNOT AFFORD TO HAVE THIS LEADERSHIP TEAM BE ORDER TAKERS. WE PAY YOU TO THINK, NOT JUST DO!
WHAT'S AT STAKE HERE IS THE SURVIVAL OF THE COMPANY!
IF YOU, OR FOR THAT MATTER, ANYONE KNOWS THAT A PROJECT WILL FAIL, I NEED YOU TO SAY SO.
BUT I NEED IT BACKED UP WITH DATA. SAYING NO JUST BASED ON A GUT FEELING ISN'T ENOUGH.

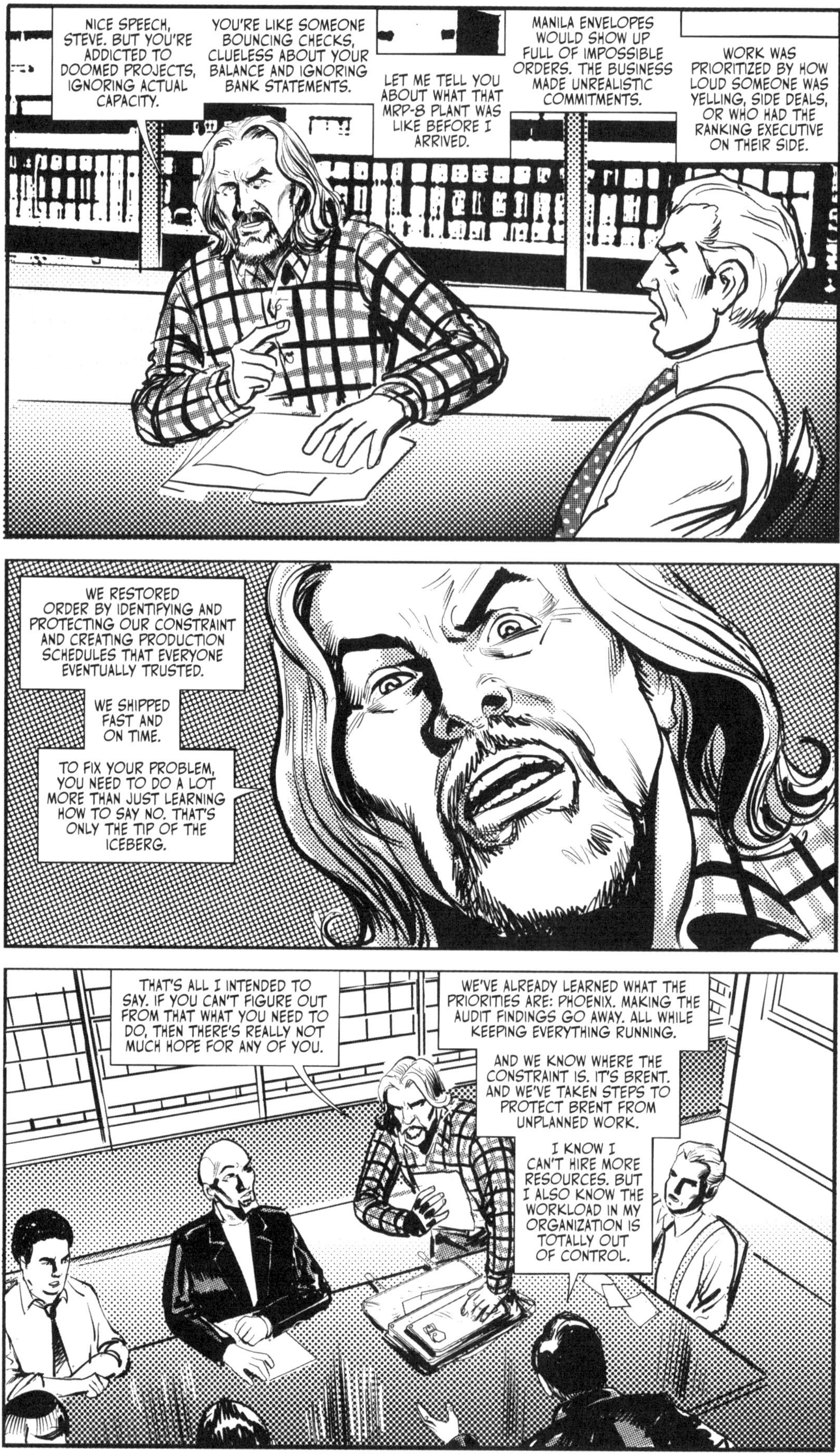

NICE SPEECH, STEVE. BUT YOU'RE ADDICTED TO DOOMED PROJECTS, IGNORING ACTUAL CAPACITY.
YOU'RE LIKE SOMEONE BOUNCING CHECKS, CLUELESS ABOUT YOUR BALANCE AND IGNORING BANK STATEMENTS.
LET ME TELL YOU ABOUT WHAT THAT MRP-8 PLANT WAS LIKE BEFORE I ARRIVED.
MANILA ENVELOPES WOULD SHOW UP FULL OF IMPOSSIBLE ORDERS. THE BUSINESS MADE UNREALISTIC COMMITMENTS.
WORK WAS PRIORITIZED BY HOW LOUD SOMEONE WAS YELLING, SIDE DEALS, OR WHO HAD THE RANKING EXECUTIVE ON THEIR SIDE.
WE RESTORED ORDER BY IDENTIFYING AND PROTECTING OUR CONSTRAINT AND CREATING PRODUCTION SCHEDULES THAT EVERYONE EVENTUALLY TRUSTED.
WE SHIPPED FAST AND ON TIME.
TO FIX YOUR PROBLEM, YOU NEED TO DO A LOT MORE THAN JUST LEARNING HOW TO SAY NO. THAT'S ONLY THE TIP OF THE ICEBERG.
THAT'S ALL I INTENDED TO SAY. IF YOU CAN'T FIGURE OUT FROM THAT WHAT YOU NEED TO DO, THEN THERE'S REALLY NOT MUCH HOPE FOR ANY OF YOU.
WE'VE ALREADY LEARNED WHAT THE PRIORITIES ARE: PHOENIX. MAKING THE AUDIT FINDINGS GO AWAY. ALL WHILE KEEPING EVERYTHING RUNNING.
AND WE KNOW WHERE THE CONSTRAINT IS. IT'S BRENT. AND WE'VE TAKEN STEPS TO PROTECT BRENT FROM UNPLANNED WORK.
I KNOW I CAN'T HIRE MORE RESOURCES. BUT I ALSO KNOW THE WORKLOAD IN MY ORGANIZATION IS TOTALLY OUT OF CONTROL.

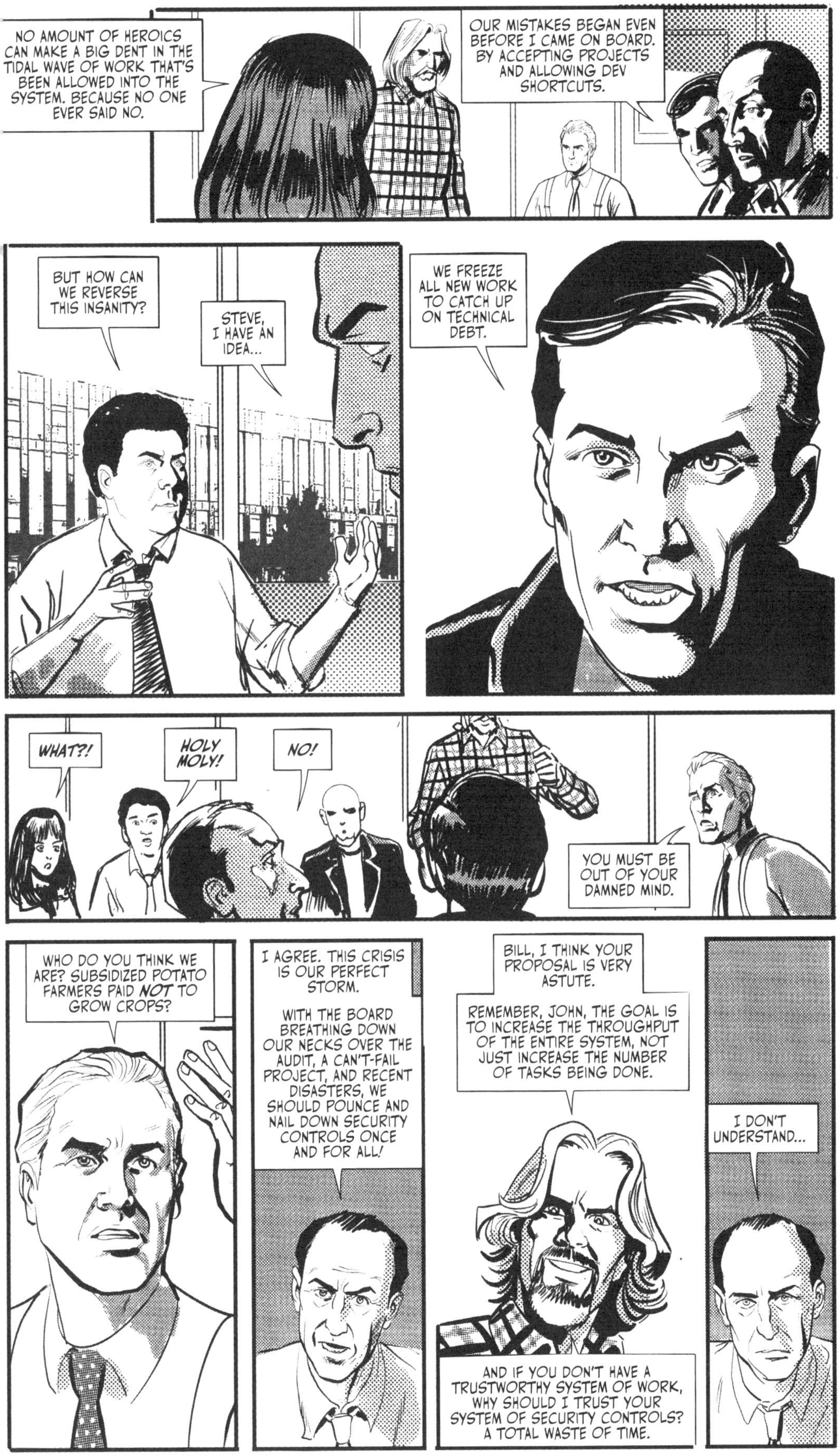
NO AMOUNT OF HEROICS CAN MAKE A BIG DENT IN THE TIDAL WAVE OF WORK THAT'S BEEN ALLOWED INTO THE SYSTEM. BECAUSE NO ONE EVER SAID NO.
OUR MISTAKES BEGAN EVEN BEFORE I CAME ON BOARD. BY ACCEPTING PROJECTS AND ALLOWING DEV SHORTCUTS.
BUT HOW CAN WE REVERSE THIS INSANITY?
STEVE, I HAVE AN IDEA...
WE FREEZE ALL NEW WORK TO CATCH UP ON TECHNICAL DEBT.
WHAT?!
HOLY MOLY!
NO!
YOU MUST BE OUT OF YOUR DAMNED MIND.
WHO DO YOU THINK WE ARE? SUBSIDIZED POTATO FARMERS PAID NOT TO GROW CROPS?
I AGREE. THIS CRISIS IS OUR PERFECT STORM.
WITH THE BOARD BREATHING DOWN OUR NECKS OVER THE AUDIT, A CAN'T-FAIL PROJECT, AND RECENT DISASTERS, WE SHOULD POUNCE AND NAIL DOWN SECURITY CONTROLS ONCE AND FOR ALL!
BILL, I THINK YOUR PROPOSAL IS VERY ASTUTE.
REMEMBER, JOHN, THE GOAL IS TO INCREASE THE THROUGHPUT OF THE ENTIRE SYSTEM, NOT JUST INCREASE THE NUMBER OF TASKS BEING DONE.
AND IF YOU DON'T HAVE A TRUSTWORTHY SYSTEM OF WORK, WHY SHOULD I TRUST YOUR SYSTEM OF SECURITY CONTROLS? A TOTAL WASTE OF TIME.
I DON'T UNDERSTAND...

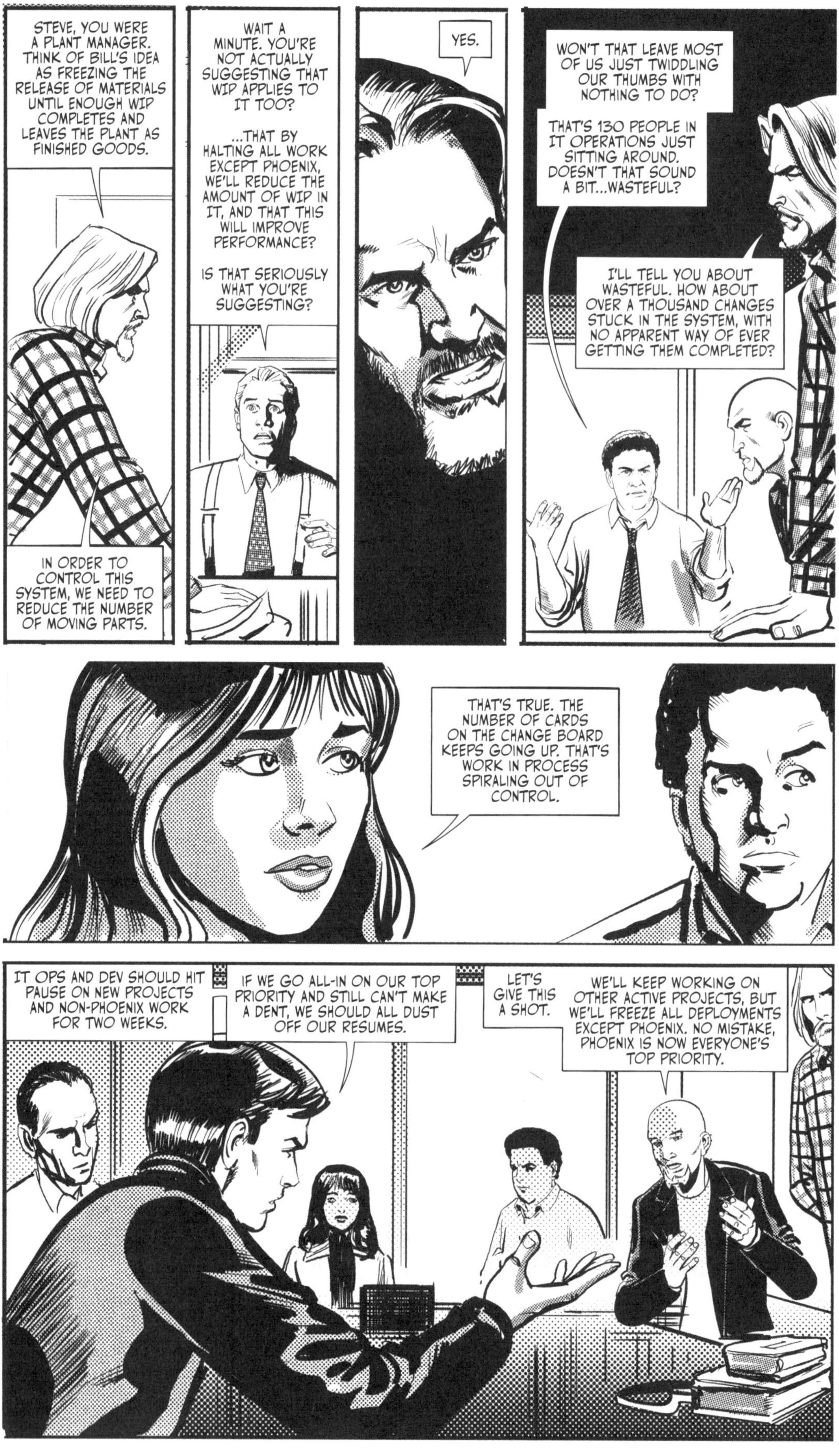

STEVE, YOU WERE A PLANT MANAGER. THINK OF BILL'S IDEA AS FREEZING THE RELEASE OF MATERIALS UNTIL ENOUGH WIP COMPLETES AND LEAVES THE PLANT AS FINISHED GOODS.
IN ORDER TO CONTROL THIS SYSTEM, WE NEED TO REDUCE THE NUMBER OF MOVING PARTS.
WAIT A MINUTE. YOU'RE NOT ACTUALLY SUGGESTING THAT WIP APPLIES TO IT TOO?
...THAT BY HALTING ALL WORK EXCEPT PHOENIX, WE'LL REDUCE THE AMOUNT OF WIP IN IT, AND THAT THIS WILL IMPROVE PERFORMANCE?
IS THAT SERIOUSLY WHAT YOU'RE SUGGESTING?
YES.
WON'T THAT LEAVE MOST OF US JUST TWIDDLING OUR THUMBS WITH NOTHING TO DO?
THAT'S 130 PEOPLE IN IT OPERATIONS JUST SITTING AROUND. DOESN'T THAT SOUND A BIT...WASTEFUL?
I'LL TELL YOU ABOUT WASTEFUL. HOW ABOUT OVER A THOUSAND CHANGES STUCK IN THE SYSTEM, WITH NO APPARENT WAY OF EVER GETTING THEM COMPLETED?
THAT'S TRUE. THE NUMBER OF CARDS ON THE CHANGE BOARD KEEPS GOING UP. THAT'S WORK IN PROCESS SPIRALING OUT OF CONTROL.
IT OPS AND DEV SHOULD HIT PAUSE ON NEW PROJECTS AND NON-PHOENIX WORK FOR TWO WEEKS.
IF WE GO ALL-IN ON OUR TOP PRIORITY AND STILL CAN'T MAKE A DENT, WE SHOULD ALL DUST OFF OUR RESUMES.
LET'S GIVE THIS A SHOT.
WE'LL KEEP WORKING ON OTHER ACTIVE PROJECTS, BUT WE'LL FREEZE ALL DEPLOYMENTS EXCEPT PHOENIX. NO MISTAKE, PHOENIX IS NOW EVERYONE'S TOP PRIORITY.

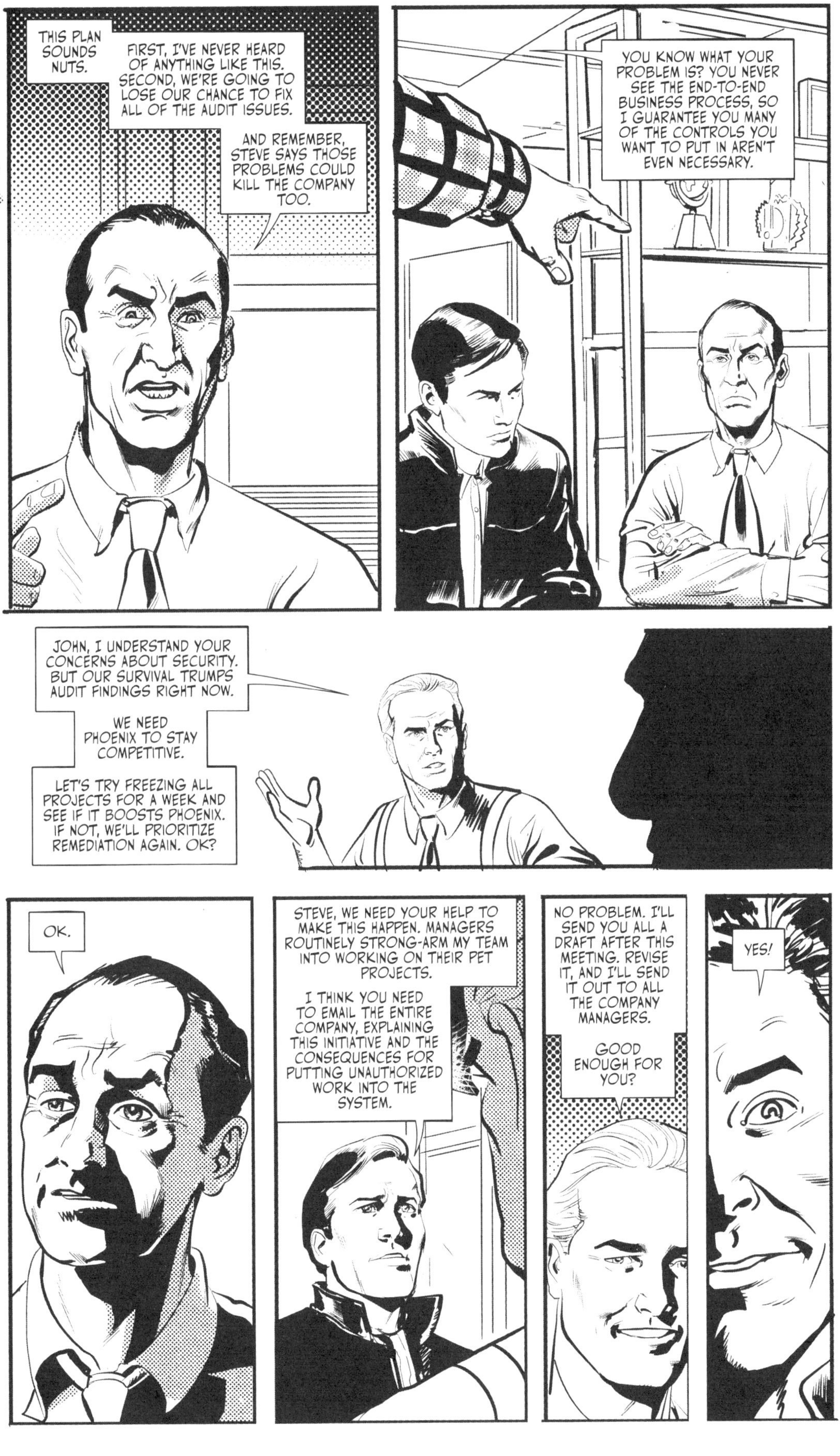
THIS PLAN SOUNDS NUTS.
FIRST, I'VE NEVER HEARD OF ANYTHING LIKE THIS. SECOND, WE'RE GOING TO LOSE OUR CHANCE TO FIX ALL OF THE AUDIT ISSUES.
AND REMEMBER, STEVE SAYS THOSE PROBLEMS COULD KILL THE COMPANY TOO.
YOU KNOW WHAT YOUR PROBLEM IS? YOU NEVER SEE THE END-TO-END BUSINESS PROCESS, SO I GUARANTEE YOU MANY OF THE CONTROLS YOU WANT TO PUT IN AREN'T EVEN NECESSARY.
JOHN, I UNDERSTAND YOUR CONCERNS ABOUT SECURITY. BUT OUR SURVIVAL TRUMPS AUDIT FINDINGS RIGHT NOW.
WE NEED PHOENIX TO STAY COMPETITIVE.
LET'S TRY FREEZING ALL PROJECTS FOR A WEEK AND SEE IF IT BOOSTS PHOENIX. IF NOT, WE'LL PRIORITIZE REMEDIATION AGAIN. OK?
OK.
STEVE, WE NEED YOUR HELP TO MAKE THIS HAPPEN. MANAGERS ROUTINELY STRONG-ARM MY TEAM INTO WORKING ON THEIR PET PROJECTS.
I THINK YOU NEED TO EMAIL THE ENTIRE COMPANY, EXPLAINING THIS INITIATIVE AND THE CONSEQUENCES FOR PUTTING UNAUTHORIZED WORK INTO THE SYSTEM.
NO PROBLEM. I'LL SEND YOU ALL A DRAFT AFTER THIS MEETING. REVISE IT, AND I'LL SEND IT OUT TO ALL THE COMPANY MANAGERS.
GOOD ENOUGH FOR YOU?
YES!

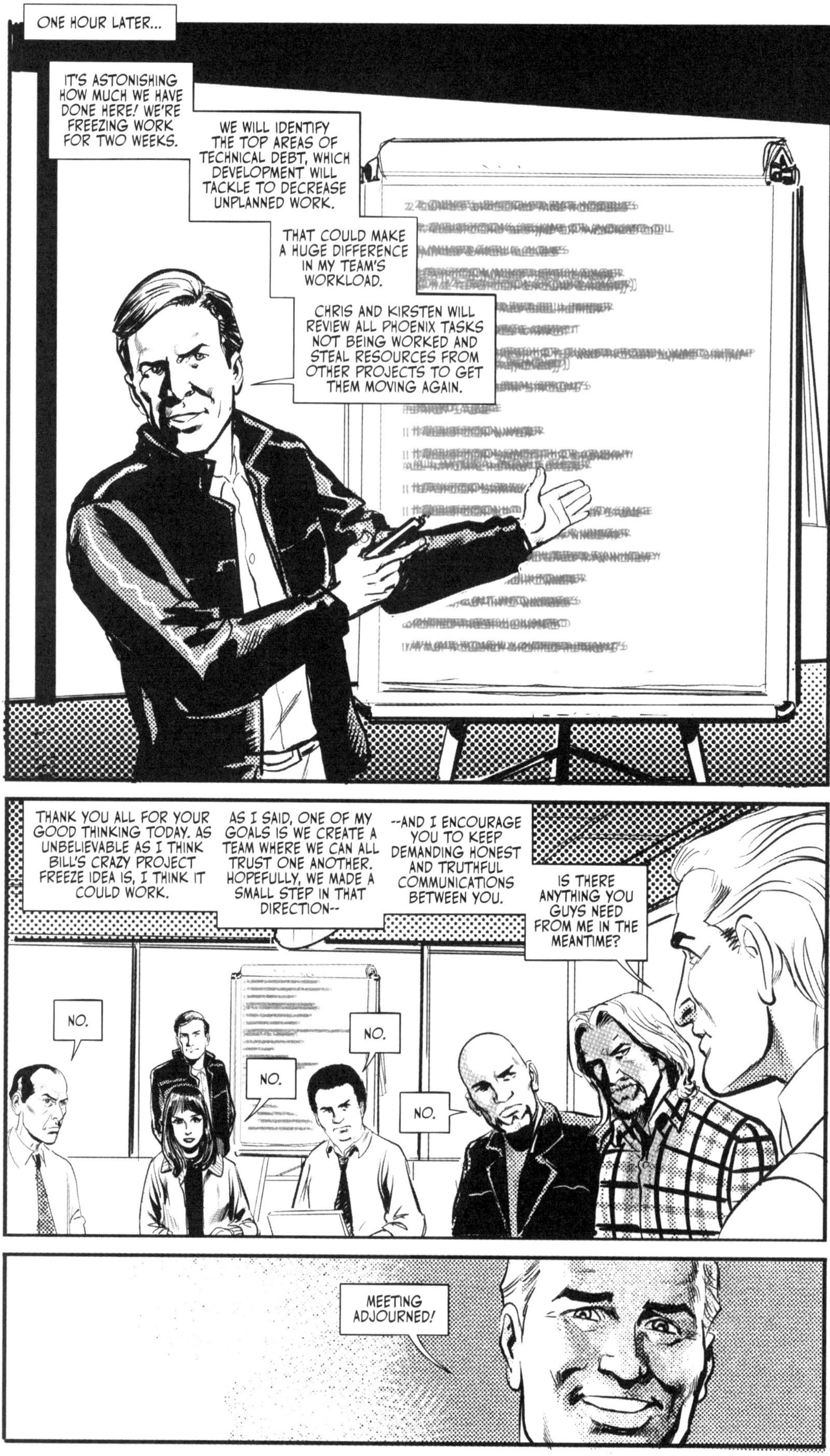
ONE HOUR LATER...
IT'S ASTONISHING HOW MUCH WE HAVE DONE HERE! WE'RE FREEZING WORK FOR TWO WEEKS.
WE WILL IDENTIFY THE TOP AREAS OF TECHNICAL DEBT, WHICH DEVELOPMENT WILL TACKLE TO DECREASE UNPLANNED WORK.
THAT COULD MAKE A HUGE DIFFERENCE IN MY TEAM'S WORKLOAD.
CHRIS AND KIRSTEN WILL REVIEW ALL PHOENIX TASKS NOT BEING WORKED AND STEAL RESOURCES FROM OTHER PROJECTS TO GET THEM MOVING AGAIN.
THANK YOU ALL FOR YOUR GOOD THINKING TODAY. AS UNBELIEVABLE AS I THINK BILL'S CRAZY PROJECT FREEZE IDEA IS, I THINK IT COULD WORK.
AS I SAID, ONE OF MY GOALS IS WE CREATE A TEAM WHERE WE CAN ALL TRUST ONE ANOTHER. HOPEFULLY, WE MADE A SMALL STEP IN THAT DIRECTION--
--AND I ENCOURAGE YOU TO KEEP DEMANDING HONEST AND TRUTHFUL COMMUNICATIONS BETWEEN YOU.
IS THERE ANYTHING YOU GUYS NEED FROM ME IN THE MEANTIME?
NO.
NO.
NO.
NO.
MEETING ADJOURNED!

CHAPTER 20 FRIDAY, SEPTEMBER 26

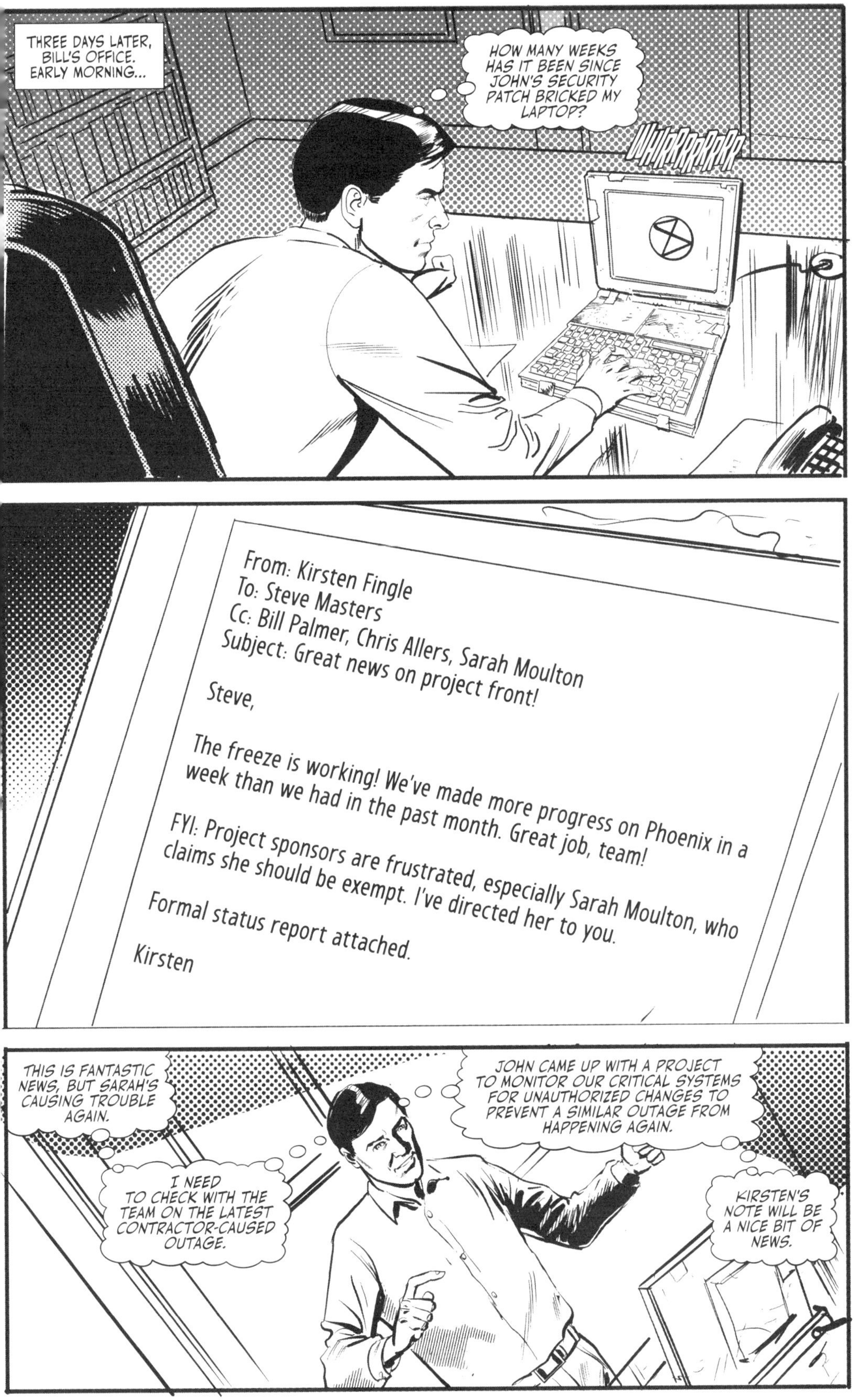
THREE DAYS LATER, BILL'S OFFICE. EARLY MORNING...
HOW MANY WEEKS HAS IT BEEN SINCE JOHN'S SECURITY PATCH BRICKED MY LAPTOP?
WHIRRRRRRR
From: Kirsten Fingle
To: Steve Masters
Cc: Bill Palmer, Chris Allers, Sarah Moulton
Subject: Great news on project front!
Steve,
The freeze is working! We've made more progress on Phoenix in a week than we had in the past month. Great job, team!
FYI: Project sponsors are frustrated, especially Sarah Moulton, who claims she should be exempt. I've directed her to you.
Formal status report attached.
Kirsten
THIS IS FANTASTIC NEWS, BUT SARAH'S CAUSING TROUBLE AGAIN.
I NEED TO CHECK WITH THE TEAM ON THE LATEST CONTRACTOR-CAUSED OUTAGE.
JOHN CAME UP WITH A PROJECT TO MONITOR OUR CRITICAL SYSTEMS FOR UNAUTHORIZED CHANGES TO PREVENT A SIMILAR OUTAGE FROM HAPPENING AGAIN.
KIRSTEN'S NOTE WILL BE A NICE BIT OF NEWS.

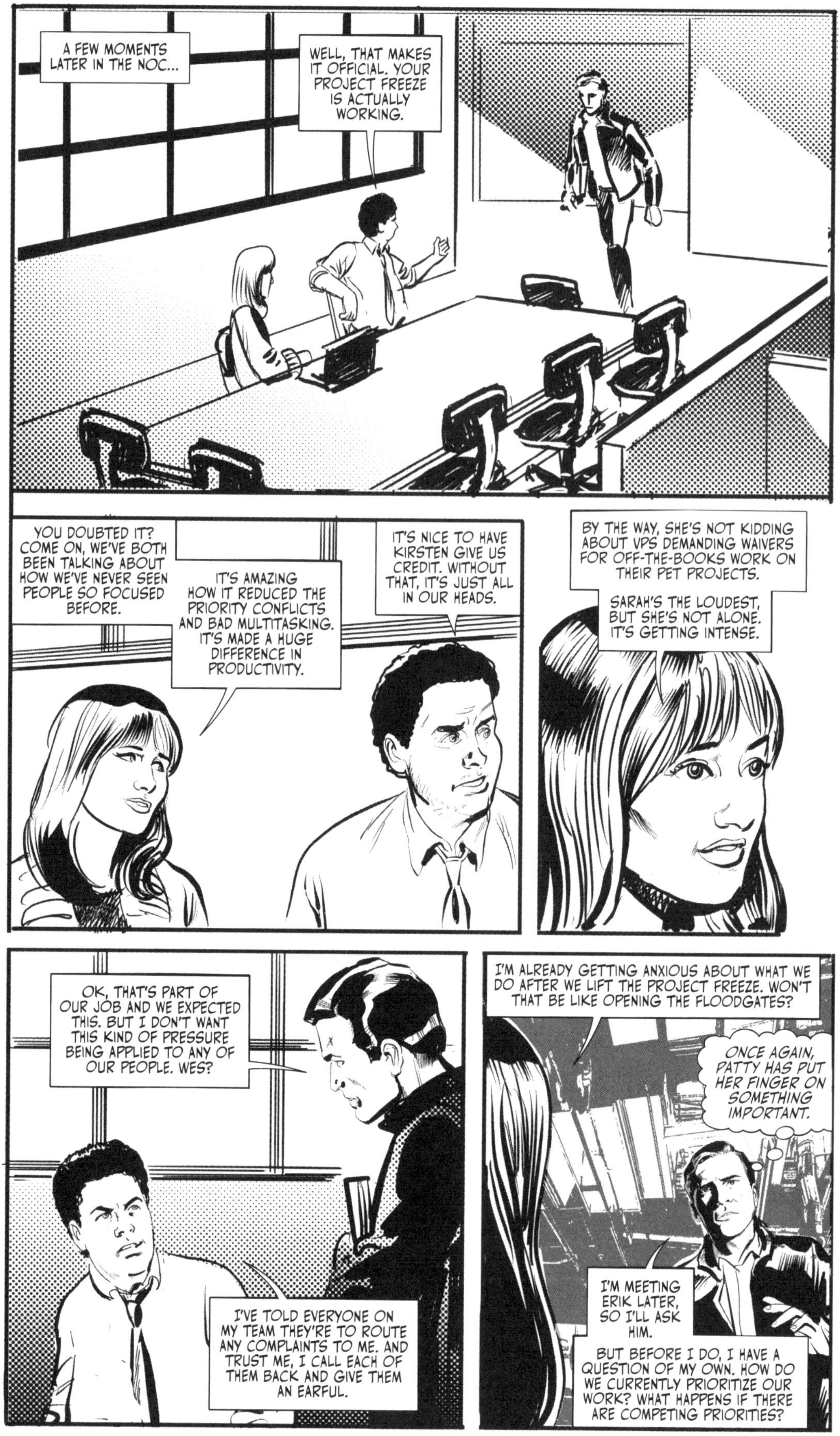
A FEW MOMENTS LATER IN THE NOC...
WELL, THAT MAKES IT OFFICIAL. YOUR PROJECT FREEZE IS ACTUALLY WORKING.
YOU DOUBTED IT? COME ON, WE'VE BOTH BEEN TALKING ABOUT HOW WE'VE NEVER SEEN PEOPLE SO FOCUSED BEFORE.
IT'S AMAZING HOW IT REDUCED THE PRIORITY CONFLICTS AND BAD MULTITASKING. IT'S MADE A HUGE DIFFERENCE IN PRODUCTIVITY.
IT'S NICE TO HAVE KIRSTEN GIVE US CREDIT. WITHOUT THAT, IT'S JUST ALL IN OUR HEADS.
BY THE WAY, SHE'S NOT KIDDING ABOUT VPS DEMANDING WAIVERS FOR OFF-THE-BOOKS WORK ON THEIR PET PROJECTS.
SARAH'S THE LOUDEST, BUT SHE'S NOT ALONE. IT'S GETTING INTENSE.
OK, THAT'S PART OF OUR JOB AND WE EXPECTED THIS. BUT I DON'T WANT THIS KIND OF PRESSURE BEING APPLIED TO ANY OF OUR PEOPLE. WES?
I'VE TOLD EVERYONE ON MY TEAM THEY'RE TO ROUTE ANY COMPLAINTS TO ME. AND TRUST ME, I CALL EACH OF THEM BACK AND GIVE THEM AN EARFUL.
I'M ALREADY GETTING ANXIOUS ABOUT WHAT WE DO AFTER WE LIFT THE PROJECT FREEZE. WON'T THAT BE LIKE OPENING THE FLOODGATES?
ONCE AGAIN, PATTY HAS PUT HER FINGER ON SOMETHING IMPORTANT.
I'M MEETING ERIK LATER, SO I'LL ASK HIM.
BUT BEFORE I DO, I HAVE A QUESTION OF MY OWN. HOW DO WE CURRENTLY PRIORITIZE OUR WORK? WHAT HAPPENS IF THERE ARE COMPETING PRIORITIES?

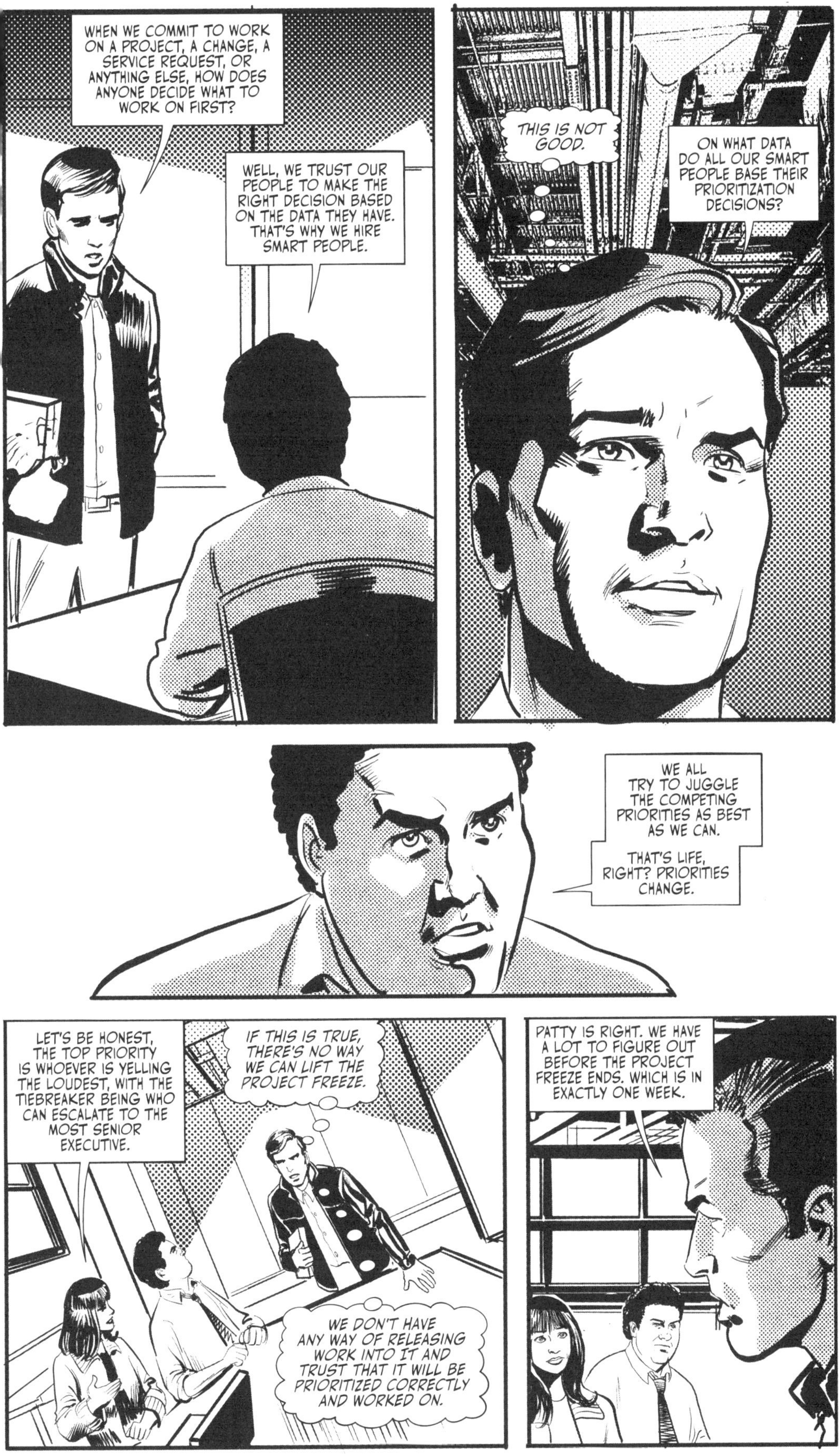
WHEN WE COMMIT TO WORK ON A PROJECT, A CHANGE, A SERVICE REQUEST, OR ANYTHING ELSE, HOW DOES ANYONE DECIDE WHAT TO WORK ON FIRST?
WELL, WE TRUST OUR PEOPLE TO MAKE THE RIGHT DECISION BASED ON THE DATA THEY HAVE. THAT'S WHY WE HIRE SMART PEOPLE.
THIS IS NOT GOOD.
ON WHAT DATA DO ALL OUR SMART PEOPLE BASE THEIR PRIORITIZATION DECISIONS?
WE ALL TRY TO JUGGLE THE COMPETING PRIORITIES AS BEST AS WE CAN.
THAT'S LIFE, RIGHT? PRIORITIES CHANGE.
LET'S BE HONEST, THE TOP PRIORITY IS WHOEVER IS YELLING THE LOUDEST, WITH THE TIEBREAKER BEING WHO CAN ESCALATE TO THE MOST SENIOR EXECUTIVE.
IF THIS IS TRUE, THERE'S NO WAY WE CAN LIFT THE PROJECT FREEZE.
WE DON'T HAVE ANY WAY OF RELEASING WORK INTO IT AND TRUST THAT IT WILL BE PRIORITIZED CORRECTLY AND WORKED ON.
PATTY IS RIGHT. WE HAVE A LOT TO FIGURE OUT BEFORE THE PROJECT FREEZE ENDS. WHICH IS IN EXACTLY ONE WEEK.

LATER THAT DAY...
SO, TELL ME WHAT YOU SEE.
SAME AS LAST TIME.
RAW MATERIALS COMING IN FROM THE LOADING DOCKS ON THE LEFT. AND ON THE RIGHT, GOODS LEAVING FROM THE OTHER SET OF LOADING DOCKS.
GOOD. AND IN BETWEEN?
WIP GOING FROM WORK CENTER TO WORK CENTER. THAT'S DICTATED BY THE BILL OF MATERIALS AND ROUTINGS. IT'S ALL ON THE JOB ORDER, WHICH WAS RELEASED AT THAT DESK OVER THERE.
CAN YOU FIND THE WORK CENTERS WHERE THE PLANT CONSTRAINTS ARE?
THE HEAT-TREAT OVENS AND PAINT-CURING BOOTHS.
GOOD. UNDER-STANDING THE FLOW OF WORK IS KEY TO ACHIEVING THE FIRST WAY.
NOW, TELL ME AGAIN WHICH WORK CENTERS YOU'VE DETERMINED ARE CONSTRAINTS IN YOUR ORGANIZATION.
BRENT. WE TALKED ABOUT THAT BEFORE.
SUDDENLY BRENT IS A ROBOTIC HEAT-TREAT OVEN? THAT MIGHT BE THE DUMBEST THING I'VE EVER HEARD.
OH, THE HEAT-TREAT OVEN IS A WORK CENTER. BRENT IS A WORKER, NOT A WORK CENTER.
I'M BETTING BRENT IS PROBABLY SUPPORTING TOO MANY ***WORK CENTERS,*** WHICH IS WHY HE'S A CONSTRAINT.

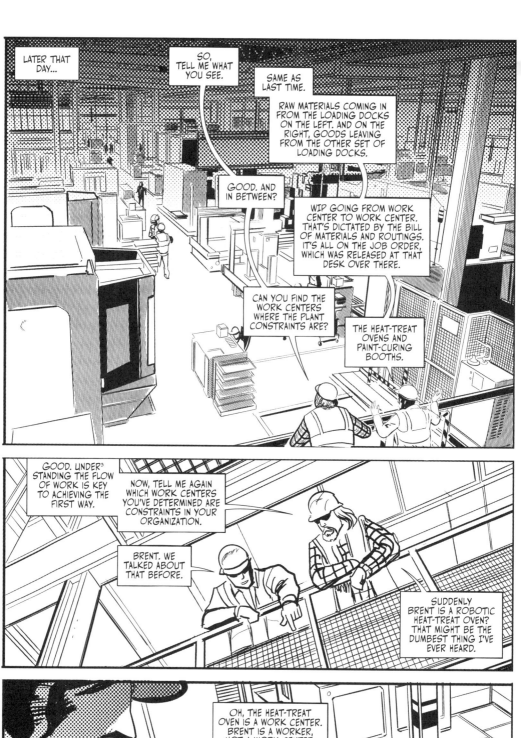

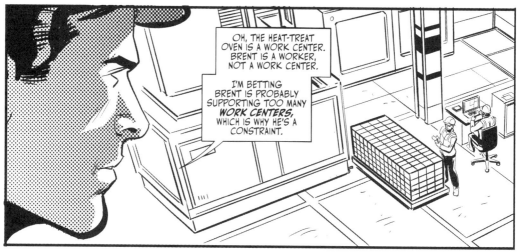

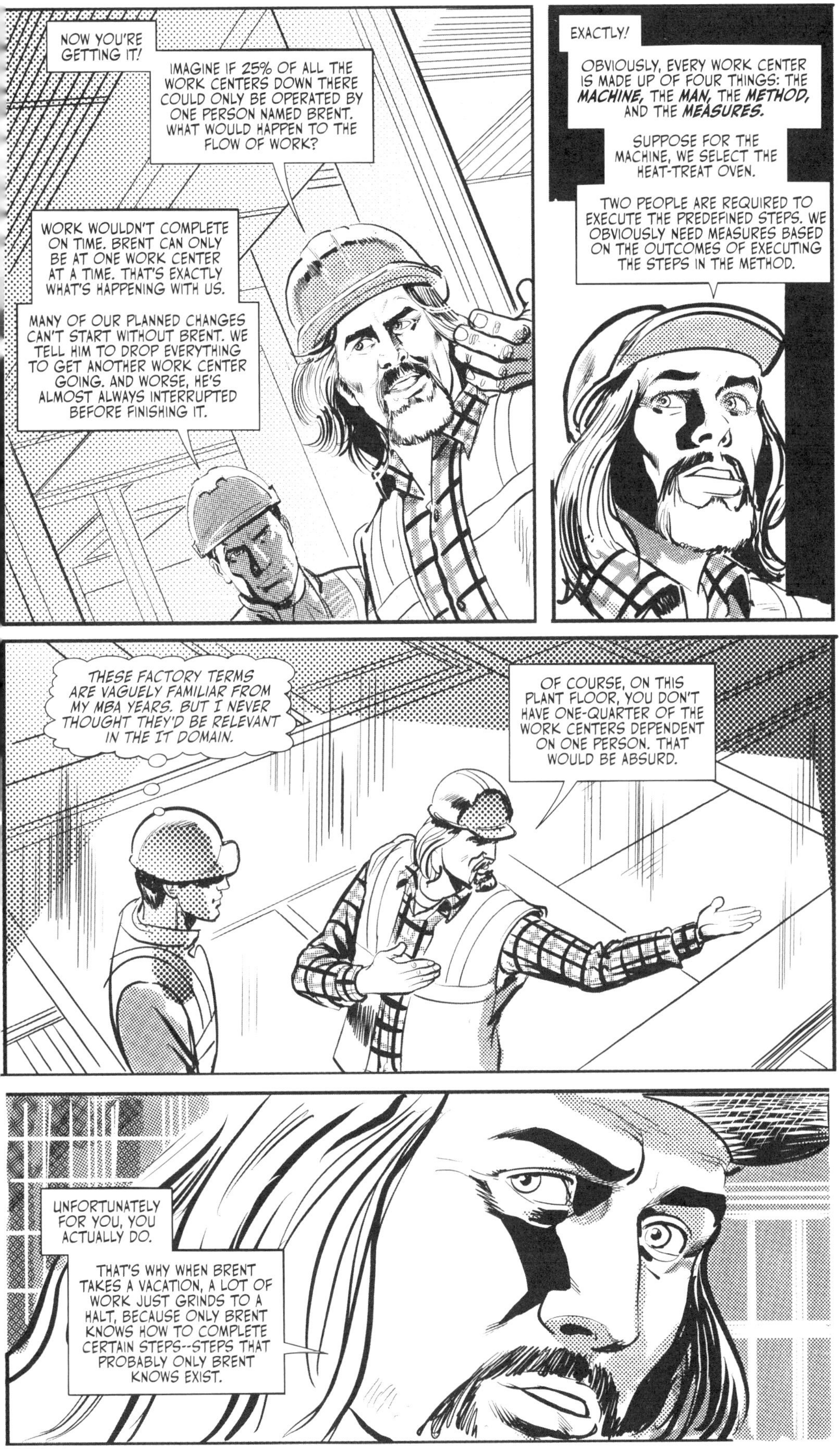
NOW YOU'RE GETTING IT!
IMAGINE IF 25% OF ALL THE WORK CENTERS DOWN THERE COULD ONLY BE OPERATED BY ONE PERSON NAMED BRENT. WHAT WOULD HAPPEN TO THE FLOW OF WORK?
WORK WOULDN'T COMPLETE ON TIME. BRENT CAN ONLY BE AT ONE WORK CENTER AT A TIME. THAT'S EXACTLY WHAT'S HAPPENING WITH US.
MANY OF OUR PLANNED CHANGES CAN'T START WITHOUT BRENT. WE TELL HIM TO DROP EVERYTHING TO GET ANOTHER WORK CENTER GOING. AND WORSE, HE'S ALMOST ALWAYS INTERRUPTED BEFORE FINISHING IT.
EXACTLY!
OBVIOUSLY, EVERY WORK CENTER IS MADE UP OF FOUR THINGS: THE ***MACHINE,*** THE ***MAN,*** THE ***METHOD,*** AND THE ***MEASURES.***
SUPPOSE FOR THE MACHINE, WE SELECT THE HEAT-TREAT OVEN.
TWO PEOPLE ARE REQUIRED TO EXECUTE THE PREDEFINED STEPS. WE OBVIOUSLY NEED MEASURES BASED ON THE OUTCOMES OF EXECUTING THE STEPS IN THE METHOD.
THESE FACTORY TERMS ARE VAGUELY FAMILIAR FROM MY MBA YEARS. BUT I NEVER THOUGHT THEY'D BE RELEVANT IN THE IT DOMAIN.
OF COURSE, ON THIS PLANT FLOOR, YOU DON'T HAVE ONE-QUARTER OF THE WORK CENTERS DEPENDENT ON ONE PERSON. THAT WOULD BE ABSURD.
UNFORTUNATELY FOR YOU, YOU ACTUALLY DO.
THAT'S WHY WHEN BRENT TAKES A VACATION, A LOT OF WORK JUST GRINDS TO A HALT, BECAUSE ONLY BRENT KNOWS HOW TO COMPLETE CERTAIN STEPS--STEPS THAT PROBABLY ONLY BRENT KNOWS EXIST.

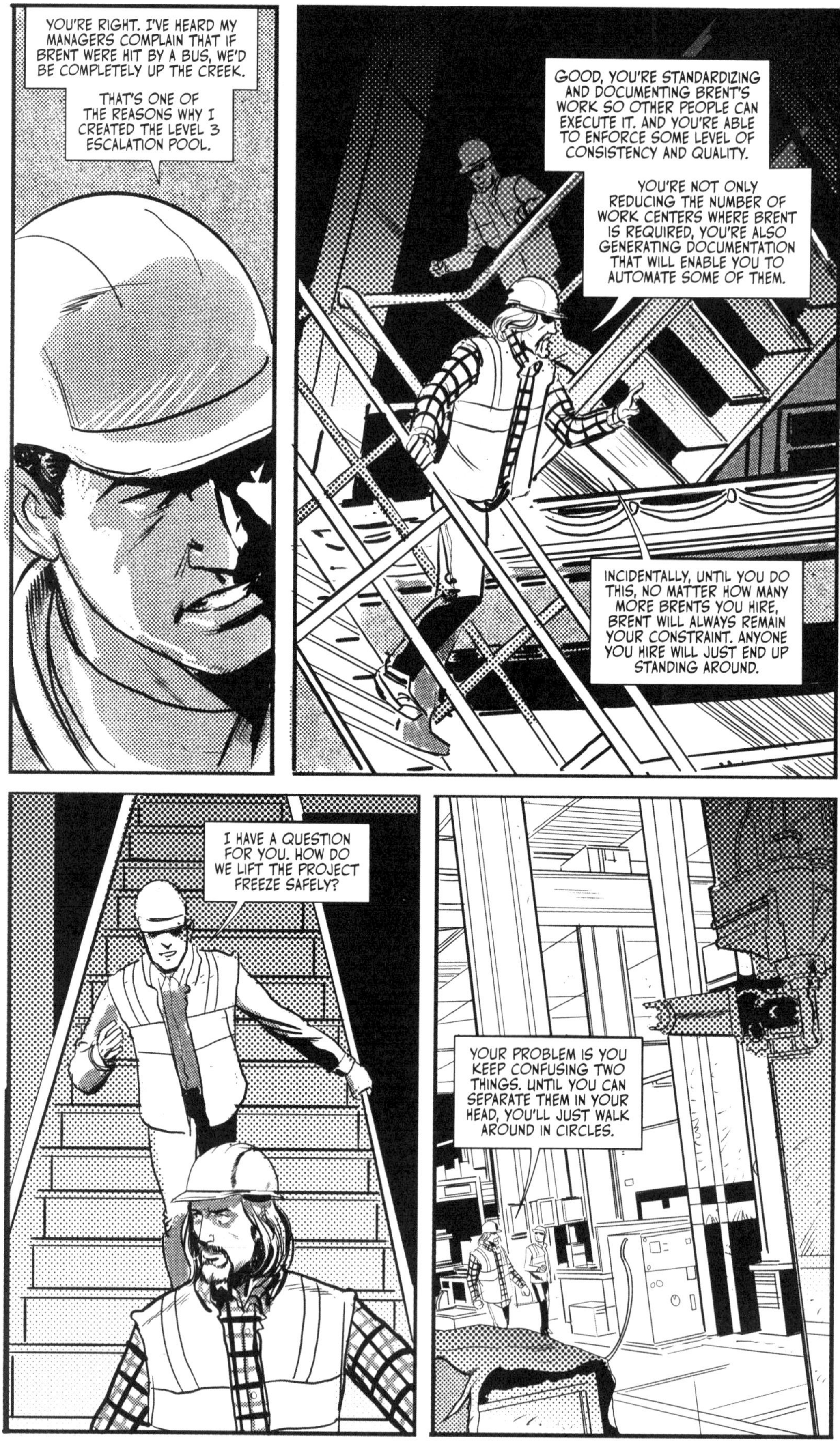
YOU'RE RIGHT. I'VE HEARD MY MANAGERS COMPLAIN THAT IF BRENT WERE HIT BY A BUS, WE'D BE COMPLETELY UP THE CREEK.
THAT'S ONE OF THE REASONS WHY I CREATED THE LEVEL 3 ESCALATION POOL.
GOOD, YOU'RE STANDARDIZING AND DOCUMENTING BRENT'S WORK SO OTHER PEOPLE CAN EXECUTE IT. AND YOU'RE ABLE TO ENFORCE SOME LEVEL OF CONSISTENCY AND QUALITY.
YOU'RE NOT ONLY REDUCING THE NUMBER OF WORK CENTERS WHERE BRENT IS REQUIRED, YOU'RE ALSO GENERATING DOCUMENTATION THAT WILL ENABLE YOU TO AUTOMATE SOME OF THEM.
INCIDENTALLY, UNTIL YOU DO THIS, NO MATTER HOW MANY MORE BRENTS YOU HIRE, BRENT WILL ALWAYS REMAIN YOUR CONSTRAINT. ANYONE YOU HIRE WILL JUST END UP STANDING AROUND.
I HAVE A QUESTION FOR YOU. HOW DO WE LIFT THE PROJECT FREEZE SAFELY?
YOUR PROBLEM IS YOU KEEP CONFUSING TWO THINGS. UNTIL YOU CAN SEPARATE THEM IN YOUR HEAD, YOU'LL JUST WALK AROUND IN CIRCLES.

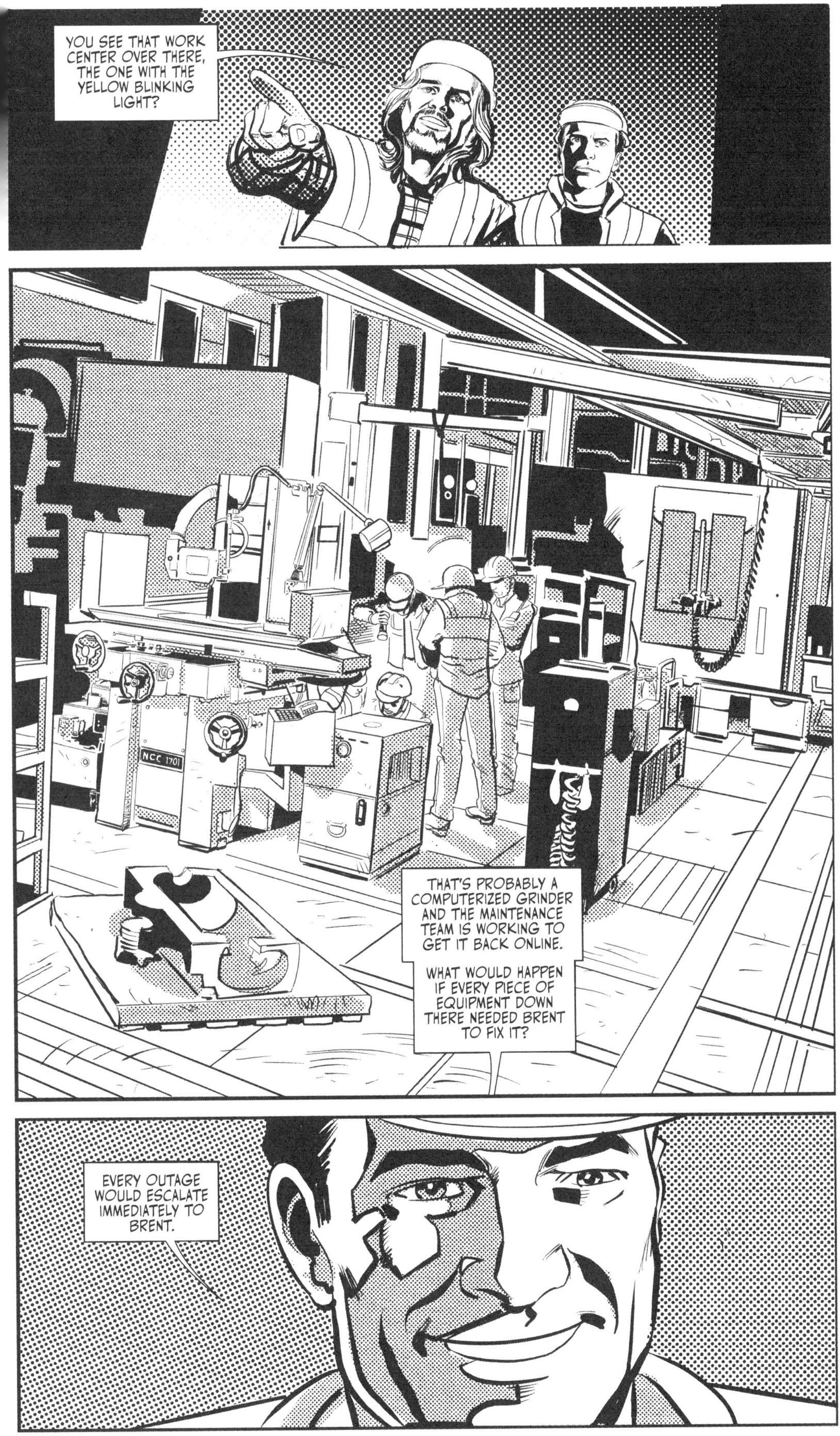
YOU SEE THAT WORK CENTER OVER THERE, THE ONE WITH THE YELLOW BLINKING LIGHT?
NCC 1701
THAT'S PROBABLY A COMPUTERIZED GRINDER AND THE MAINTENANCE TEAM IS WORKING TO GET IT BACK ONLINE.
WHAT WOULD HAPPEN IF EVERY PIECE OF EQUIPMENT DOWN THERE NEEDED BRENT TO FIX IT?
EVERY OUTAGE WOULD ESCALATE IMMEDIATELY TO BRENT.

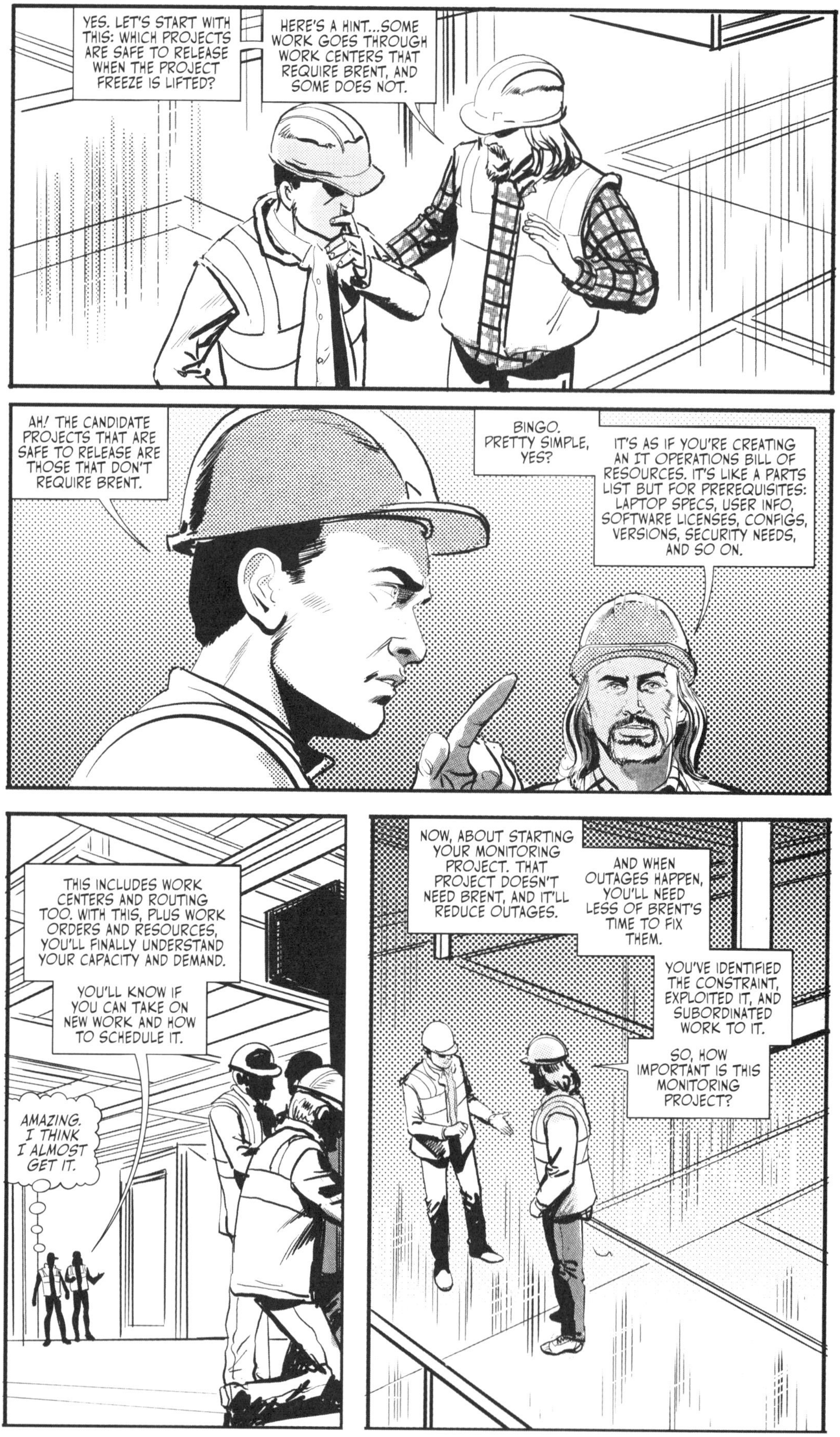
YES. LET'S START WITH THIS: WHICH PROJECTS ARE SAFE TO RELEASE WHEN THE PROJECT FREEZE IS LIFTED?
HERE'S A HINT...SOME WORK GOES THROUGH WORK CENTERS THAT REQUIRE BRENT, AND SOME DOES NOT.
AH! THE CANDIDATE PROJECTS THAT ARE SAFE TO RELEASE ARE THOSE THAT DON'T REQUIRE BRENT.
BINGO. PRETTY SIMPLE, YES?
IT'S AS IF YOU'RE CREATING AN IT OPERATIONS BILL OF RESOURCES. IT'S LIKE A PARTS LIST BUT FOR PREREQUISITES: LAPTOP SPECS, USER INFO, SOFTWARE LICENSES, CONFIGS, VERSIONS, SECURITY NEEDS, AND SO ON.
THIS INCLUDES WORK CENTERS AND ROUTING TOO. WITH THIS, PLUS WORK ORDERS AND RESOURCES, YOU'LL FINALLY UNDERSTAND YOUR CAPACITY AND DEMAND.
YOU'LL KNOW IF YOU CAN TAKE ON NEW WORK AND HOW TO SCHEDULE IT.
AMAZING. I THINK I ALMOST GET IT.
NOW, ABOUT STARTING YOUR MONITORING PROJECT. THAT PROJECT DOESN'T NEED BRENT, AND IT'LL REDUCE OUTAGES.
AND WHEN OUTAGES HAPPEN, YOU'LL NEED LESS OF BRENT'S TIME TO FIX THEM.
YOU'VE IDENTIFIED THE CONSTRAINT, EXPLOITED IT, AND SUBORDINATED WORK TO IT.
SO, HOW IMPORTANT IS THIS MONITORING PROJECT?

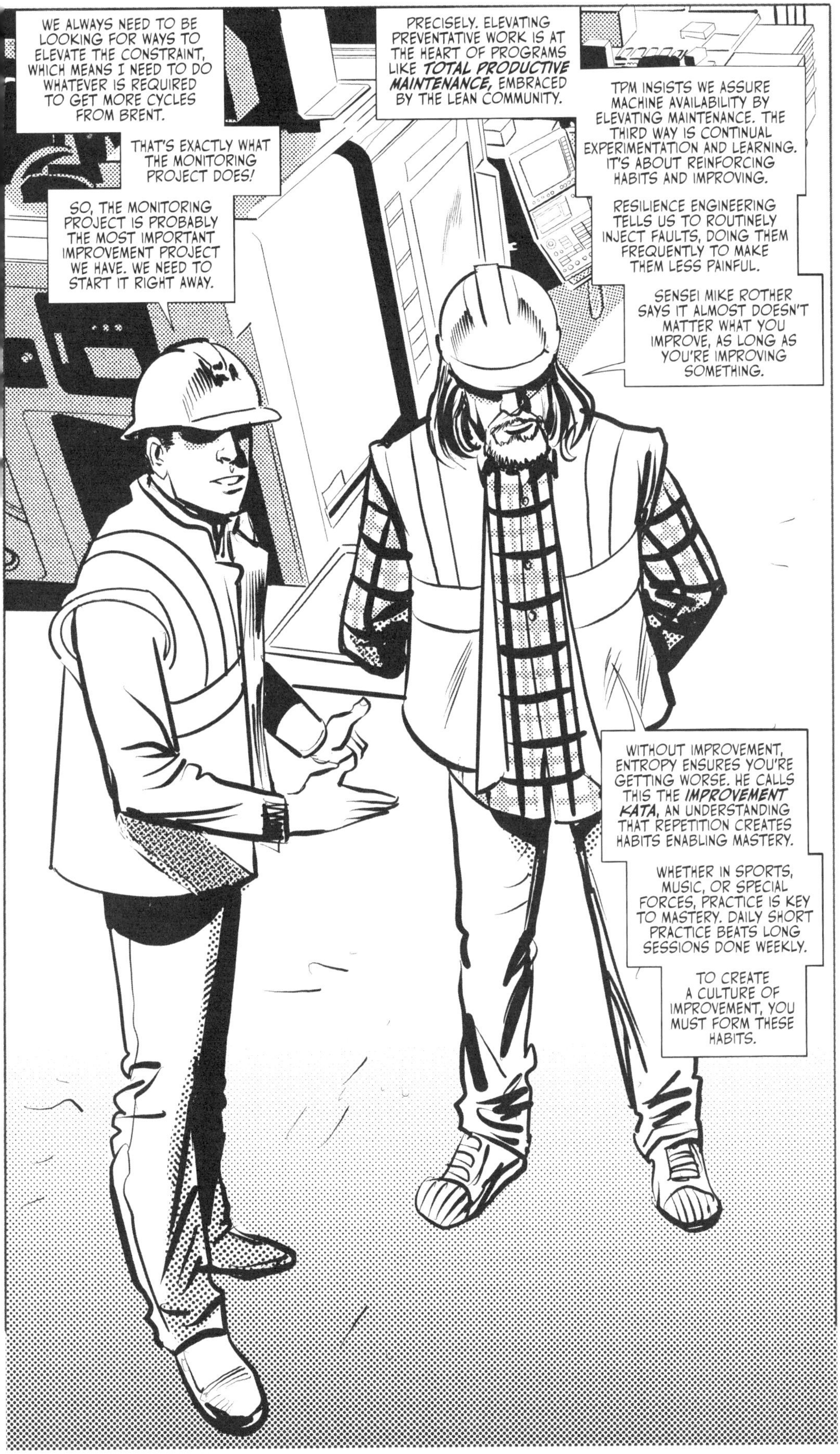
WE ALWAYS NEED TO BE LOOKING FOR WAYS TO ELEVATE THE CONSTRAINT, WHICH MEANS I NEED TO DO WHATEVER IS REQUIRED TO GET MORE CYCLES FROM BRENT.
PRECISELY. ELEVATING PREVENTATIVE WORK IS AT THE HEART OF PROGRAMS LIKE ***TOTAL PRODUCTIVE MAINTENANCE,*** EMBRACED BY THE LEAN COMMUNITY.
TPM INSISTS WE ASSURE MACHINE AVAILABILITY BY ELEVATING MAINTENANCE. THE THIRD WAY IS CONTINUAL EXPERIMENTATION AND LEARNING. IT'S ABOUT REINFORCING HABITS AND IMPROVING.
RESILIENCE ENGINEERING TELLS US TO ROUTINELY INJECT FAULTS, DOING THEM FREQUENTLY TO MAKE THEM LESS PAINFUL.
THAT'S EXACTLY WHAT THE MONITORING PROJECT DOES!
SO, THE MONITORING PROJECT IS PROBABLY THE MOST IMPORTANT IMPROVEMENT PROJECT WE HAVE. WE NEED TO START IT RIGHT AWAY.
SENSEI MIKE ROTHER SAYS IT ALMOST DOESN'T MATTER WHAT YOU IMPROVE, AS LONG AS YOU'RE IMPROVING SOMETHING.
WITHOUT IMPROVEMENT, ENTROPY ENSURES YOU'RE GETTING WORSE. HE CALLS THIS THE ***IMPROVEMENT KATA***, AN UNDERSTANDING THAT REPETITION CREATES HABITS ENABLING MASTERY.
WHETHER IN SPORTS, MUSIC, OR SPECIAL FORCES, PRACTICE IS KEY TO MASTERY. DAILY SHORT PRACTICE BEATS LONG SESSIONS DONE WEEKLY.
TO CREATE A CULTURE OF IMPROVEMENT, YOU MUST FORM THESE HABITS.

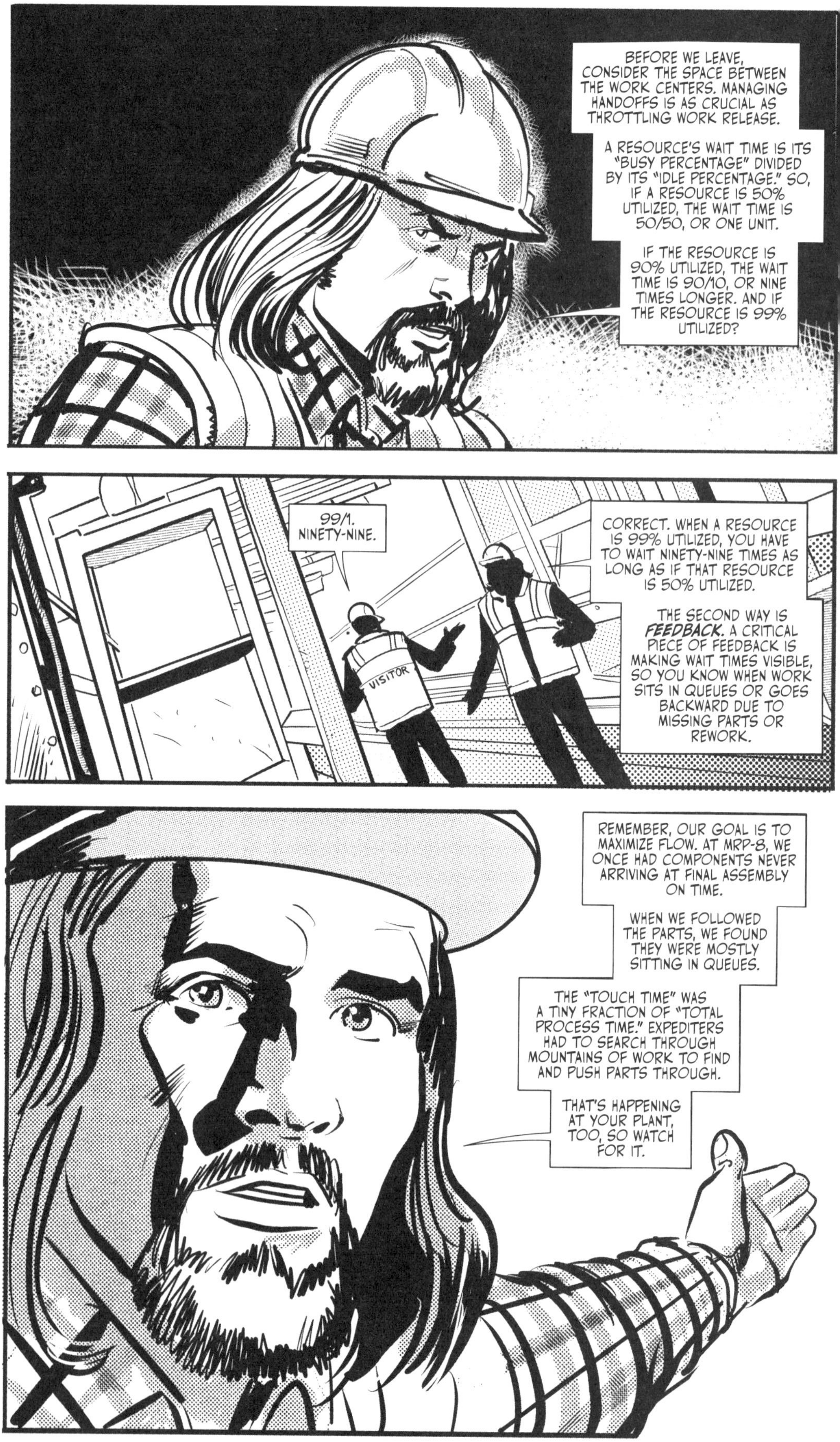
BEFORE WE LEAVE, CONSIDER THE SPACE BETWEEN THE WORK CENTERS. MANAGING HANDOFFS IS AS CRUCIAL AS THROTTLING WORK RELEASE.
A RESOURCE'S WAIT TIME IS ITS "BUSY PERCENTAGE" DIVIDED BY ITS "IDLE PERCENTAGE." SO, IF A RESOURCE IS 50% UTILIZED, THE WAIT TIME IS 50/50, OR ONE UNIT.
IF THE RESOURCE IS 90% UTILIZED, THE WAIT TIME IS 90/10, OR NINE TIMES LONGER. AND IF THE RESOURCE IS 99% UTILIZED?
99/1. NINETY-NINE.
CORRECT. WHEN A RESOURCE IS 99% UTILIZED, YOU HAVE TO WAIT NINETY-NINE TIMES AS LONG AS IF THAT RESOURCE IS 50% UTILIZED.
THE SECOND WAY IS ***FEEDBACK.*** A CRITICAL PIECE OF FEEDBACK IS MAKING WAIT TIMES VISIBLE, SO YOU KNOW WHEN WORK SITS IN QUEUES OR GOES BACKWARD DUE TO MISSING PARTS OR REWORK.
VISITOR
REMEMBER, OUR GOAL IS TO MAXIMIZE FLOW. AT MRP-8, WE ONCE HAD COMPONENTS NEVER ARRIVING AT FINAL ASSEMBLY ON TIME.
WHEN WE FOLLOWED THE PARTS, WE FOUND THEY WERE MOSTLY SITTING IN QUEUES.
THE "TOUCH TIME" WAS A TINY FRACTION OF "TOTAL PROCESS TIME." EXPEDITERS HAD TO SEARCH THROUGH MOUNTAINS OF WORK TO FIND AND PUSH PARTS THROUGH.
THAT'S HAPPENING AT YOUR PLANT, TOO, SO WATCH FOR IT.

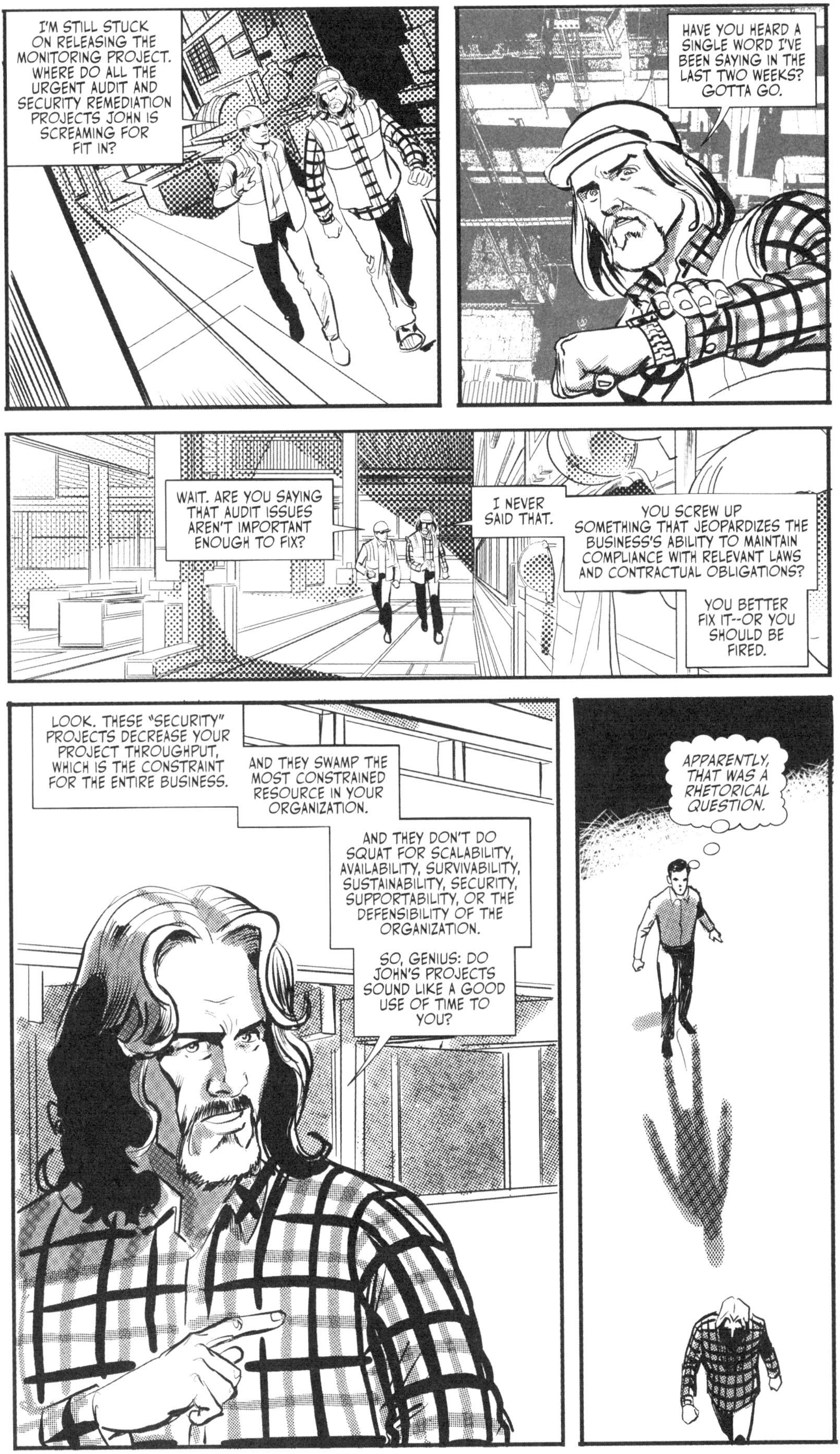

I'M STILL STUCK ON RELEASING THE MONITORING PROJECT. WHERE DO ALL THE URGENT AUDIT AND SECURITY REMEDIATION PROJECTS JOHN IS SCREAMING FOR FIT IN?
HAVE YOU HEARD A SINGLE WORD I'VE BEEN SAYING IN THE LAST TWO WEEKS? GOTTA GO.
WAIT. ARE YOU SAYING THAT AUDIT ISSUES AREN'T IMPORTANT ENOUGH TO FIX?
I NEVER SAID THAT.
YOU SCREW UP SOMETHING THAT JEOPARDIZES THE BUSINESS'S ABILITY TO MAINTAIN COMPLIANCE WITH RELEVANT LAWS AND CONTRACTUAL OBLIGATIONS?
YOU BETTER FIX IT--OR YOU SHOULD BE FIRED.
LOOK. THESE "SECURITY" PROJECTS DECREASE YOUR PROJECT THROUGHPUT, WHICH IS THE CONSTRAINT FOR THE ENTIRE BUSINESS.
AND THEY SWAMP THE MOST CONSTRAINED RESOURCE IN YOUR ORGANIZATION.
AND THEY DON'T DO SQUAT FOR SCALABILITY, AVAILABILITY, SURVIVABILITY, SUSTAINABILITY, SECURITY, SUPPORTABILITY, OR THE DEFENSIBILITY OF THE ORGANIZATION.
SO, GENIUS: DO JOHN'S PROJECTS SOUND LIKE A GOOD USE OF TIME TO YOU?
APPARENTLY, THAT WAS A RHETORICAL QUESTION.

CHAPTER 21 FRIDAY, SEPTEMBER 26

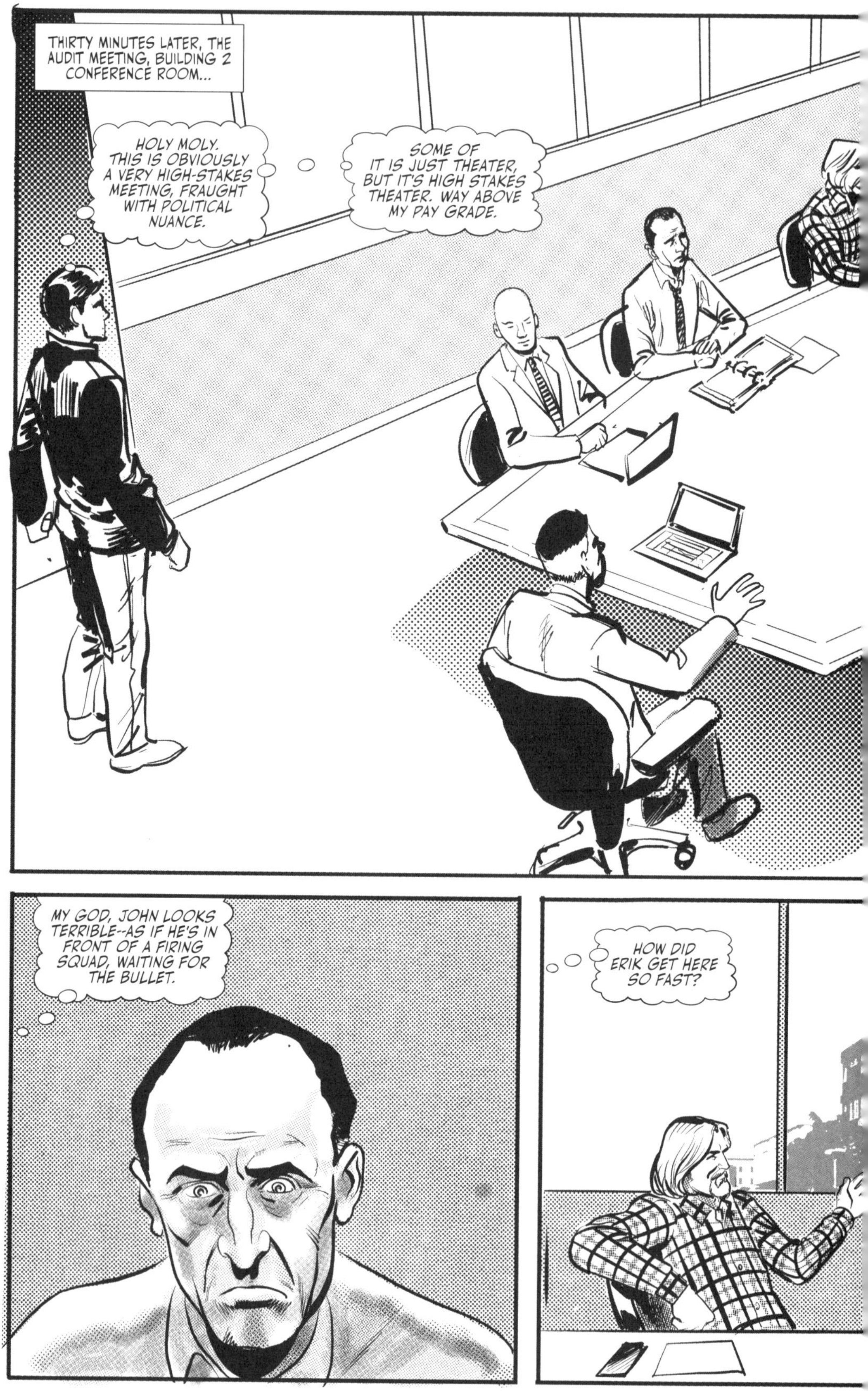

THIRTY MINUTES LATER, THE AUDIT MEETING, BUILDING 2 CONFERENCE ROOM...
HOLY MOLY. THIS IS OBVIOUSLY A VERY HIGH-STAKES MEETING, FRAUGHT WITH POLITICAL NUANCE.
SOME OF IT IS JUST THEATER, BUT IT'S HIGH STAKES THEATER. WAY ABOVE MY PAY GRADE.
MY GOD, JOHN LOOKS TERRIBLE--AS IF HE'S IN FRONT OF A FIRING SQUAD, WAITING FOR THE BULLET.
HOW DID ERIK GET HERE SO FAST?

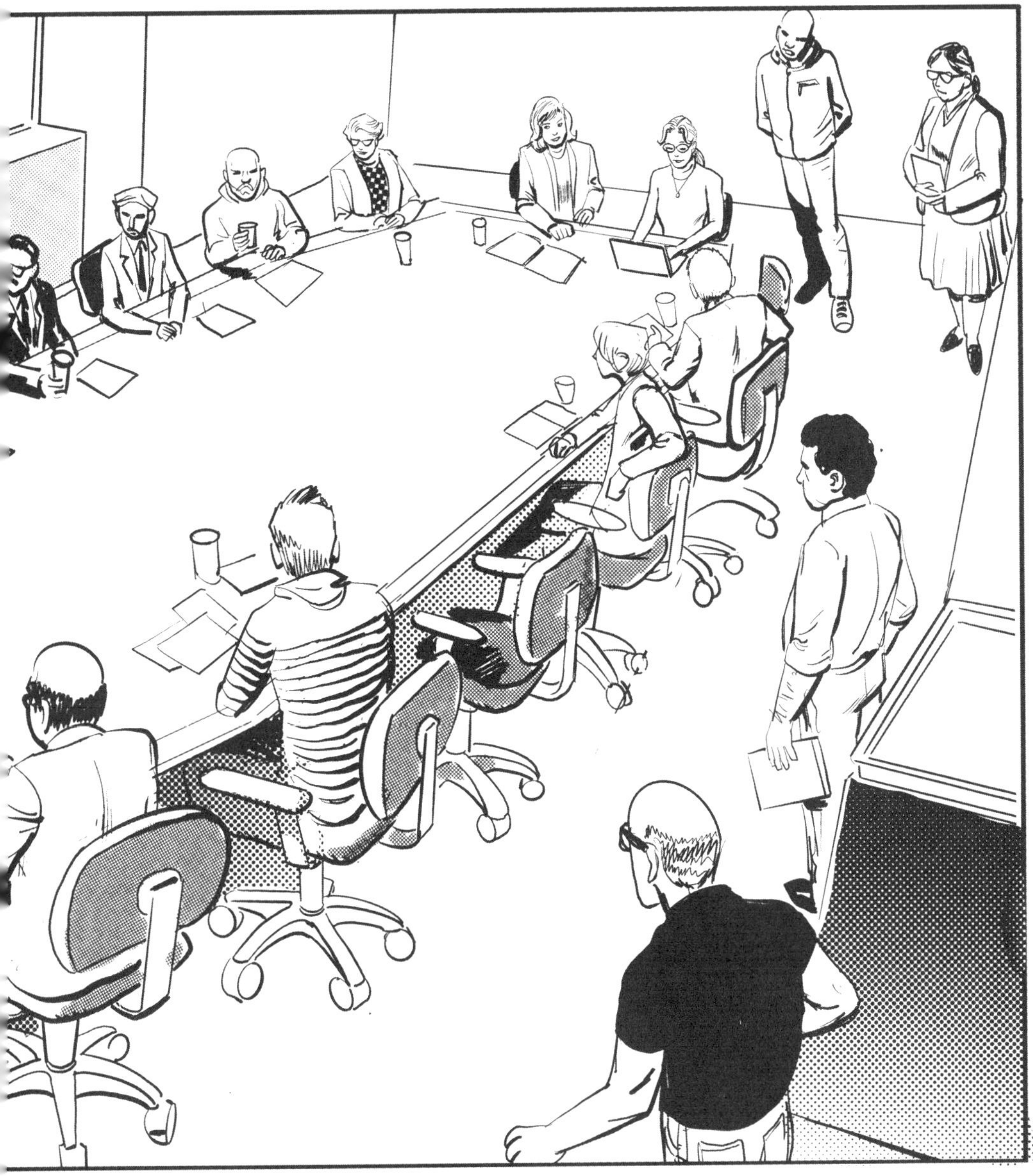

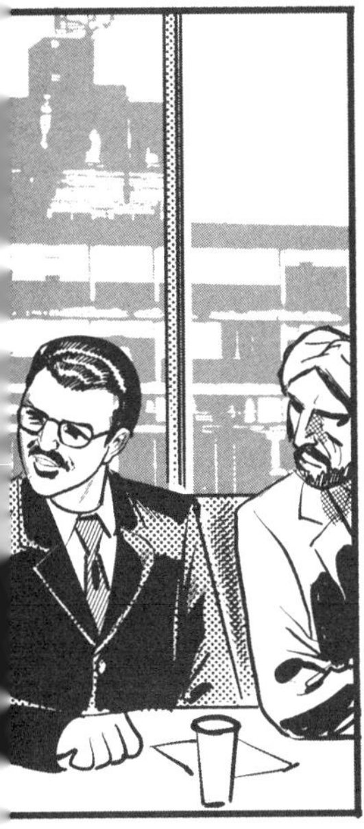

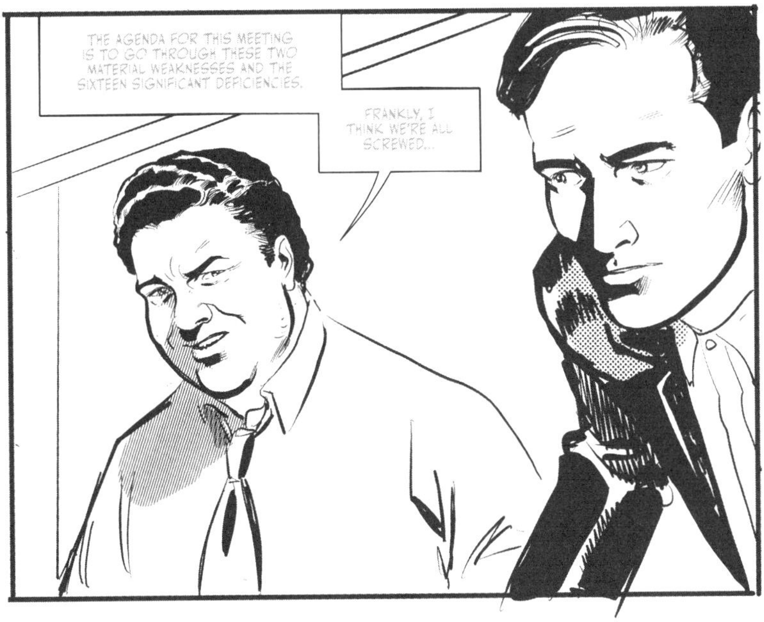
THE AGENDA FOR THIS MEETING IS TO GO THROUGH THESE TWO MATERIAL WEAKNESSES AND THE SIXTEEN SIGNIFICANT DEFICIENCIES.
FRANKLY, I THINK WE'RE ALL SCREWED...

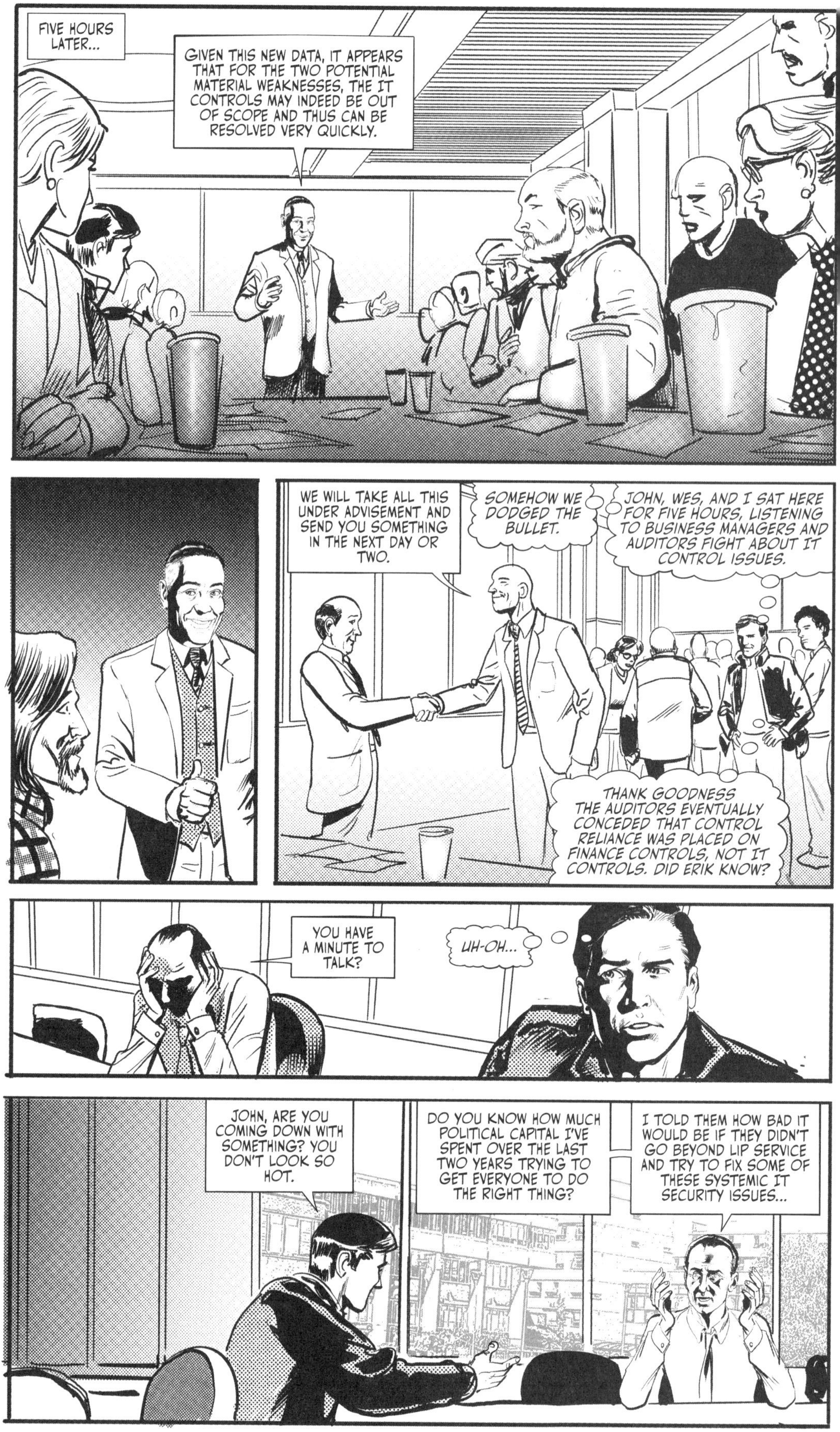

FIVE HOURS LATER...
GIVEN THIS NEW DATA, IT APPEARS THAT FOR THE TWO POTENTIAL MATERIAL WEAKNESSES, THE IT CONTROLS MAY INDEED BE OUT OF SCOPE AND THUS CAN BE RESOLVED VERY QUICKLY.
WE WILL TAKE ALL THIS UNDER ADVISEMENT AND SEND YOU SOMETHING IN THE NEXT DAY OR TWO.
SOMEHOW WE DODGED THE BULLET.
JOHN, WES, AND I SAT HERE FOR FIVE HOURS, LISTENING TO BUSINESS MANAGERS AND AUDITORS FIGHT ABOUT IT CONTROL ISSUES.
THANK GOODNESS THE AUDITORS EVENTUALLY CONCEDED THAT CONTROL RELIANCE WAS PLACED ON FINANCE CONTROLS, NOT IT CONTROLS. DID ERIK KNOW?
YOU HAVE A MINUTE TO TALK?
UH-OH...
JOHN, ARE YOU COMING DOWN WITH SOMETHING? YOU DON'T LOOK SO HOT.
DO YOU KNOW HOW MUCH POLITICAL CAPITAL I'VE SPENT OVER THE LAST TWO YEARS TRYING TO GET EVERYONE TO DO THE RIGHT THING?
I TOLD THEM HOW BAD IT WOULD BE IF THEY DIDN'T GO BEYOND LIP SERVICE AND TRY TO FIX SOME OF THESE SYSTEMIC IT SECURITY ISSUES...

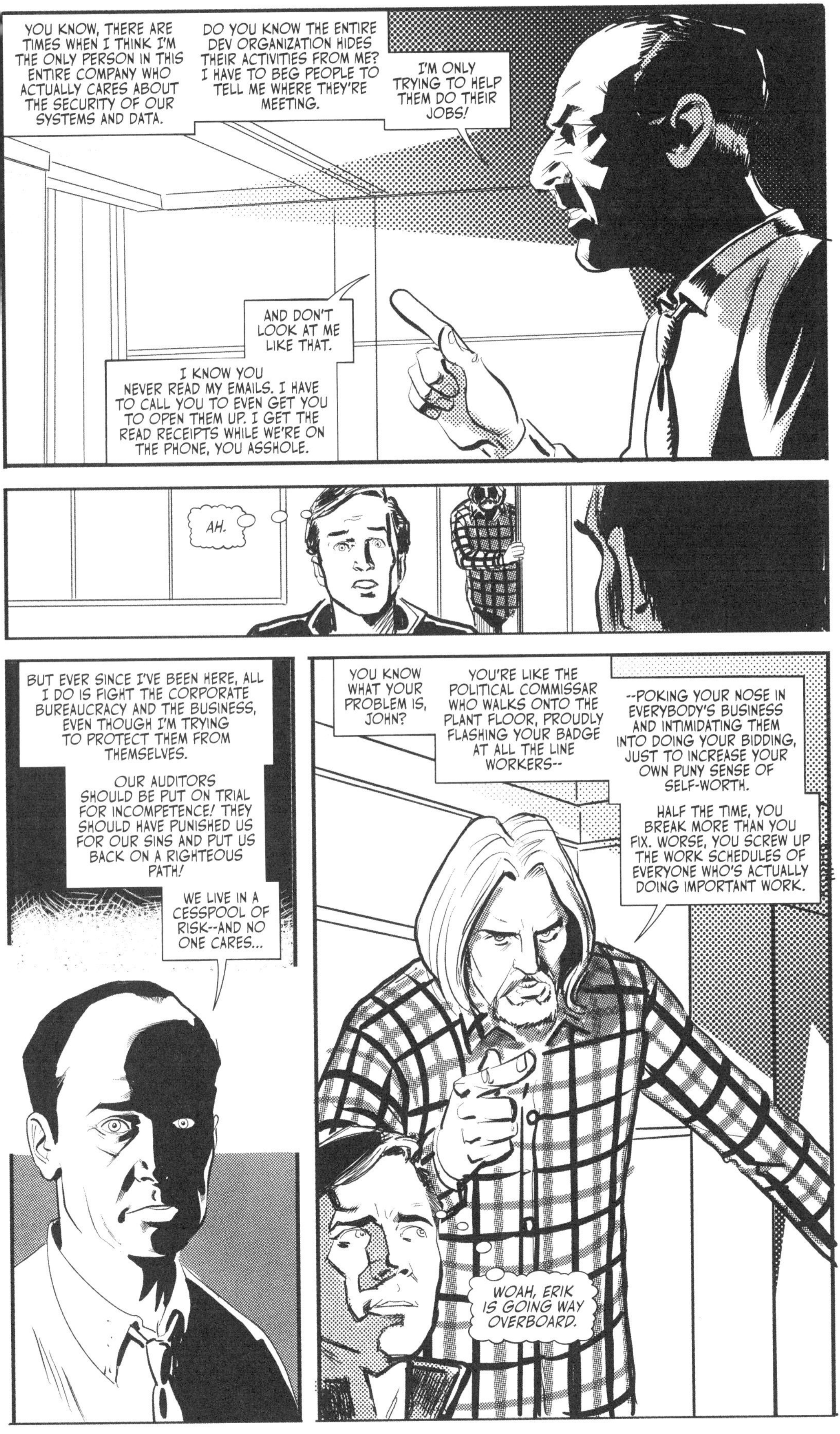
YOU KNOW, THERE ARE TIMES WHEN I THINK I'M THE ONLY PERSON IN THIS ENTIRE COMPANY WHO ACTUALLY CARES ABOUT THE SECURITY OF OUR SYSTEMS AND DATA.
DO YOU KNOW THE ENTIRE DEV ORGANIZATION HIDES THEIR ACTIVITIES FROM ME? I HAVE TO BEG PEOPLE TO TELL ME WHERE THEY'RE MEETING.
I'M ONLY TRYING TO HELP THEM DO THEIR JOBS!
AND DON'T LOOK AT ME LIKE THAT.
I KNOW YOU NEVER READ MY EMAILS. I HAVE TO CALL YOU TO EVEN GET YOU TO OPEN THEM UP. I GET THE READ RECEIPTS WHILE WE'RE ON THE PHONE, YOU ASSHOLE.
AH.
BUT EVER SINCE I'VE BEEN HERE, ALL I DO IS FIGHT THE CORPORATE BUREAUCRACY AND THE BUSINESS, EVEN THOUGH I'M TRYING TO PROTECT THEM FROM THEMSELVES.
OUR AUDITORS SHOULD BE PUT ON TRIAL FOR INCOMPETENCE! THEY SHOULD HAVE PUNISHED US FOR OUR SINS AND PUT US BACK ON A RIGHTEOUS PATH!
WE LIVE IN A CESSPOOL OF RISK--AND NO ONE CARES...
YOU KNOW WHAT YOUR PROBLEM IS, JOHN?
YOU'RE LIKE THE POLITICAL COMMISSAR WHO WALKS ONTO THE PLANT FLOOR, PROUDLY FLASHING YOUR BADGE AT ALL THE LINE WORKERS--
--POKING YOUR NOSE IN EVERYBODY'S BUSINESS AND INTIMIDATING THEM INTO DOING YOUR BIDDING, JUST TO INCREASE YOUR OWN PUNY SENSE OF SELF-WORTH.
HALF THE TIME, YOU BREAK MORE THAN YOU FIX. WORSE, YOU SCREW UP THE WORK SCHEDULES OF EVERYONE WHO'S ACTUALLY DOING IMPORTANT WORK.
WOAH, ERIK IS GOING WAY OVERBOARD.

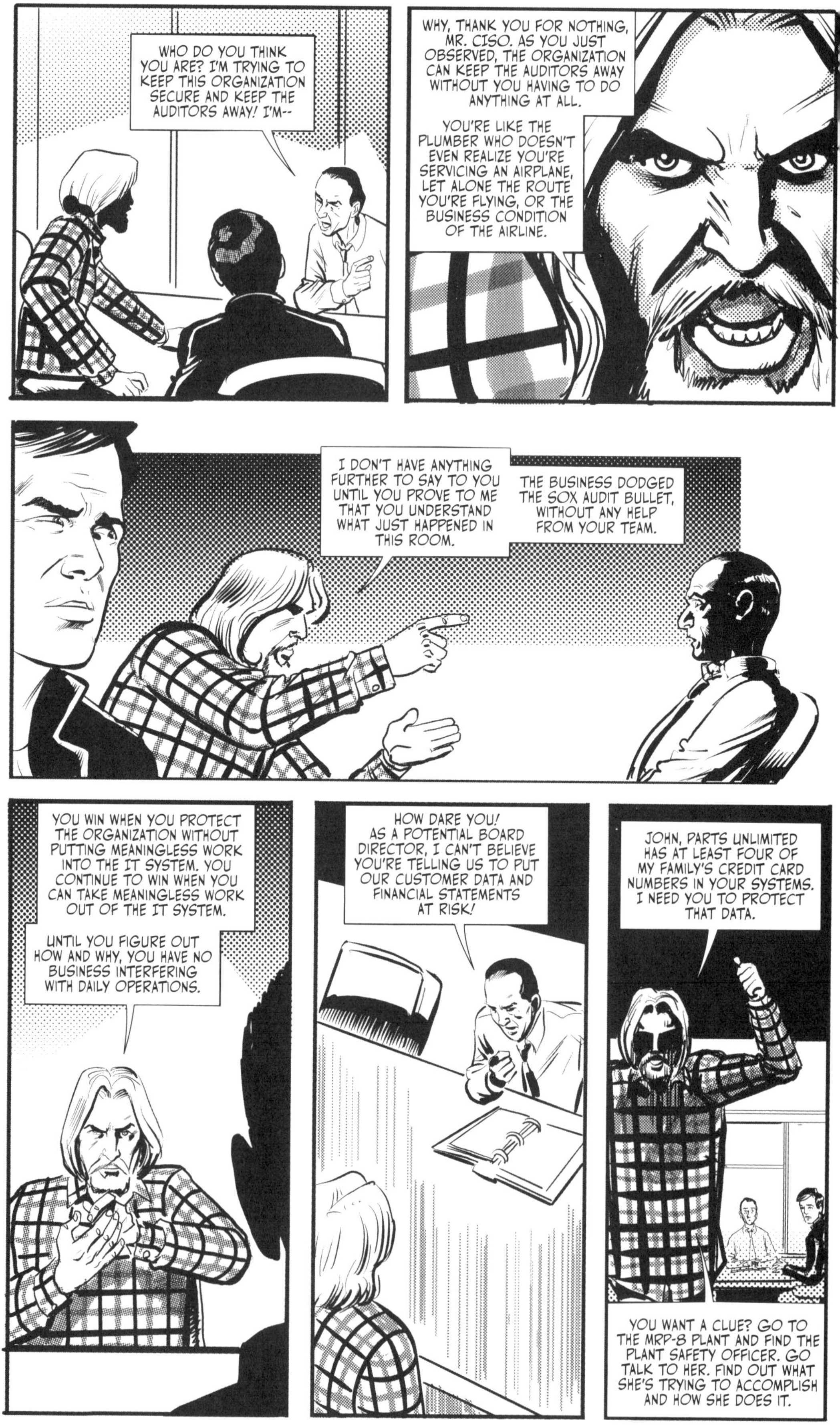

WHO DO YOU THINK YOU ARE? I'M TRYING TO KEEP THIS ORGANIZATION SECURE AND KEEP THE AUDITORS AWAY! I'M--
WHY, THANK YOU FOR NOTHING, MR. CISO. AS YOU JUST OBSERVED, THE ORGANIZATION CAN KEEP THE AUDITORS AWAY WITHOUT YOU HAVING TO DO ANYTHING AT ALL.
YOU'RE LIKE THE PLUMBER WHO DOESN'T EVEN REALIZE YOU'RE SERVICING AN AIRPLANE, LET ALONE THE ROUTE YOU'RE FLYING, OR THE BUSINESS CONDITION OF THE AIRLINE.
THE BUSINESS DODGED THE SOX AUDIT BULLET, WITHOUT ANY HELP FROM YOUR TEAM.
I DON'T HAVE ANYTHING FURTHER TO SAY TO YOU UNTIL YOU PROVE TO ME THAT YOU UNDERSTAND WHAT JUST HAPPENED IN THIS ROOM.
YOU WIN WHEN YOU PROTECT THE ORGANIZATION WITHOUT PUTTING MEANINGLESS WORK INTO THE IT SYSTEM. YOU CONTINUE TO WIN WHEN YOU CAN TAKE MEANINGLESS WORK OUT OF THE IT SYSTEM.
UNTIL YOU FIGURE OUT HOW AND WHY, YOU HAVE NO BUSINESS INTERFERING WITH DAILY OPERATIONS.
HOW DARE YOU! AS A POTENTIAL BOARD DIRECTOR, I CAN'T BELIEVE YOU'RE TELLING US TO PUT OUR CUSTOMER DATA AND FINANCIAL STATEMENTS AT RISK!
JOHN, PARTS UNLIMITED HAS AT LEAST FOUR OF MY FAMILY'S CREDIT CARD NUMBERS IN YOUR SYSTEMS. I NEED YOU TO PROTECT THAT DATA.
YOU WANT A CLUE? GO TO THE MRP-8 PLANT AND FIND THE PLANT SAFETY OFFICER. GO TALK TO HER. FIND OUT WHAT SHE'S TRYING TO ACCOMPLISH AND HOW SHE DOES IT.

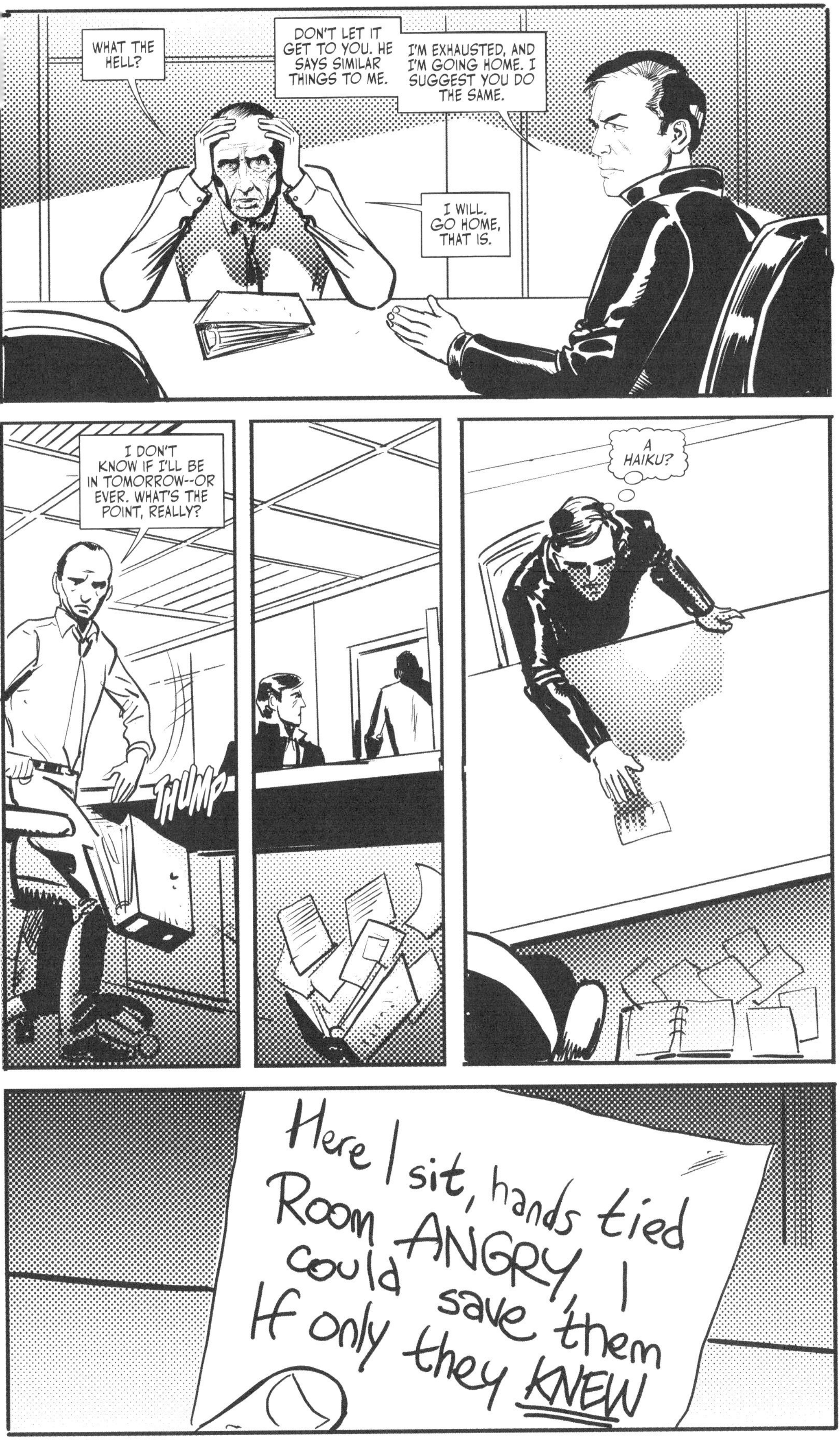
WHAT THE HELL?
DON'T LET IT GET TO YOU. HE SAYS SIMILAR THINGS TO ME.
I'M EXHAUSTED, AND I'M GOING HOME. I SUGGEST YOU DO THE SAME.
I WILL. GO HOME, THAT IS.
I DON'T KNOW IF I'LL BE IN TOMORROW--OR EVER. WHAT'S THE POINT, REALLY?
THUMP
A HAIKU?
Here I sit, hands tied
Room ANGRY, I could save them
If only they KNEW

CHAPTER 22 MONDAY, SEPTEMBER 29

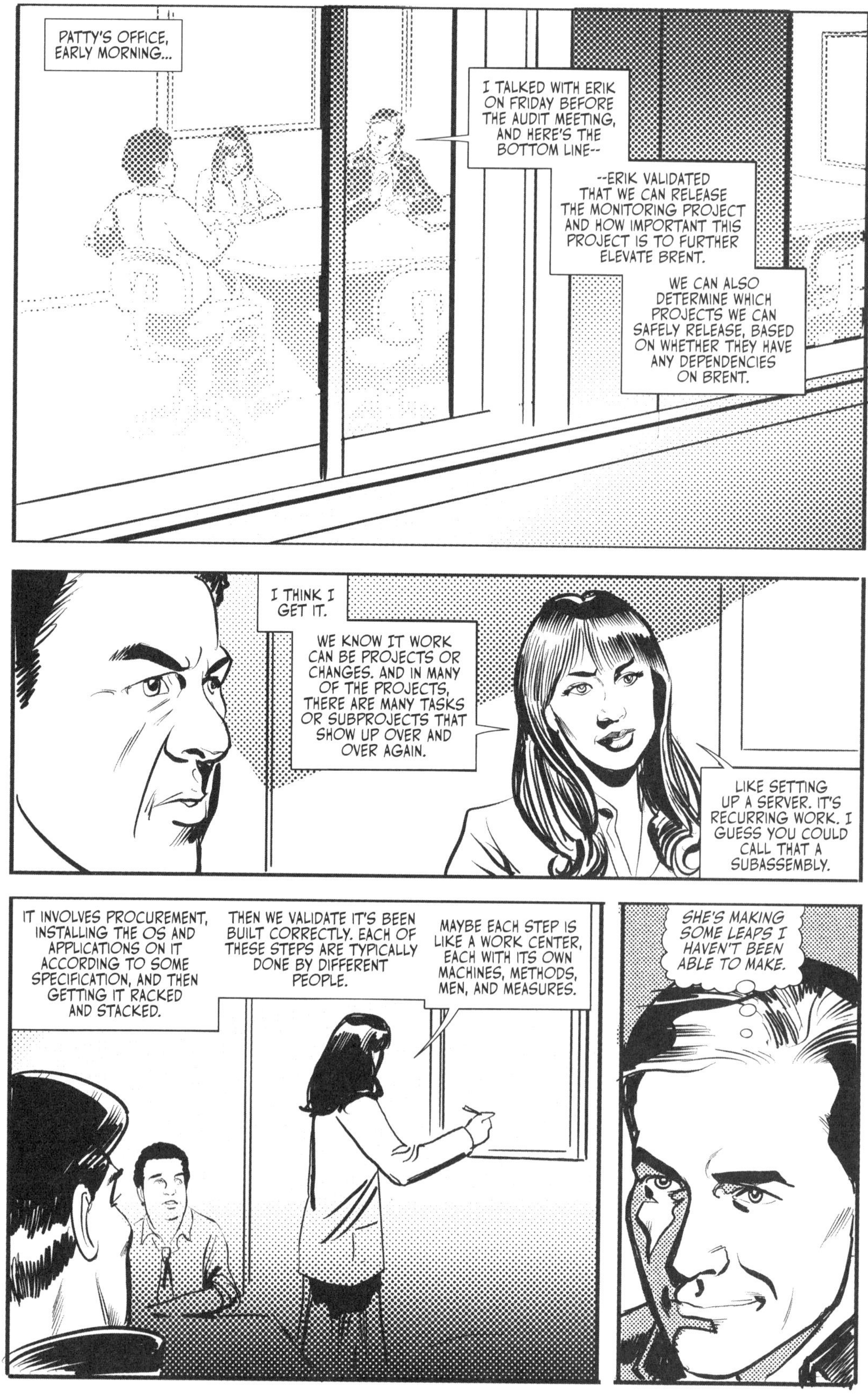

PATTY'S OFFICE, EARLY MORNING...
I TALKED WITH ERIK ON FRIDAY BEFORE THE AUDIT MEETING, AND HERE'S THE BOTTOM LINE--
--ERIK VALIDATED THAT WE CAN RELEASE THE MONITORING PROJECT AND HOW IMPORTANT THIS PROJECT IS TO FURTHER ELEVATE BRENT.
WE CAN ALSO DETERMINE WHICH PROJECTS WE CAN SAFELY RELEASE, BASED ON WHETHER THEY HAVE ANY DEPENDENCIES ON BRENT.
I THINK I GET IT.
WE KNOW IT WORK CAN BE PROJECTS OR CHANGES. AND IN MANY OF THE PROJECTS, THERE ARE MANY TASKS OR SUBPROJECTS THAT SHOW UP OVER AND OVER AGAIN.
LIKE SETTING UP A SERVER. IT'S RECURRING WORK. I GUESS YOU COULD CALL THAT A SUBASSEMBLY.
IT INVOLVES PROCUREMENT, INSTALLING THE OS AND APPLICATIONS ON IT ACCORDING TO SOME SPECIFICATION, AND THEN GETTING IT RACKED AND STACKED.
THEN WE VALIDATE IT'S BEEN BUILT CORRECTLY. EACH OF THESE STEPS ARE TYPICALLY DONE BY DIFFERENT PEOPLE.
MAYBE EACH STEP IS LIKE A WORK CENTER, EACH WITH ITS OWN MACHINES, METHODS, MEN, AND MEASURES.
SHE'S MAKING SOME LEAPS I HAVEN'T BEEN ABLE TO MAKE.

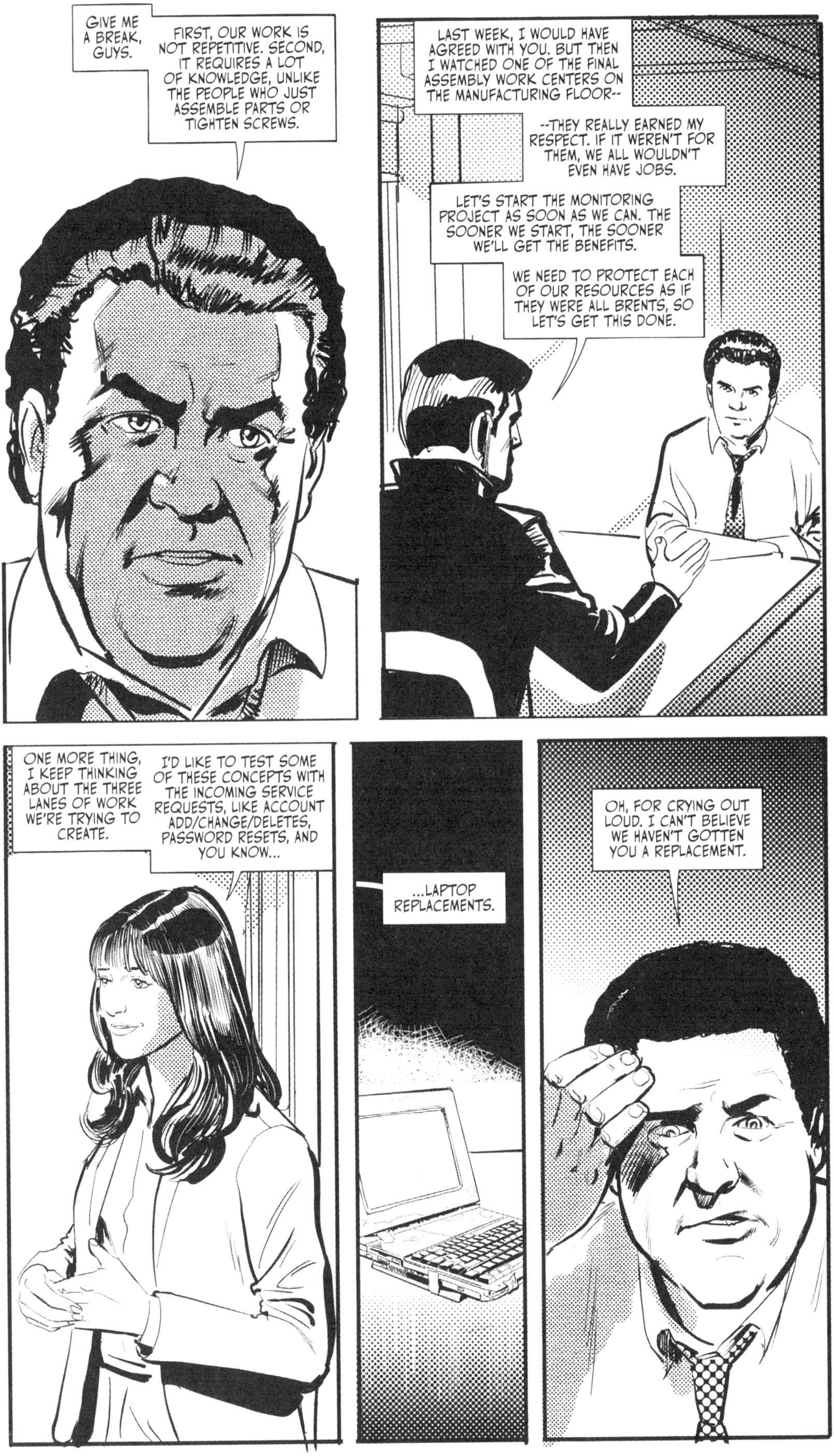
GIVE ME A BREAK, GUYS.
FIRST, OUR WORK IS NOT REPETITIVE. SECOND, IT REQUIRES A LOT OF KNOWLEDGE, UNLIKE THE PEOPLE WHO JUST ASSEMBLE PARTS OR TIGHTEN SCREWS.
LAST WEEK, I WOULD HAVE AGREED WITH YOU. BUT THEN I WATCHED ONE OF THE FINAL ASSEMBLY WORK CENTERS ON THE MANUFACTURING FLOOR--
--THEY REALLY EARNED MY RESPECT. IF IT WEREN'T FOR THEM, WE ALL WOULDN'T EVEN HAVE JOBS.
LET'S START THE MONITORING PROJECT AS SOON AS WE CAN. THE SOONER WE START, THE SOONER WE'LL GET THE BENEFITS.
WE NEED TO PROTECT EACH OF OUR RESOURCES AS IF THEY WERE ALL BRENTS, SO LET'S GET THIS DONE.
ONE MORE THING, I KEEP THINKING ABOUT THE THREE LANES OF WORK WE'RE TRYING TO CREATE.
I'D LIKE TO TEST SOME OF THESE CONCEPTS WITH THE INCOMING SERVICE REQUESTS, LIKE ACCOUNT ADD/CHANGE/DELETES, PASSWORD RESETS, AND YOU KNOW...
...LAPTOP REPLACEMENTS.
OH, FOR CRYING OUT LOUD. I CAN'T BELIEVE WE HAVEN'T GOTTEN YOU A REPLACEMENT.

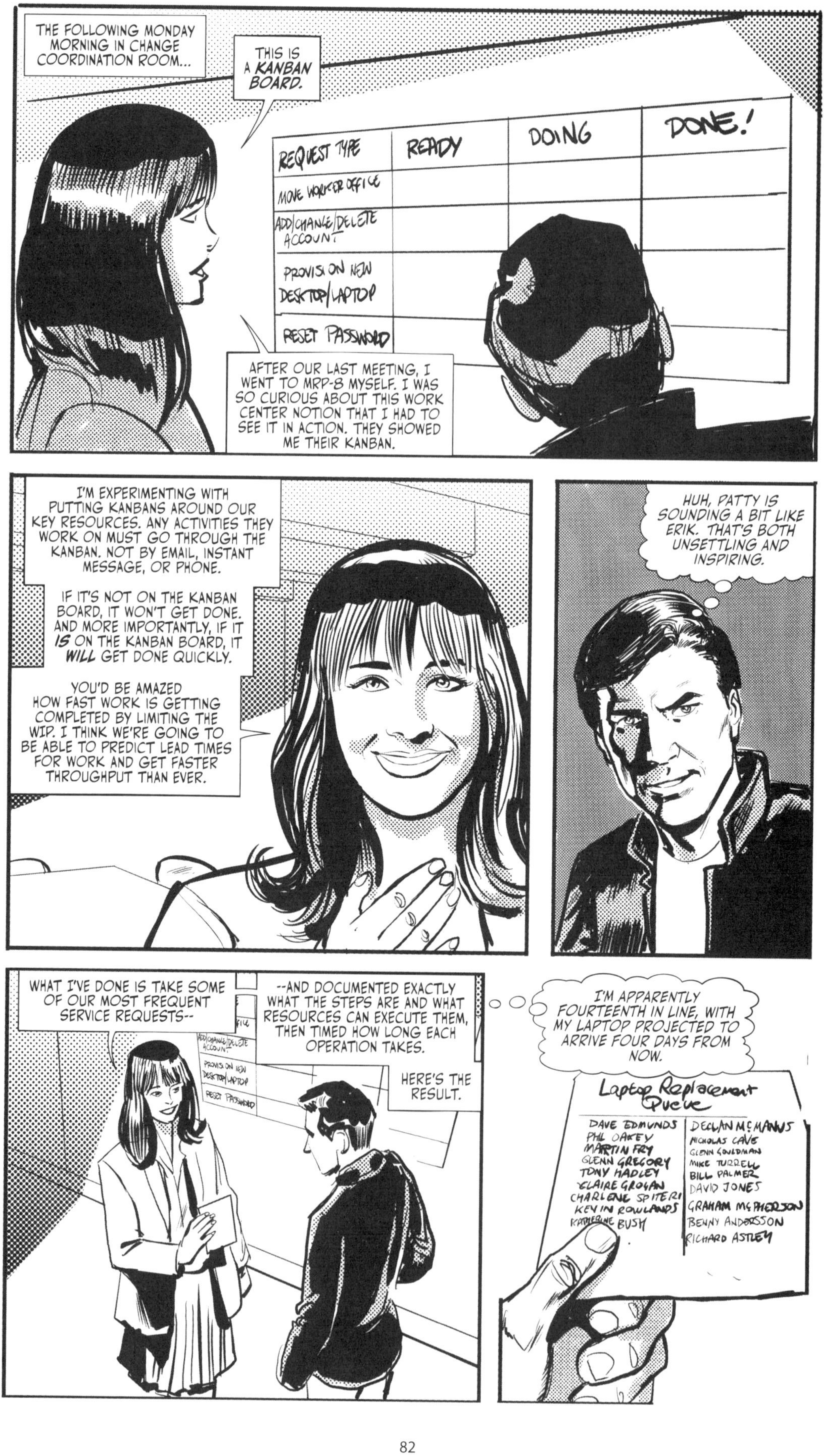
THE FOLLOWING MONDAY MORNING IN CHANGE COORDINATION ROOM...
THIS IS A KANBAN BOARD.
REQUEST TYPE
READY
DOING
DONE!
MOVE WORKER OFFICE
ADD/CHANGE/DELETE ACCOUNT
PROVISION NEW DESKTOP/LAPTOP
RESET PASSWORD
AFTER OUR LAST MEETING, I WENT TO MRP-8 MYSELF. I WAS SO CURIOUS ABOUT THIS WORK CENTER NOTION THAT I HAD TO SEE IT IN ACTION. THEY SHOWED ME THEIR KANBAN.
I'M EXPERIMENTING WITH PUTTING KANBANS AROUND OUR KEY RESOURCES. ANY ACTIVITIES THEY WORK ON MUST GO THROUGH THE KANBAN. NOT BY EMAIL, INSTANT MESSAGE, OR PHONE.
IF IT'S NOT ON THE KANBAN BOARD, IT WON'T GET DONE. AND MORE IMPORTANTLY, IF IT *IS* ON THE KANBAN BOARD, IT *WILL* GET DONE QUICKLY.
YOU'D BE AMAZED HOW FAST WORK IS GETTING COMPLETED BY LIMITING THE WIP. I THINK WE'RE GOING TO BE ABLE TO PREDICT LEAD TIMES FOR WORK AND GET FASTER THROUGHPUT THAN EVER.
HUH, PATTY IS SOUNDING A BIT LIKE ERIK. THAT'S BOTH UNSETTLING AND INSPIRING.
WHAT I'VE DONE IS TAKE SOME OF OUR MOST FREQUENT SERVICE REQUESTS--
--AND DOCUMENTED EXACTLY WHAT THE STEPS ARE AND WHAT RESOURCES CAN EXECUTE THEM, THEN TIMED HOW LONG EACH OPERATION TAKES.
HERE'S THE RESULT.
I'M APPARENTLY FOURTEENTH IN LINE, WITH MY LAPTOP PROJECTED TO ARRIVE FOUR DAYS FROM NOW.
Laptop Replacement Queue
DAVE EDMUNDS
PHIL OAKEY
MARTIN FRY
GLENN GREGORY
TONY HADLEY
CLAIRE GROGAN
CHARLENE SPITERI
KEVIN ROWLANDS
KATHERINE BUSH
DECLAN McMANUS
NICHOLAS CAVE
GLENN GOLDMAN
MIKE TURRELL
BILL PALMER
DAVID JONES
GRAHAM McPHERSON
BENNY ANDERSSON
RICHARD ASTLEY

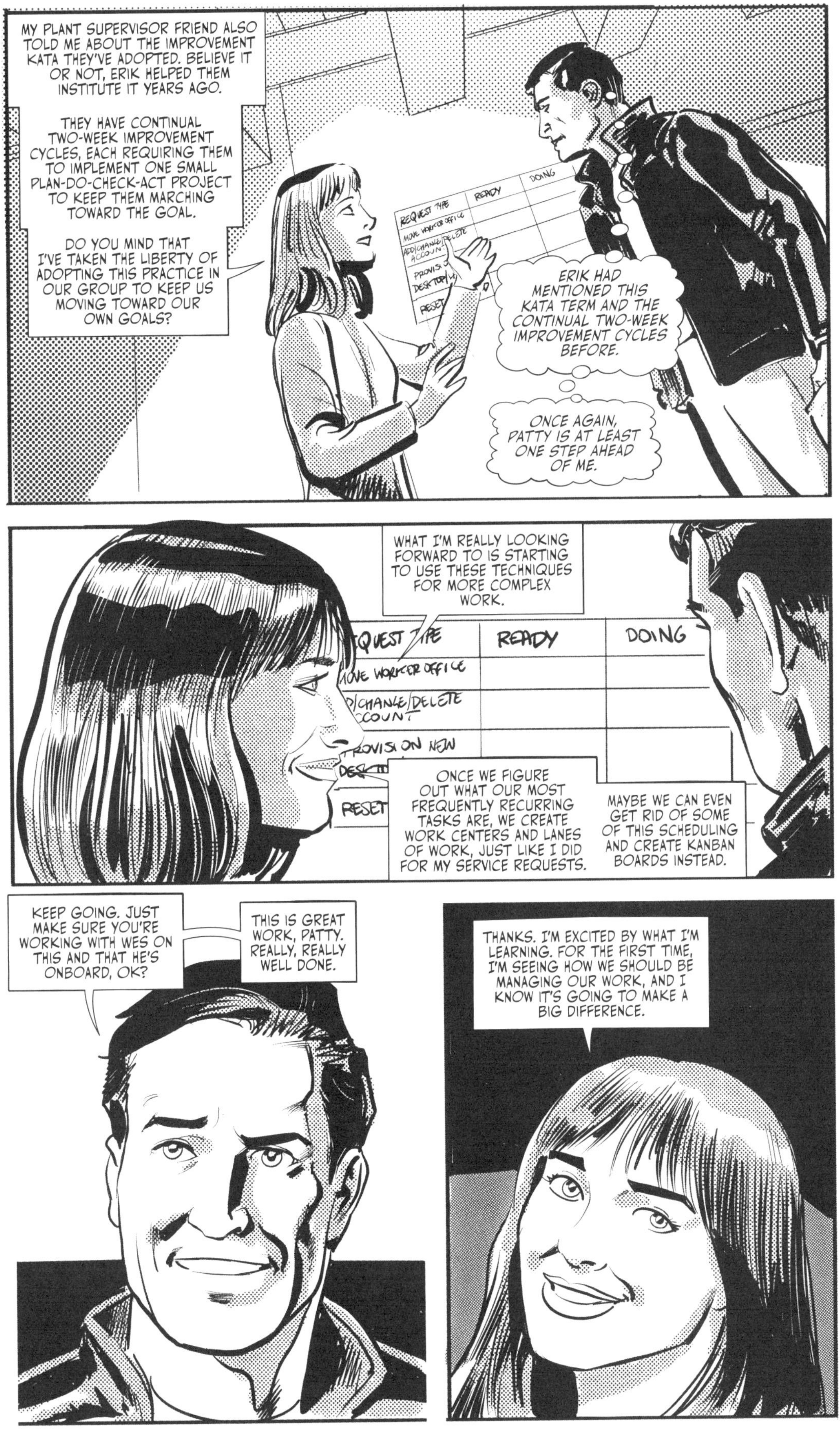
MY PLANT SUPERVISOR FRIEND ALSO TOLD ME ABOUT THE IMPROVEMENT KATA THEY'VE ADOPTED. BELIEVE IT OR NOT, ERIK HELPED THEM INSTITUTE IT YEARS AGO.
THEY HAVE CONTINUAL TWO-WEEK IMPROVEMENT CYCLES, EACH REQUIRING THEM TO IMPLEMENT ONE SMALL PLAN-DO-CHECK-ACT PROJECT TO KEEP THEM MARCHING TOWARD THE GOAL.
DO YOU MIND THAT I'VE TAKEN THE LIBERTY OF ADOPTING THIS PRACTICE IN OUR GROUP TO KEEP US MOVING TOWARD OUR OWN GOALS?
ERIK HAD MENTIONED THIS KATA TERM AND THE CONTINUAL TWO-WEEK IMPROVEMENT CYCLES BEFORE.
ONCE AGAIN, PATTY IS AT LEAST ONE STEP AHEAD OF ME.
WHAT I'M REALLY LOOKING FORWARD TO IS STARTING TO USE THESE TECHNIQUES FOR MORE COMPLEX WORK.
READY
DOING
ONCE WE FIGURE OUT WHAT OUR MOST FREQUENTLY RECURRING TASKS ARE, WE CREATE WORK CENTERS AND LANES OF WORK, JUST LIKE I DID FOR MY SERVICE REQUESTS.
MAYBE WE CAN EVEN GET RID OF SOME OF THIS SCHEDULING AND CREATE KANBAN BOARDS INSTEAD.
KEEP GOING. JUST MAKE SURE YOU'RE WORKING WITH WES ON THIS AND THAT HE'S ONBOARD, OK?
THIS IS GREAT WORK, PATTY. REALLY, REALLY WELL DONE.
THANKS. I'M EXCITED BY WHAT I'M LEARNING. FOR THE FIRST TIME, I'M SEEING HOW WE SHOULD BE MANAGING OUR WORK, AND I KNOW IT'S GOING TO MAKE A BIG DIFFERENCE.

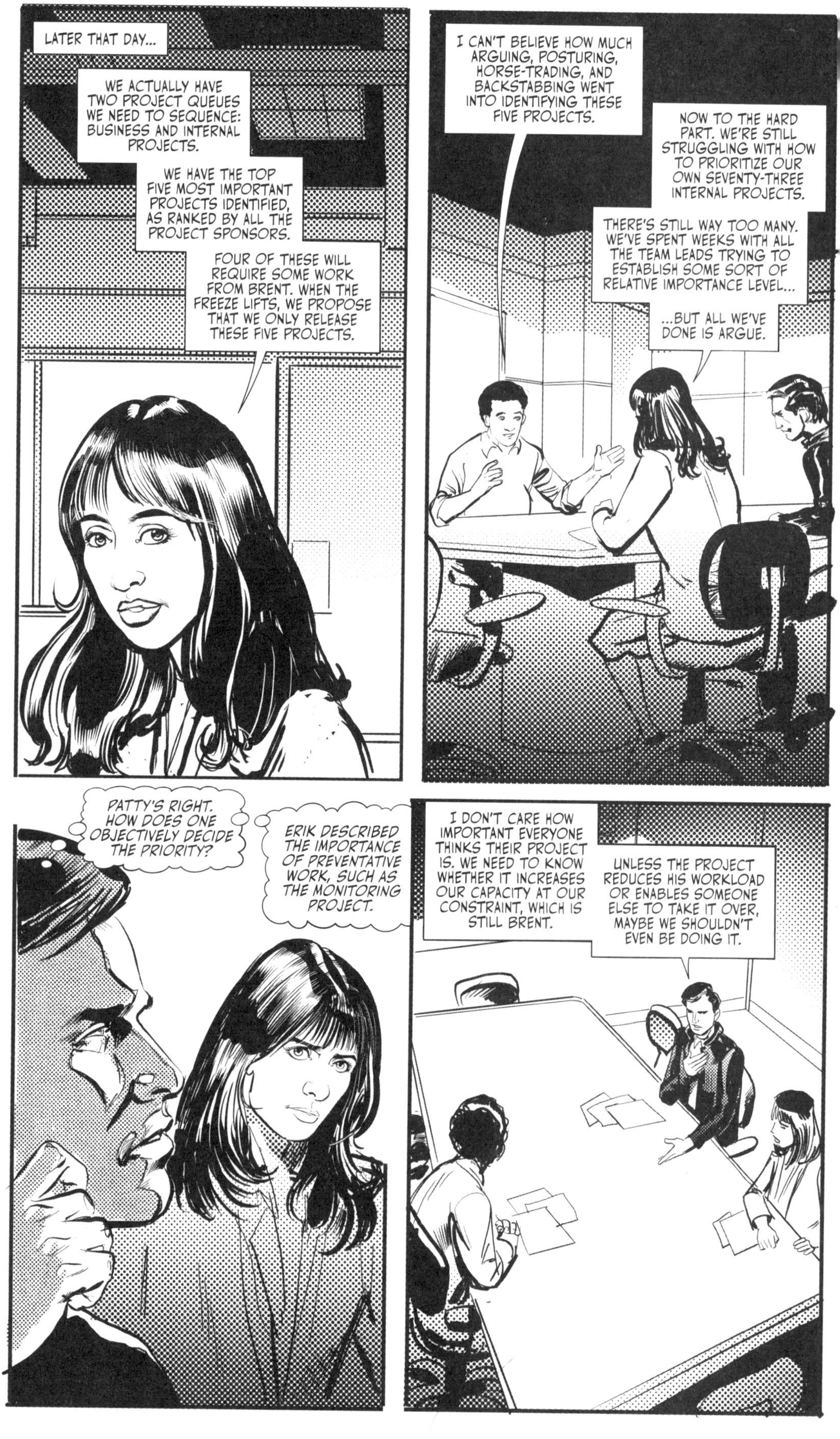
LATER THAT DAY...
WE ACTUALLY HAVE TWO PROJECT QUEUES WE NEED TO SEQUENCE: BUSINESS AND INTERNAL PROJECTS.
WE HAVE THE TOP FIVE MOST IMPORTANT PROJECTS IDENTIFIED, AS RANKED BY ALL THE PROJECT SPONSORS.
FOUR OF THESE WILL REQUIRE SOME WORK FROM BRENT. WHEN THE FREEZE LIFTS, WE PROPOSE THAT WE ONLY RELEASE THESE FIVE PROJECTS.
I CAN'T BELIEVE HOW MUCH ARGUING, POSTURING, HORSE-TRADING, AND BACKSTABBING WENT INTO IDENTIFYING THESE FIVE PROJECTS.
NOW TO THE HARD PART. WE'RE STILL STRUGGLING WITH HOW TO PRIORITIZE OUR OWN SEVENTY-THREE INTERNAL PROJECTS.
THERE'S STILL WAY TOO MANY. WE'VE SPENT WEEKS WITH ALL THE TEAM LEADS TRYING TO ESTABLISH SOME SORT OF RELATIVE IMPORTANCE LEVEL...
...BUT ALL WE'VE DONE IS ARGUE.
PATTY'S RIGHT. HOW DOES ONE OBJECTIVELY DECIDE THE PRIORITY?
ERIK DESCRIBED THE IMPORTANCE OF PREVENTATIVE WORK, SUCH AS THE MONITORING PROJECT.
I DON'T CARE HOW IMPORTANT EVERYONE THINKS THEIR PROJECT IS. WE NEED TO KNOW WHETHER IT INCREASES OUR CAPACITY AT OUR CONSTRAINT, WHICH IS STILL BRENT.
UNLESS THE PROJECT REDUCES HIS WORKLOAD OR ENABLES SOMEONE ELSE TO TAKE IT OVER, MAYBE WE SHOULDN'T EVEN BE DOING IT.

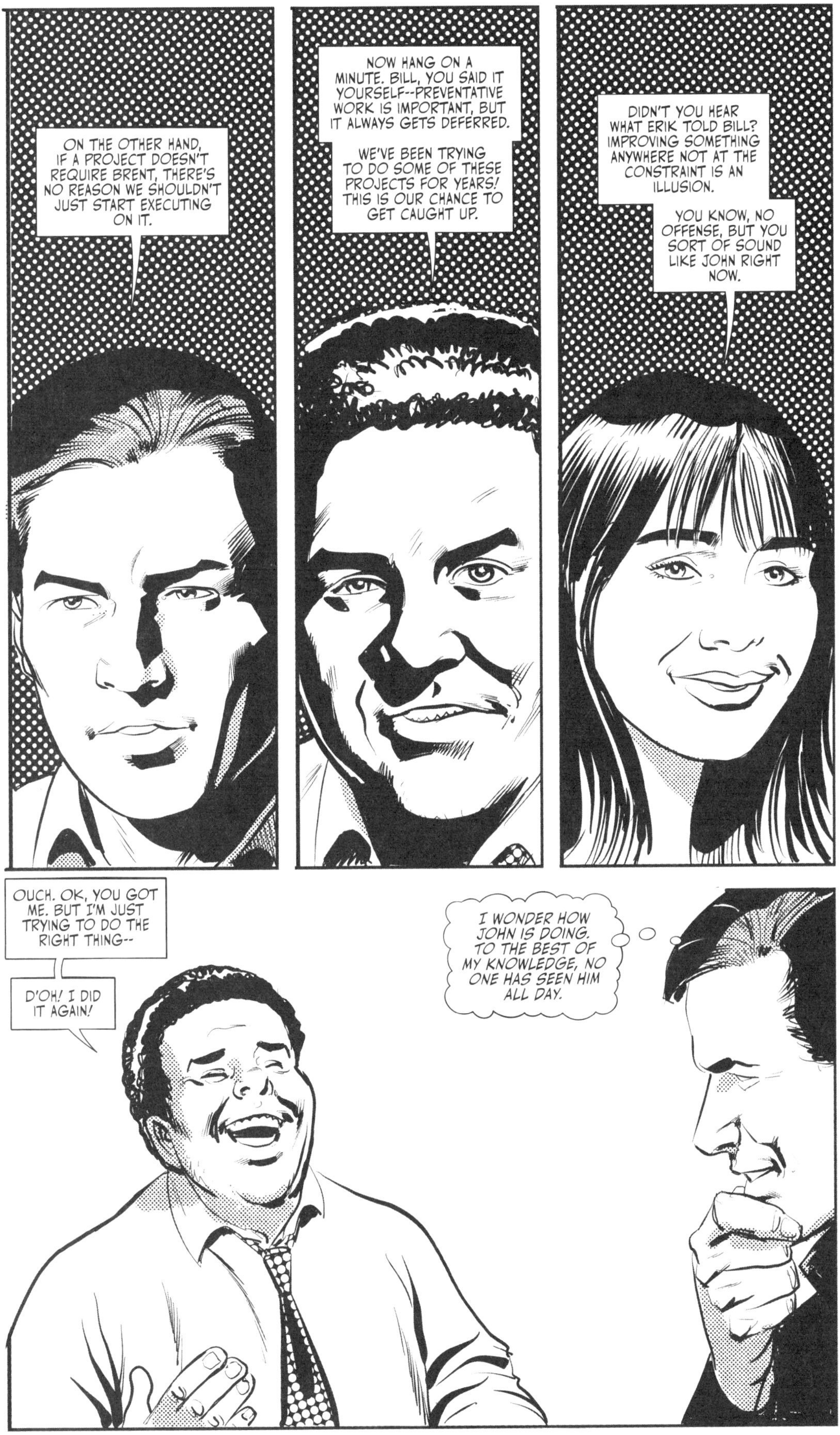
ON THE OTHER HAND, IF A PROJECT DOESN'T REQUIRE BRENT, THERE'S NO REASON WE SHOULDN'T JUST START EXECUTING ON IT.
NOW HANG ON A MINUTE. BILL, YOU SAID IT YOURSELF--PREVENTATIVE WORK IS IMPORTANT, BUT IT ALWAYS GETS DEFERRED.
WE'VE BEEN TRYING TO DO SOME OF THESE PROJECTS FOR YEARS! THIS IS OUR CHANCE TO GET CAUGHT UP.
DIDN'T YOU HEAR WHAT ERIK TOLD BILL? IMPROVING SOMETHING ANYWHERE NOT AT THE CONSTRAINT IS AN ILLUSION.
YOU KNOW, NO OFFENSE, BUT YOU SORT OF SOUND LIKE JOHN RIGHT NOW.
OUCH. OK, YOU GOT ME. BUT I'M JUST TRYING TO DO THE RIGHT THING--
D'OH! I DID IT AGAIN!
I WONDER HOW JOHN IS DOING. TO THE BEST OF MY KNOWLEDGE, NO ONE HAS SEEN HIM ALL DAY.

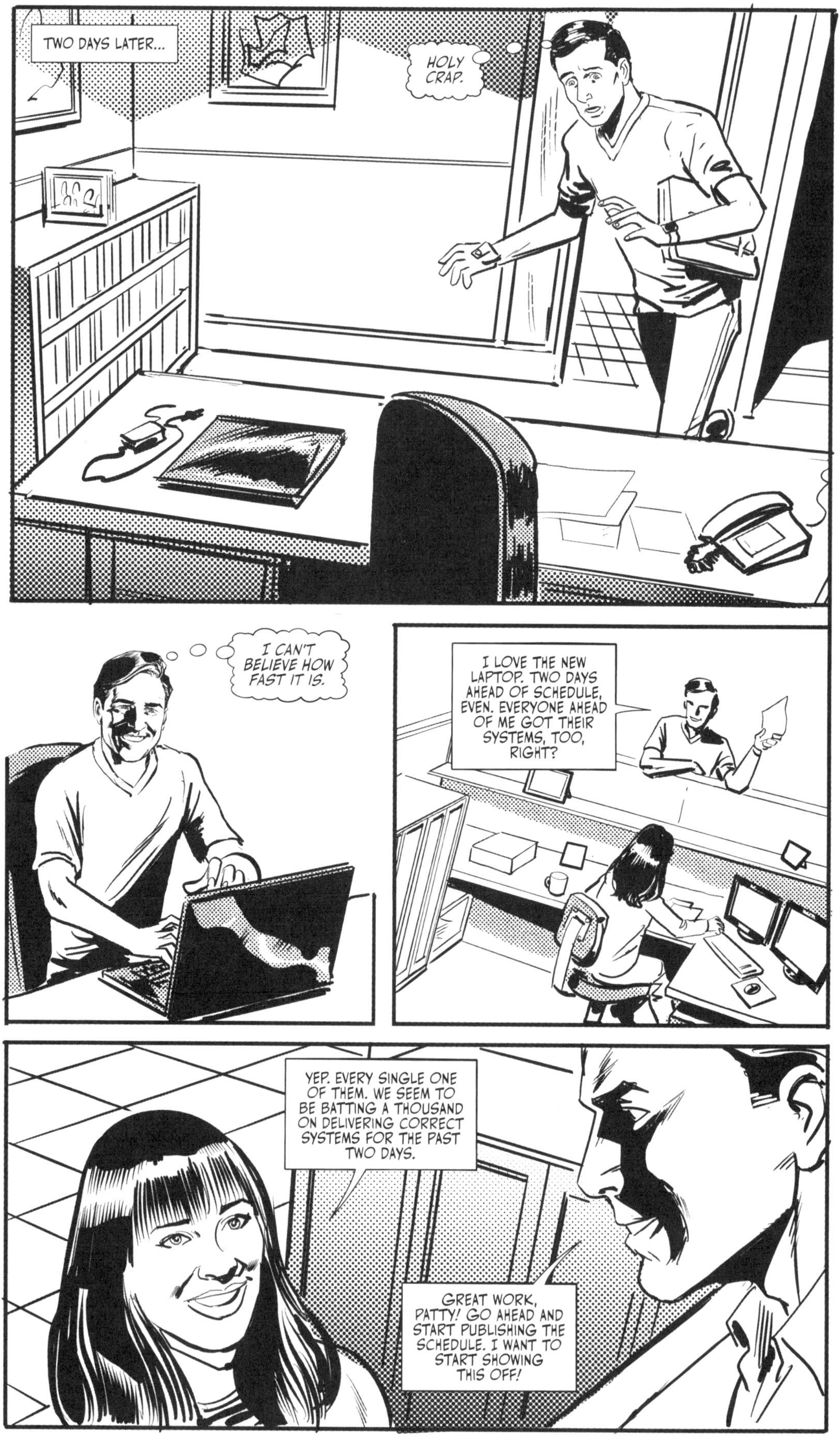
TWO DAYS LATER...
HOLY CRAP.
I CAN'T BELIEVE HOW FAST IT IS.
I LOVE THE NEW LAPTOP. TWO DAYS AHEAD OF SCHEDULE, EVEN. EVERYONE AHEAD OF ME GOT THEIR SYSTEMS, TOO, RIGHT?
YEP. EVERY SINGLE ONE OF THEM. WE SEEM TO BE BATTING A THOUSAND ON DELIVERING CORRECT SYSTEMS FOR THE PAST TWO DAYS.
GREAT WORK, PATTY! GO AHEAD AND START PUBLISHING THE SCHEDULE. I WANT TO START SHOWING THIS OFF!

CHAPTER 23 TUESDAY, OCTOBER 7

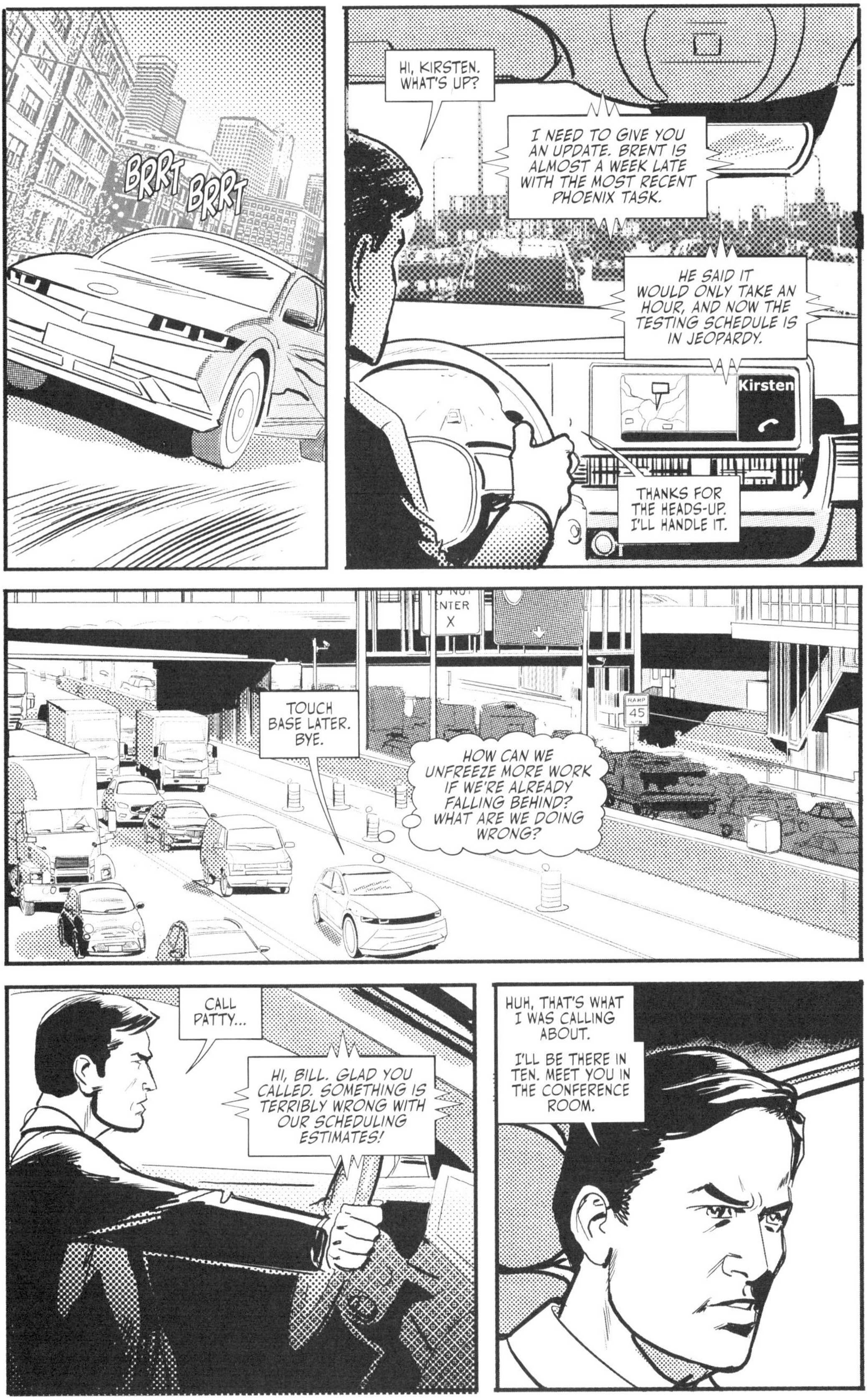
BRRT BRRT
HI, KIRSTEN. WHAT'S UP?
I NEED TO GIVE YOU AN UPDATE. BRENT IS ALMOST A WEEK LATE WITH THE MOST RECENT PHOENIX TASK.
HE SAID IT WOULD ONLY TAKE AN HOUR, AND NOW THE TESTING SCHEDULE IS IN JEOPARDY.
Kirsten
THANKS FOR THE HEADS-UP. I'LL HANDLE IT.
RAMP 45
TOUCH BASE LATER. BYE.
HOW CAN WE UNFREEZE MORE WORK IF WE'RE ALREADY FALLING BEHIND? WHAT ARE WE DOING WRONG?
CALL PATTY...
HI, BILL. GLAD YOU CALLED. SOMETHING IS TERRIBLY WRONG WITH OUR SCHEDULING ESTIMATES!
HUH, THAT'S WHAT I WAS CALLING ABOUT.
I'LL BE THERE IN TEN. MEET YOU IN THE CONFERENCE ROOM.

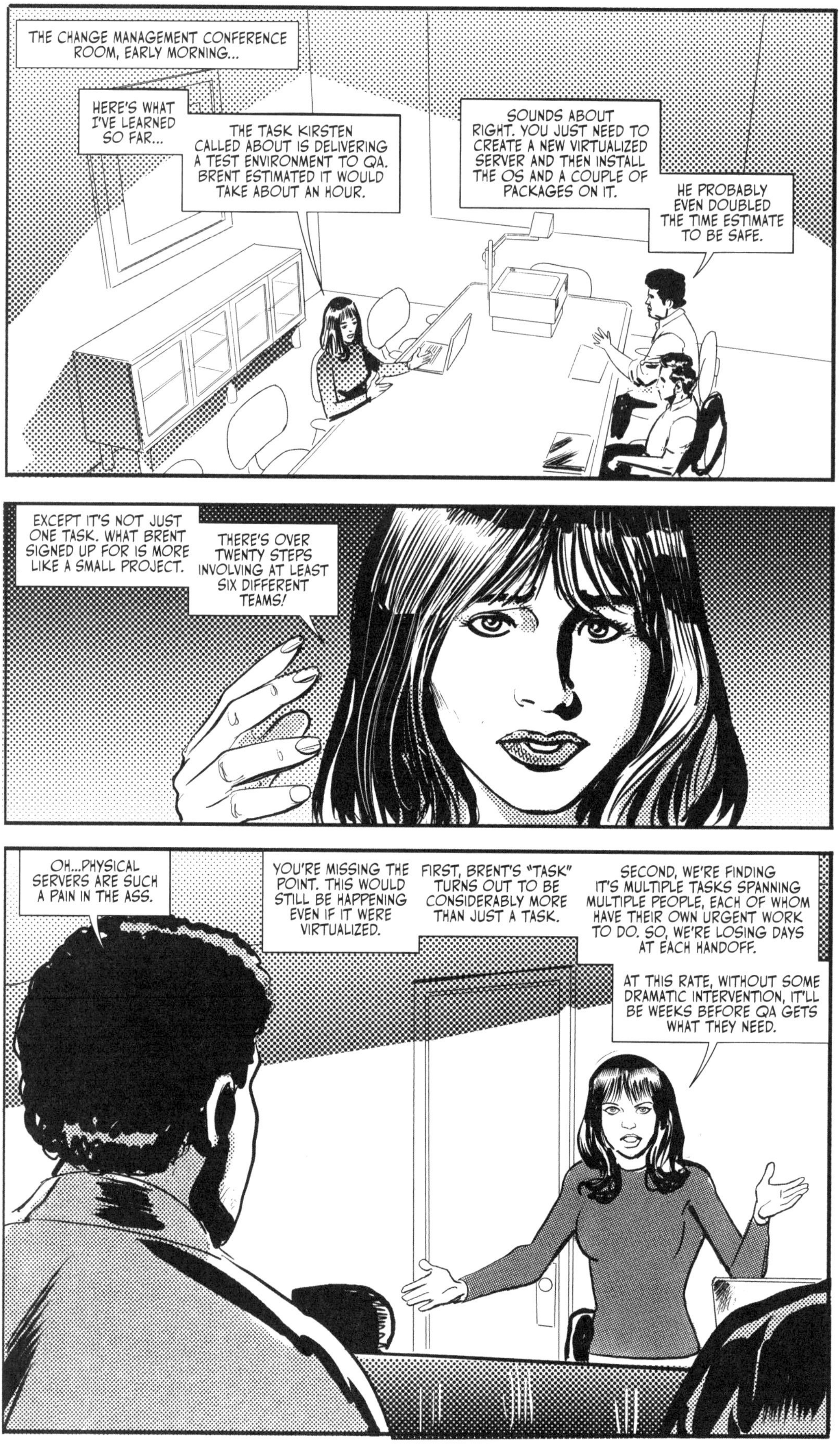
THE CHANGE MANAGEMENT CONFERENCE ROOM, EARLY MORNING...
HERE'S WHAT I'VE LEARNED SO FAR...
THE TASK KIRSTEN CALLED ABOUT IS DELIVERING A TEST ENVIRONMENT TO QA. BRENT ESTIMATED IT WOULD TAKE ABOUT AN HOUR.
SOUNDS ABOUT RIGHT. YOU JUST NEED TO CREATE A NEW VIRTUALIZED SERVER AND THEN INSTALL THE OS AND A COUPLE OF PACKAGES ON IT.
HE PROBABLY EVEN DOUBLED THE TIME ESTIMATE TO BE SAFE.
EXCEPT IT'S NOT JUST ONE TASK. WHAT BRENT SIGNED UP FOR IS MORE LIKE A SMALL PROJECT.
THERE'S OVER TWENTY STEPS INVOLVING AT LEAST SIX DIFFERENT TEAMS!
OH...PHYSICAL SERVERS ARE SUCH A PAIN IN THE ASS.
YOU'RE MISSING THE POINT. THIS WOULD STILL BE HAPPENING EVEN IF IT WERE VIRTUALIZED.
FIRST, BRENT'S "TASK" TURNS OUT TO BE CONSIDERABLY MORE THAN JUST A TASK.
SECOND, WE'RE FINDING IT'S MULTIPLE TASKS SPANNING MULTIPLE PEOPLE, EACH OF WHOM HAVE THEIR OWN URGENT WORK TO DO. SO, WE'RE LOSING DAYS AT EACH HANDOFF.
AT THIS RATE, WITHOUT SOME DRAMATIC INTERVENTION, IT'LL BE WEEKS BEFORE QA GETS WHAT THEY NEED.

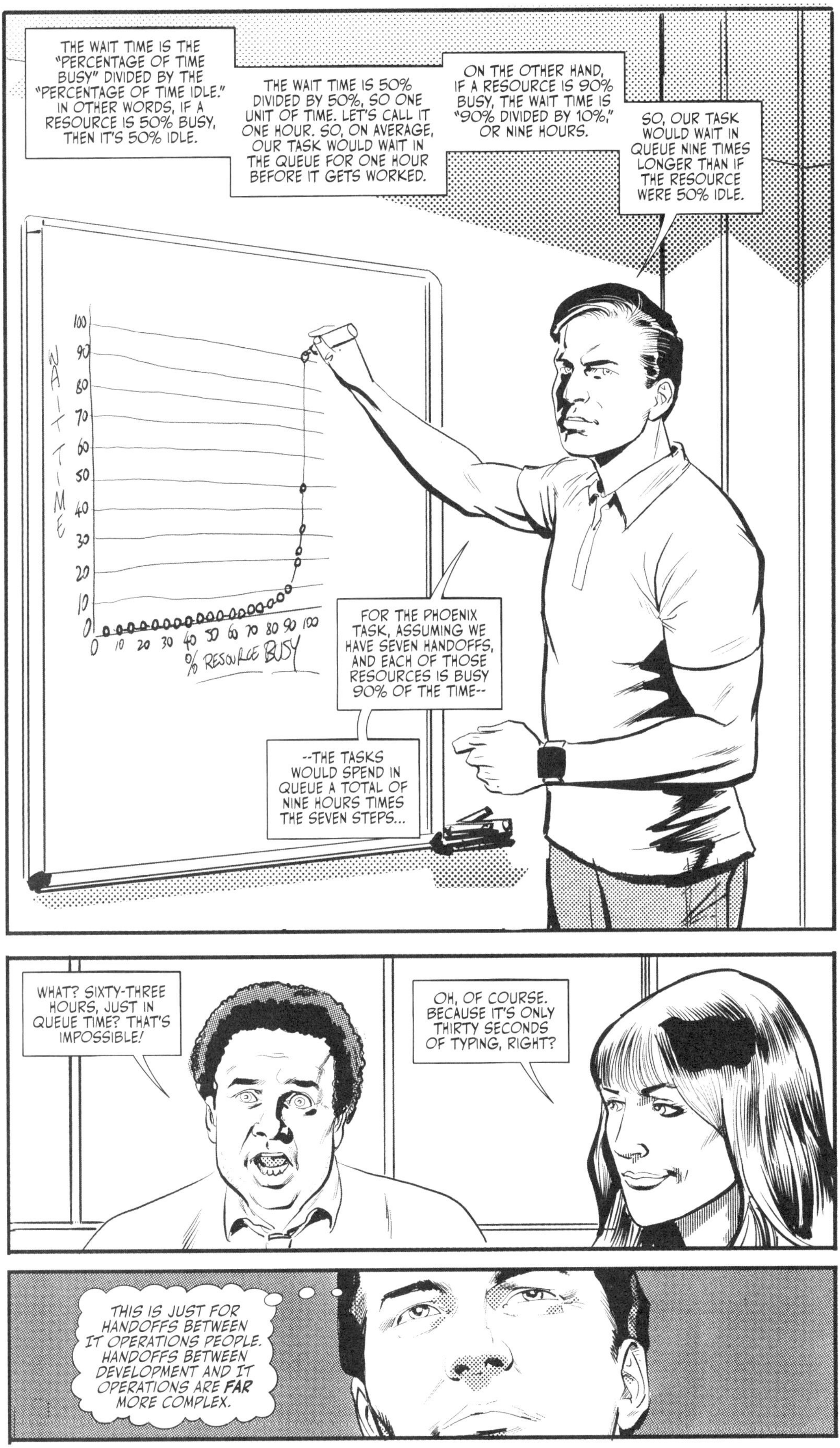

THE WAIT TIME IS THE "PERCENTAGE OF TIME BUSY" DIVIDED BY THE "PERCENTAGE OF TIME IDLE." IN OTHER WORDS, IF A RESOURCE IS 50% BUSY, THEN IT'S 50% IDLE.
THE WAIT TIME IS 50% DIVIDED BY 50%, SO ONE UNIT OF TIME. LET'S CALL IT ONE HOUR. SO, ON AVERAGE, OUR TASK WOULD WAIT IN THE QUEUE FOR ONE HOUR BEFORE IT GETS WORKED.
ON THE OTHER HAND, IF A RESOURCE IS 90% BUSY, THE WAIT TIME IS "90% DIVIDED BY 10%," OR NINE HOURS.
SO, OUR TASK WOULD WAIT IN QUEUE NINE TIMES LONGER THAN IF THE RESOURCE WERE 50% IDLE.
WAIT TIME
100
90
80
70
60
50
40
30
20
10
0
0 10 20 30 40 50 60 70 80 90 100
% RESOURCE BUSY
FOR THE PHOENIX TASK, ASSUMING WE HAVE SEVEN HANDOFFS, AND EACH OF THOSE RESOURCES IS BUSY 90% OF THE TIME--
--THE TASKS WOULD SPEND IN QUEUE A TOTAL OF NINE HOURS TIMES THE SEVEN STEPS...
WHAT? SIXTY-THREE HOURS, JUST IN QUEUE TIME? THAT'S IMPOSSIBLE!
OH, OF COURSE. BECAUSE IT'S ONLY THIRTY SECONDS OF TYPING, RIGHT?
THIS IS JUST FOR HANDOFFS BETWEEN IT OPERATIONS PEOPLE. HANDOFFS BETWEEN DEVELOPMENT AND IT OPERATIONS ARE FAR MORE COMPLEX.

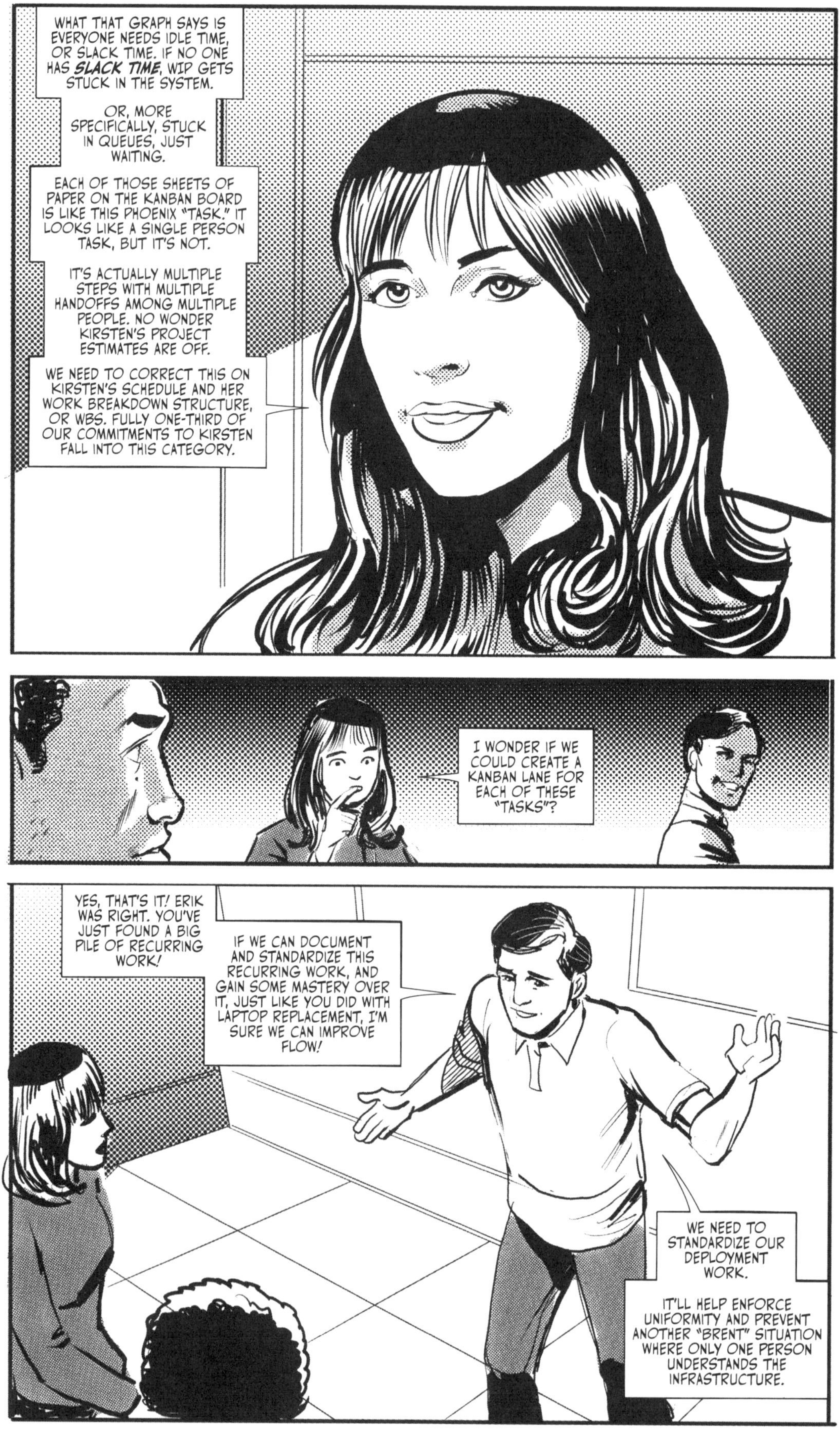
WHAT THAT GRAPH SAYS IS EVERYONE NEEDS IDLE TIME, OR SLACK TIME. IF NO ONE HAS **SLACK TIME**, WIP GETS STUCK IN THE SYSTEM.
OR, MORE SPECIFICALLY, STUCK IN QUEUES, JUST WAITING.
EACH OF THOSE SHEETS OF PAPER ON THE KANBAN BOARD IS LIKE THIS PHOENIX "TASK." IT LOOKS LIKE A SINGLE PERSON TASK, BUT IT'S NOT.
IT'S ACTUALLY MULTIPLE STEPS WITH MULTIPLE HANDOFFS AMONG MULTIPLE PEOPLE. NO WONDER KIRSTEN'S PROJECT ESTIMATES ARE OFF.
WE NEED TO CORRECT THIS ON KIRSTEN'S SCHEDULE AND HER WORK BREAKDOWN STRUCTURE, OR WBS. FULLY ONE-THIRD OF OUR COMMITMENTS TO KIRSTEN FALL INTO THIS CATEGORY.
I WONDER IF WE COULD CREATE A KANBAN LANE FOR EACH OF THESE "TASKS"?
YES, THAT'S IT! ERIK WAS RIGHT. YOU'VE JUST FOUND A BIG PILE OF RECURRING WORK!
IF WE CAN DOCUMENT AND STANDARDIZE THIS RECURRING WORK, AND GAIN SOME MASTERY OVER IT, JUST LIKE YOU DID WITH LAPTOP REPLACEMENT, I'M SURE WE CAN IMPROVE FLOW!
WE NEED TO STANDARDIZE OUR DEPLOYMENT WORK.
IT'LL HELP ENFORCE UNIFORMITY AND PREVENT ANOTHER "BRENT" SITUATION WHERE ONLY ONE PERSON UNDERSTANDS THE INFRASTRUCTURE.

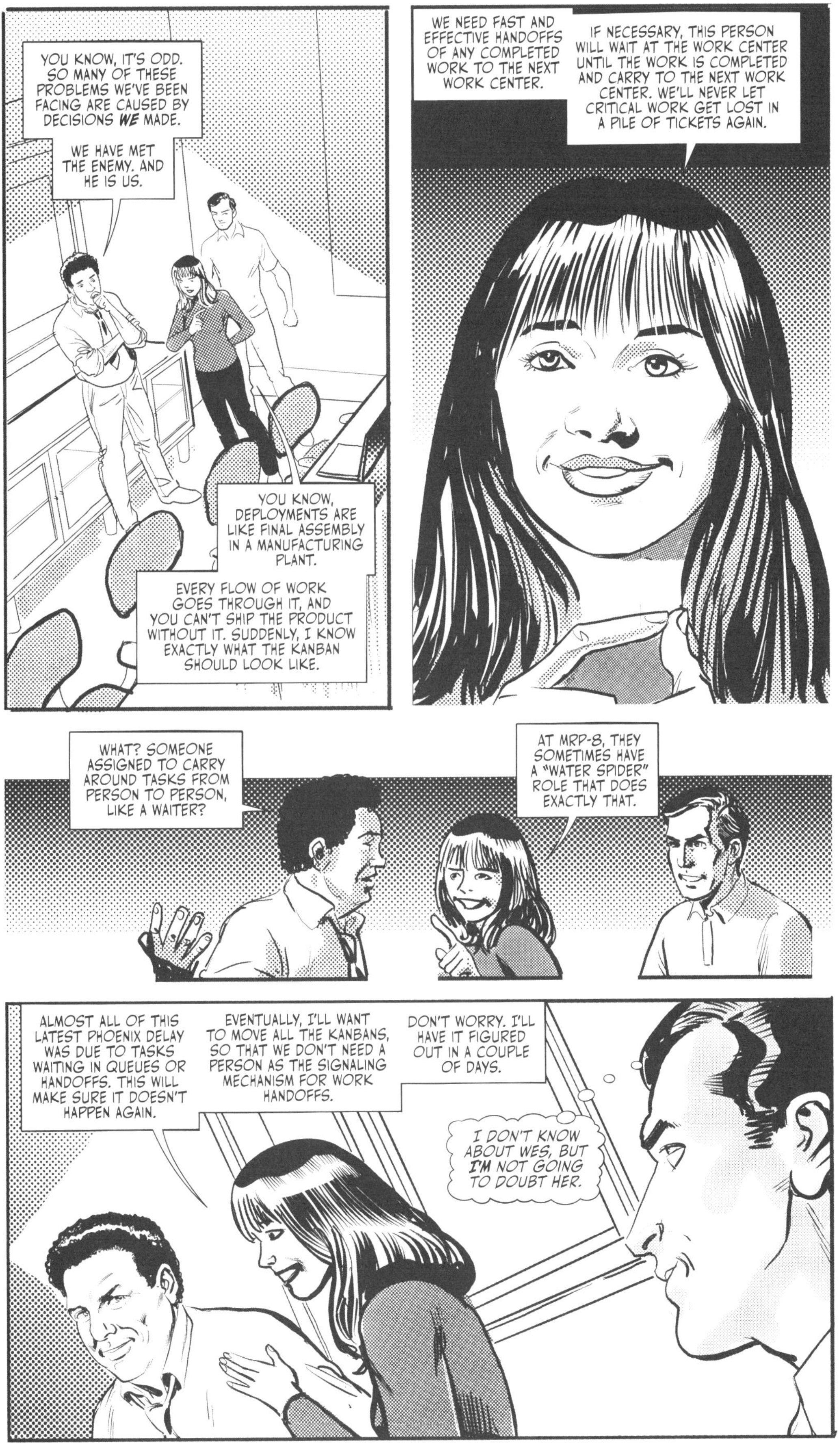
YOU KNOW, IT'S ODD. SO MANY OF THESE PROBLEMS WE'VE BEEN FACING ARE CAUSED BY DECISIONS **WE** MADE.
WE HAVE MET THE ENEMY. AND HE IS US.
YOU KNOW, DEPLOYMENTS ARE LIKE FINAL ASSEMBLY IN A MANUFACTURING PLANT.
EVERY FLOW OF WORK GOES THROUGH IT, AND YOU CAN'T SHIP THE PRODUCT WITHOUT IT. SUDDENLY, I KNOW EXACTLY WHAT THE KANBAN SHOULD LOOK LIKE.
WE NEED FAST AND EFFECTIVE HANDOFFS OF ANY COMPLETED WORK TO THE NEXT WORK CENTER.
IF NECESSARY, THIS PERSON WILL WAIT AT THE WORK CENTER UNTIL THE WORK IS COMPLETED AND CARRY TO THE NEXT WORK CENTER. WE'LL NEVER LET CRITICAL WORK GET LOST IN A PILE OF TICKETS AGAIN.
WHAT? SOMEONE ASSIGNED TO CARRY AROUND TASKS FROM PERSON TO PERSON, LIKE A WAITER?
AT MRP-8, THEY SOMETIMES HAVE A "WATER SPIDER" ROLE THAT DOES EXACTLY THAT.
ALMOST ALL OF THIS LATEST PHOENIX DELAY WAS DUE TO TASKS WAITING IN QUEUES OR HANDOFFS. THIS WILL MAKE SURE IT DOESN'T HAPPEN AGAIN.
EVENTUALLY, I'LL WANT TO MOVE ALL THE KANBANS, SO THAT WE DON'T NEED A PERSON AS THE SIGNALING MECHANISM FOR WORK HANDOFFS.
DON'T WORRY. I'LL HAVE IT FIGURED OUT IN A COUPLE OF DAYS.
*I DON'T KNOW ABOUT WES, BUT **I'M** NOT GOING TO DOUBT HER.*

CHAPTER 24 SATURDAY, OCTOBER 11

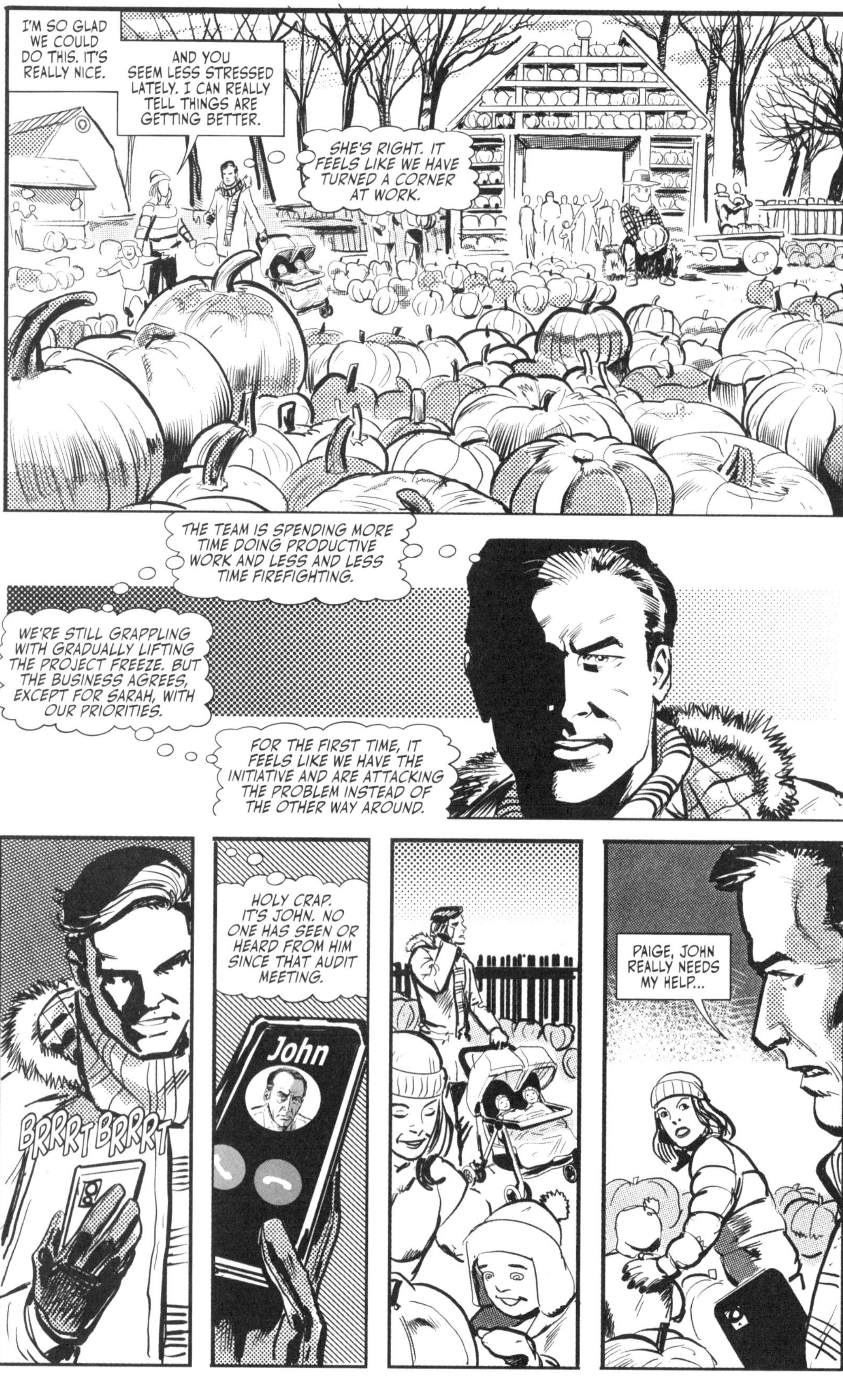

I'M SO GLAD WE COULD DO THIS. IT'S REALLY NICE.
AND YOU SEEM LESS STRESSED LATELY. I CAN REALLY TELL THINGS ARE GETTING BETTER.
SHE'S RIGHT. IT FEELS LIKE WE HAVE TURNED A CORNER AT WORK.
THE TEAM IS SPENDING MORE TIME DOING PRODUCTIVE WORK AND LESS AND LESS TIME FIREFIGHTING.
WE'RE STILL GRAPPLING WITH GRADUALLY LIFTING THE PROJECT FREEZE. BUT THE BUSINESS AGREES, EXCEPT FOR SARAH, WITH OUR PRIORITIES.
FOR THE FIRST TIME, IT FEELS LIKE WE HAVE THE INITIATIVE AND ARE ATTACKING THE PROBLEM INSTEAD OF THE OTHER WAY AROUND.
BRRRT BRRRT
HOLY CRAP. IT'S JOHN. NO ONE HAS SEEN OR HEARD FROM HIM SINCE THAT AUDIT MEETING.
John
PAIGE, JOHN REALLY NEEDS MY HELP...

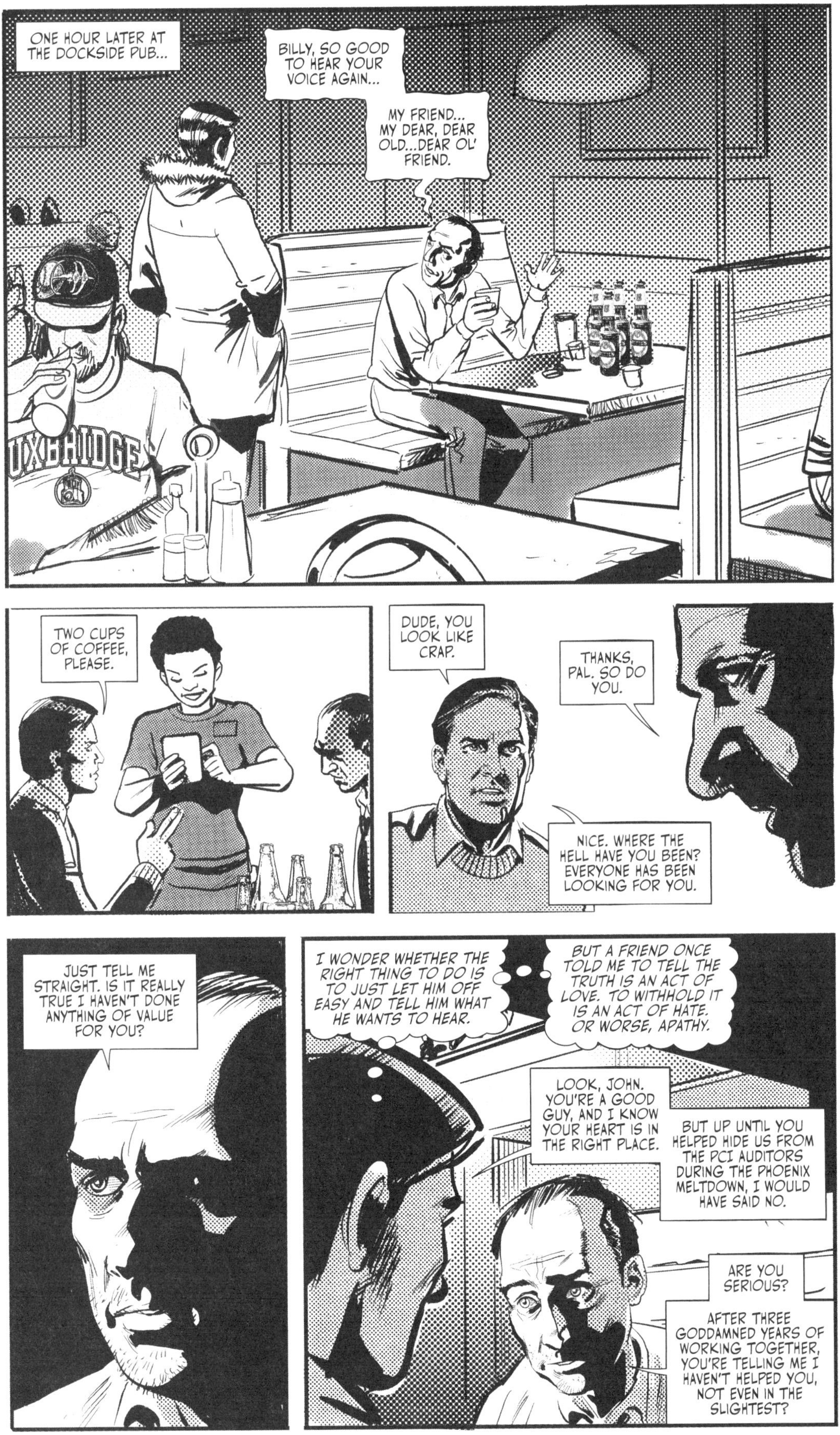

ONE HOUR LATER AT THE DOCKSIDE PUB...
BILLY, SO GOOD TO HEAR YOUR VOICE AGAIN...
MY FRIEND... MY DEAR, DEAR OLD...DEAR OL' FRIEND.
UXBRIDGE
TWO CUPS OF COFFEE, PLEASE.
DUDE, YOU LOOK LIKE CRAP.
THANKS, PAL. SO DO YOU.
NICE. WHERE THE HELL HAVE YOU BEEN? EVERYONE HAS BEEN LOOKING FOR YOU.
JUST TELL ME STRAIGHT. IS IT REALLY TRUE I HAVEN'T DONE ANYTHING OF VALUE FOR YOU?
I WONDER WHETHER THE RIGHT THING TO DO IS TO JUST LET HIM OFF EASY AND TELL HIM WHAT HE WANTS TO HEAR.
BUT A FRIEND ONCE TOLD ME TO TELL THE TRUTH IS AN ACT OF LOVE. TO WITHHOLD IT IS AN ACT OF HATE. OR WORSE, APATHY.
LOOK, JOHN. YOU'RE A GOOD GUY, AND I KNOW YOUR HEART IS IN THE RIGHT PLACE.
BUT UP UNTIL YOU HELPED HIDE US FROM THE PCI AUDITORS DURING THE PHOENIX MELTDOWN, I WOULD HAVE SAID NO.
ARE YOU SERIOUS?
AFTER THREE GODDAMNED YEARS OF WORKING TOGETHER, YOU'RE TELLING ME I HAVEN'T HELPED YOU, NOT EVEN IN THE SLIGHTEST?

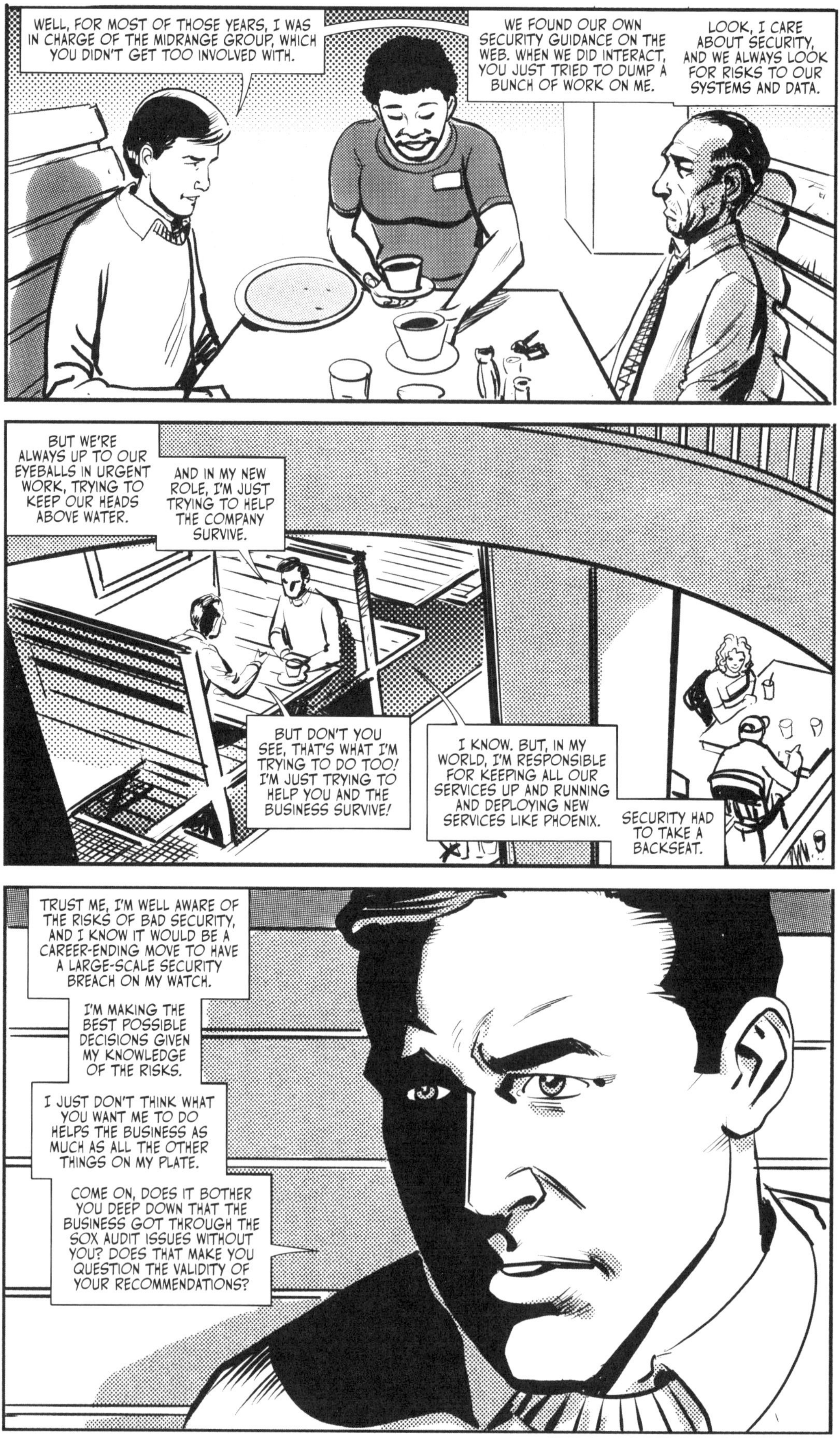
WELL, FOR MOST OF THOSE YEARS, I WAS IN CHARGE OF THE MIDRANGE GROUP, WHICH YOU DIDN'T GET TOO INVOLVED WITH.
WE FOUND OUR OWN SECURITY GUIDANCE ON THE WEB. WHEN WE DID INTERACT, YOU JUST TRIED TO DUMP A BUNCH OF WORK ON ME.
LOOK, I CARE ABOUT SECURITY, AND WE ALWAYS LOOK FOR RISKS TO OUR SYSTEMS AND DATA.
BUT WE'RE ALWAYS UP TO OUR EYEBALLS IN URGENT WORK, TRYING TO KEEP OUR HEADS ABOVE WATER.
AND IN MY NEW ROLE, I'M JUST TRYING TO HELP THE COMPANY SURVIVE.
BUT DON'T YOU SEE, THAT'S WHAT I'M TRYING TO DO TOO! I'M JUST TRYING TO HELP YOU AND THE BUSINESS SURVIVE!
I KNOW. BUT, IN MY WORLD, I'M RESPONSIBLE FOR KEEPING ALL OUR SERVICES UP AND RUNNING AND DEPLOYING NEW SERVICES LIKE PHOENIX.
SECURITY HAD TO TAKE A BACKSEAT.
TRUST ME, I'M WELL AWARE OF THE RISKS OF BAD SECURITY, AND I KNOW IT WOULD BE A CAREER-ENDING MOVE TO HAVE A LARGE-SCALE SECURITY BREACH ON MY WATCH.
I'M MAKING THE BEST POSSIBLE DECISIONS GIVEN MY KNOWLEDGE OF THE RISKS.
I JUST DON'T THINK WHAT YOU WANT ME TO DO HELPS THE BUSINESS AS MUCH AS ALL THE OTHER THINGS ON MY PLATE.
COME ON, DOES IT BOTHER YOU DEEP DOWN THAT THE BUSINESS GOT THROUGH THE SOX AUDIT ISSUES WITHOUT YOU? DOES THAT MAKE YOU QUESTION THE VALIDITY OF YOUR RECOMMENDATIONS?

CHECK, PLEASE? AND CALL A CAB?
OF COURSE.
I FEEL SORRY FOR HIM.
HEY!
OUR WAITRESS IS TIPPING OUT, AND YOU ARE NOT DRIVING IN YOUR STATE. A CAB IS ON THE WAY.
I WONDER WHEN I'M GOING TO SEE HIM NEXT.
Dockside
TAXI

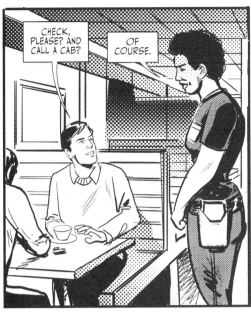

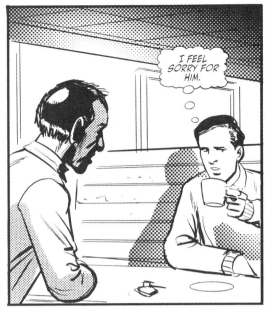

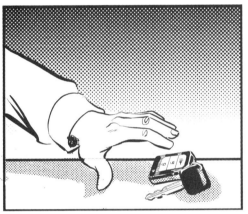

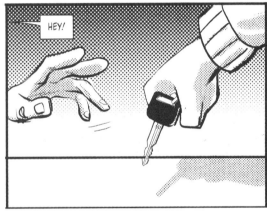

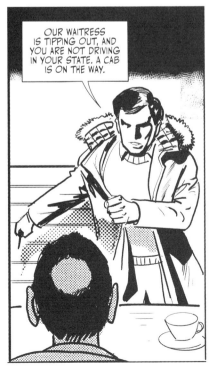

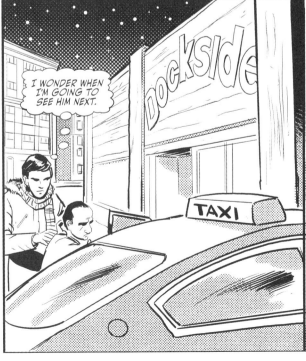

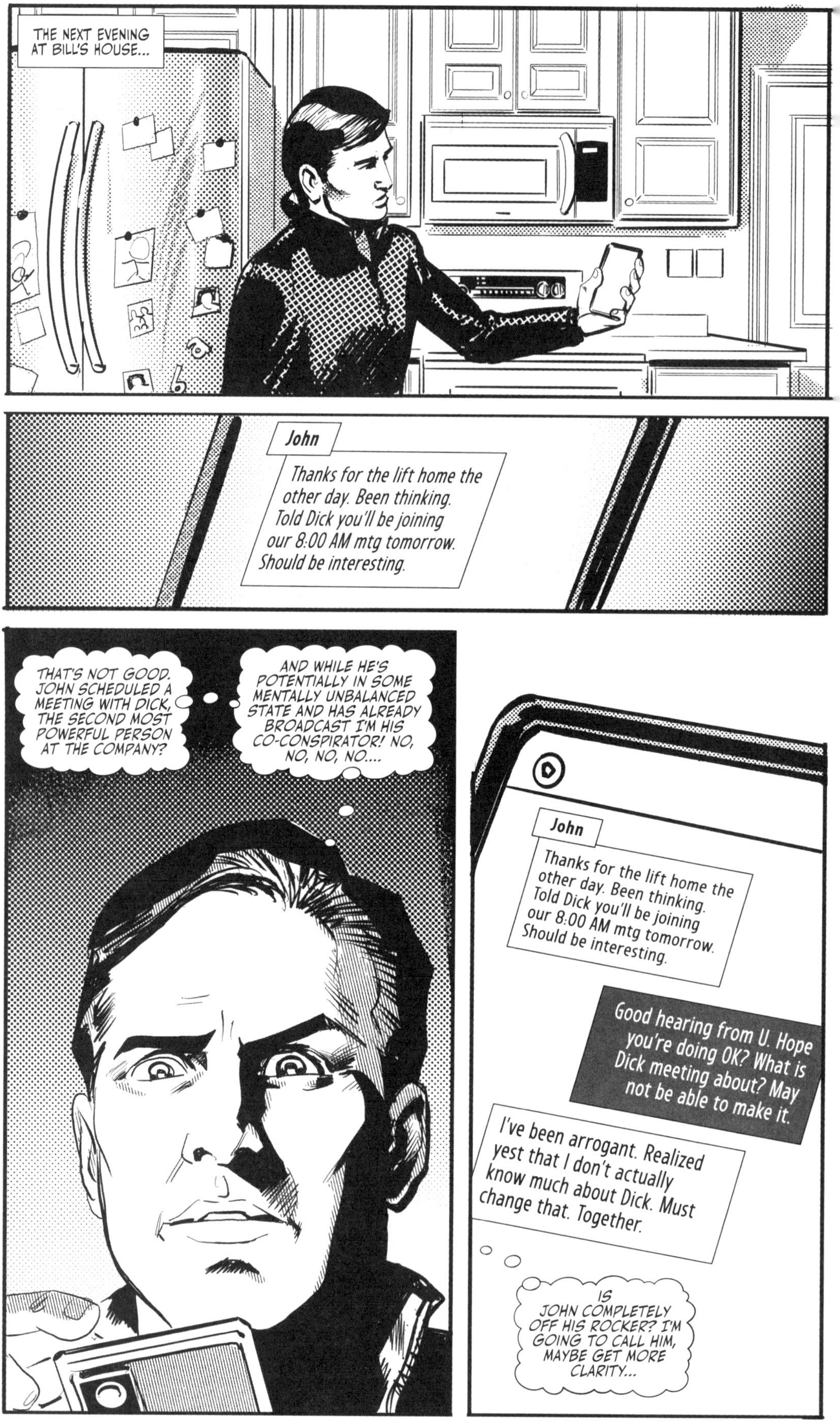
THE NEXT EVENING AT BILL'S HOUSE...
John
Thanks for the lift home the other day. Been thinking. Told Dick you'll be joining our 8:00 AM mtg tomorrow. Should be interesting.
THAT'S NOT GOOD. JOHN SCHEDULED A MEETING WITH DICK, THE SECOND MOST POWERFUL PERSON AT THE COMPANY?
AND WHILE HE'S POTENTIALLY IN SOME MENTALLY UNBALANCED STATE AND HAS ALREADY BROADCAST I'M HIS CO-CONSPIRATOR! NO, NO, NO, NO....
John
Thanks for the lift home the other day. Been thinking. Told Dick you'll be joining our 8:00 AM mtg tomorrow. Should be interesting.
Good hearing from U. Hope you're doing OK? What is Dick meeting about? May not be able to make it.
I've been arrogant. Realized yest that I don't actually know much about Dick. Must change that. Together.
IS JOHN COMPLETELY OFF HIS ROCKER? I'M GOING TO CALL HIM, MAYBE GET MORE CLARITY...

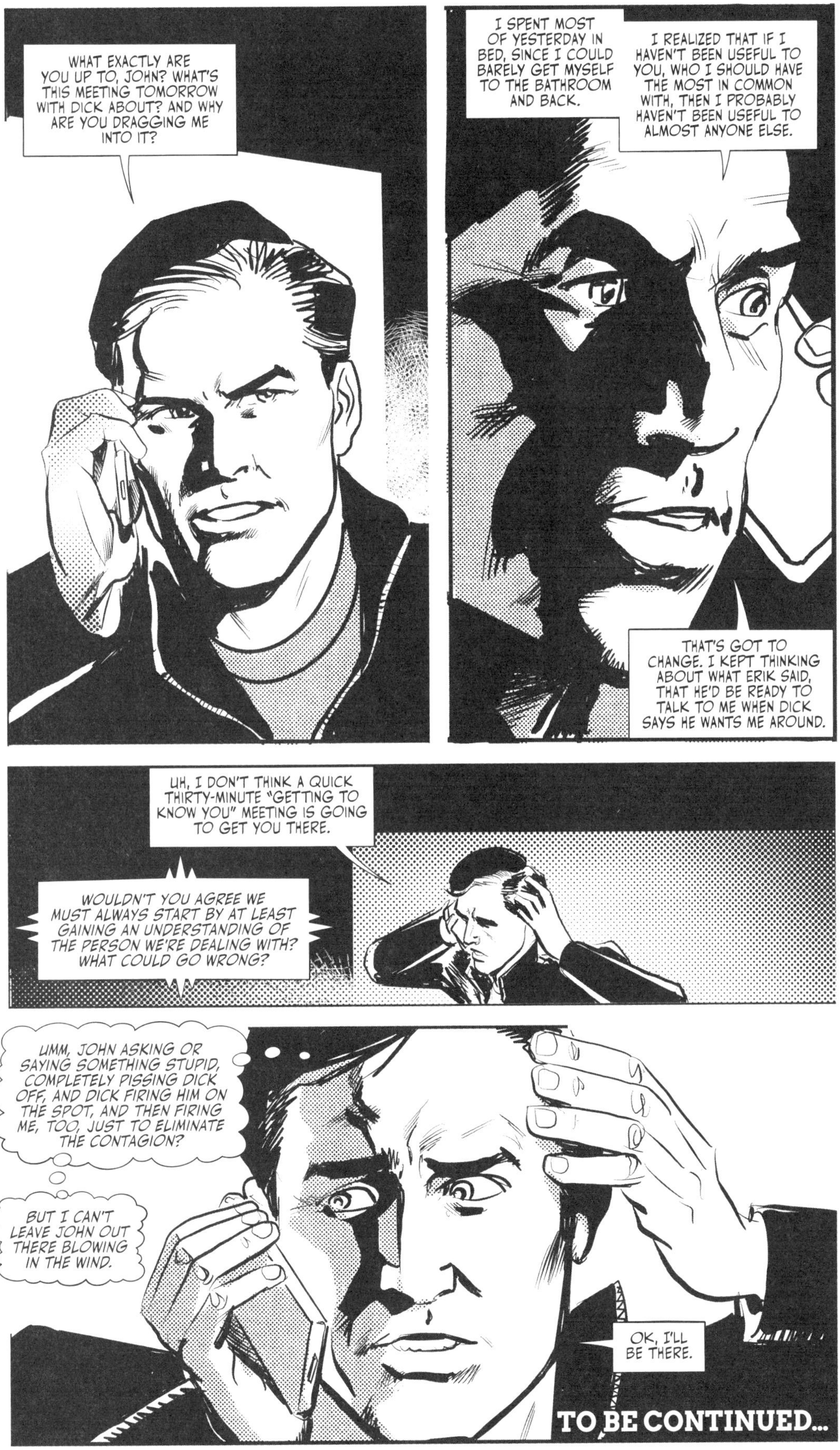
WHAT EXACTLY ARE YOU UP TO, JOHN? WHAT'S THIS MEETING TOMORROW WITH DICK ABOUT? AND WHY ARE YOU DRAGGING ME INTO IT?
I SPENT MOST OF YESTERDAY IN BED, SINCE I COULD BARELY GET MYSELF TO THE BATHROOM AND BACK.
I REALIZED THAT IF I HAVEN'T BEEN USEFUL TO YOU, WHO I SHOULD HAVE THE MOST IN COMMON WITH, THEN I PROBABLY HAVEN'T BEEN USEFUL TO ALMOST ANYONE ELSE.
THAT'S GOT TO CHANGE. I KEPT THINKING ABOUT WHAT ERIK SAID, THAT HE'D BE READY TO TALK TO ME WHEN DICK SAYS HE WANTS ME AROUND.
UH, I DON'T THINK A QUICK THIRTY-MINUTE "GETTING TO KNOW YOU" MEETING IS GOING TO GET YOU THERE.
WOULDN'T YOU AGREE WE MUST ALWAYS START BY AT LEAST GAINING AN UNDERSTANDING OF THE PERSON WE'RE DEALING WITH? WHAT COULD GO WRONG?
UMM, JOHN ASKING OR SAYING SOMETHING STUPID, COMPLETELY PISSING DICK OFF, AND DICK FIRING HIM ON THE SPOT, AND THEN FIRING ME, TOO, JUST TO ELIMINATE THE CONTAGION?
BUT I CAN'T LEAVE JOHN OUT THERE BLOWING IN THE WIND.
OK, I'LL BE THERE.
TO BE CONTINUED...

The Three Ways

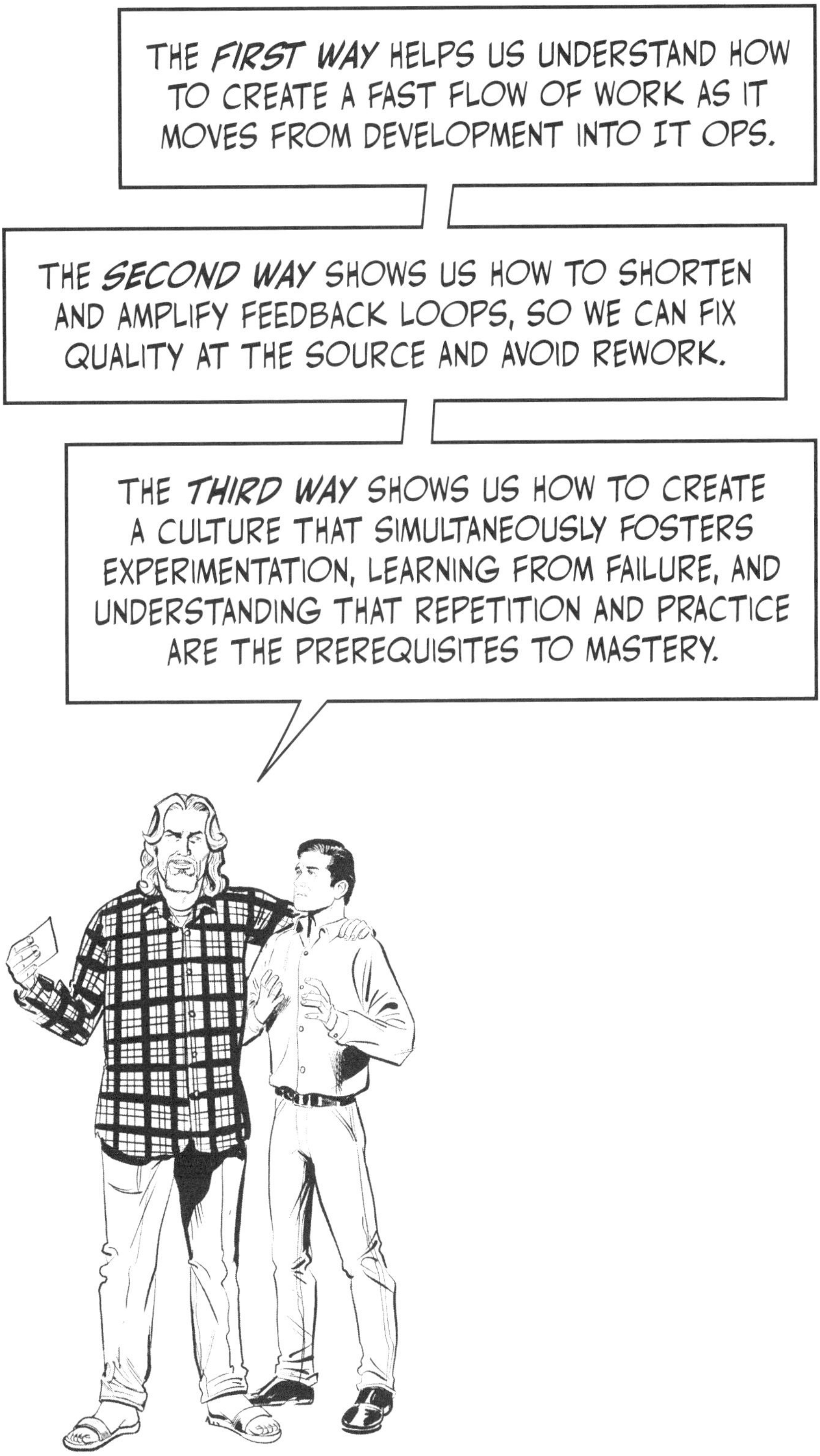
THE *FIRST WAY* HELPS US UNDERSTAND HOW TO CREATE A FAST FLOW OF WORK AS IT MOVES FROM DEVELOPMENT INTO IT OPS.
THE *SECOND WAY* SHOWS US HOW TO SHORTEN AND AMPLIFY FEEDBACK LOOPS, SO WE CAN FIX QUALITY AT THE SOURCE AND AVOID REWORK.
THE *THIRD WAY* SHOWS US HOW TO CREATE A CULTURE THAT SIMULTANEOUSLY FOSTERS EXPERIMENTATION, LEARNING FROM FAILURE, AND UNDERSTANDING THAT REPETITION AND PRACTICE ARE THE PREREQUISITES TO MASTERY.

About the Publisher

IT Revolution is an independent publisher of books for enterprise technology leaders. For over a decade, IT Revolution has published bestselling and award-winning books on DevOps, business agility, organizational design and culture, and leadership strategies.